This remarkable book touches my hea ~~the years – "invest in local leaders." As~~ much I was shaped and transformed b, ~~.... ...~~ designer" approach is what we need in the Arab World.

The Most Rev. Dr. Mouneer Hanna Anis
Archbishop,
Anglican Province of Alexandria, Egypt

Throughout the Arab world, the Lord is receiving praise from the lips of an increasing number of Christian brothers and sisters. Some of these Christians come from a long heritage of Christian faith and practice, while others are new believers coming to faith from various backgrounds. In light of this growing Arab Christian population, the need for raising up Arab leaders in MENA's churches is both immediately pressing and missiologically fruitful. In response to this exciting reality, Joseph Nehemiah's book, *Leadership Training in the Hands of the Church*, provides a welcome contribution to the global understanding of the task of encouraging the development of Arab Christian leaders. Writing at the intersection of educational research, pedagogical best-practices, and intimate personal knowledge of the dynamics of the MENA region, Nehemiah's work offers a posture and approach to delivering transformative leadership training that will contribute to the strengthening of the Arab church across the region.

Matthew Bennett, PhD
Assistant Professor of Missions and Theology,
Cedarville University, Cedarville, Ohio, USA

This book reveals a bright pathway to effective and reproducible leadership training for the great variety of churches in the Middle East and North Africa. Joseph Nehemiah has done a superb job of bringing together the best insights of adult learning, cultural contextualization, and practical long-term planning into something unique – a handbook for current church leaders and those who have come alongside them to become trainers of trainers. *Leadership Training in the Hands of the Church* is grounded throughout by real-life experience – by the author's own many years of experience teaching in the region, and even more importantly, by his diligent gleaning of first-hand insights of current leaders there. The elements of learning that have been most impactful in their own development are captured well in the book's appendix and effectively distilled in the practical suggestions provided to current and future trainers. A book like this has been urgently needed for some time, so it is thrilling to know that it will be available in Arabic as well as English from the start. May God use it mightily in training effective leaders for the churches he is building throughout the region!

Gary R. Corwin
Missiologist
Former Editor, *Evangelical Missions Quarterly*

Leadership Training in the Hands of the Church is an excellent resource for those who are training leaders in the MENA region. It has a strong biblical foundation, well-researched insights from adult learning theory, and is guided by the voices of many MENA regional leaders. This is a unique treasure that will serve the church well for years to come.

Lloyd Kim, PhD
Coordinator, Mission to the World

The author's long history in the Middle East and North Africa provides an invaluable resource in the best tradition of missiological study – an engaged practitioner motivated by love for the people he serves. Nehemiah's world is that of Athanasius, Augustine and Tertullian. Yet today it is an Islamic context, with inherent risks for those who teach the values, concepts and skills of Christian ministry. As one who has taught extensively in this context, I was often underlining points in agreement as Nehemiah analyzed the educational culture of the Arab world.

Sustainability is a critical concern in this part of world where institutional approaches are impractical and unattainable. Nehemiah suggests "*shura*-based education," derived from the consultative process often led by tribal sheikhs in decision-making and leadership. It is a culturally adaptive means of balancing the student's need of assurance that the trainer or teacher is knowledgeable (a high power-distance index), while inviting the student into the participative process of learning (valuing collectivism). The process is delightfully labeled "sheikhocratic." If we are to draw from Jesus's approach to discipleship and Paul's traveling ministry team, we may find that Nehemiah is returning us to a more biblical model – an indigenous, interactive and experiential educational process. Perhaps it is time for the West to learn from this and similar contextualized approaches to Christian leadership development. As all education is cross-cultural at some point, this book is valuable for all educators. For those who seek to assist servant-leaders in cultures other than their own, *Leadership Training in the Hands of the Church* is a vital resource.

Michael F. Kuhn, PhD
International Theological Education Network
Adjunct Professor, Arab Baptist Theological Seminary, Beirut, Lebanon

This book is the fruit of more than twenty years of the author's love and perseverance as a reflective practitioner. Joseph Nehemiah's *Leadership Training in the Hands of the Church* brilliantly unveils a framework that trains thoughtful and effective Arab shepherd-leaders, particularly those from the region's majority faith. This study provides a scaffolding for generations of Arab leaders to multiply themselves through designing leadership training that adapts individualistic and student-centric Western adult education principles to collective, hierarchical, teacher-centric and "honour/shame" contexts such as Arab society. Nehemiah equips leaders in biblical application, problem-solving and real-life ministry skills amid potential security challenges and limited training options and materials appropriate to their context. Anyone who desires to see godly leaders developed anywhere in the world can benefit from the biblical, educational and contextual wisdom found in these pages. I highly commend both the author and this valuable contribution to missiology, intercultural adult education, leadership and discipleship development, and ministry in Arab and other non-Western contexts.

Lanver Mak, PhD
Lecturer in Islamic Studies,
All Nations Christian College, Ware, UK

All learning and teaching happens in a particular context and this is so important for gospel relevance and impact. In this publication, Joseph Nehemiah brings this vividly to our imagination as he delves into how this happens in the MENA regional context with general application to other contexts. This is for both students and teachers who take context seriously.

Victor Nakah
International Director for Sub-Saharan Africa,
Mission to the World

Joseph Nehemiah is not a novice theoretician but rather a seasoned Christian educator writing on a subject of his expertise. Nehemiah has spent years serving in Arab nations observing teaching and learning principles. In this well-written book Nehemiah highlights several cultural norms that influence Arab teaching styles: the professor is an authoritarian figure; tolerance for ambiguity is low; rote memorization is emphasized; verbal interaction in classes is minimal.

Nehemiah suggest an alternative style he describes as the professor being a "servant-leader." In this paradigm the teacher seeks to become maximally relational with the students. Classroom interaction is encouraged, being careful to avoid student embarrassment: the professor becomes a facilitator to draw out opinions and creative thinking.

Nehemiah expands these themes into a well-researched tome that has the potential of making a major impact on the Arab world of education.

Phil Parshall
SIM, Retired

Why is it that a good number of church leaders who have gone through leadership training are ineffectual? Dr. Nehemiah has produced a most valuable gift to those concerned with better leadership development for the church in the Arab world. The combination of solid insights from the Bible, sound educational theories of adult education, and well-researched Arab cultural values makes the book important and unique. In addition, captivating interviews with Arab leaders reinforce theological, educational and cultural insights.

James E. Plueddemann
Former Professor of Intercultural Studies,
Trinity Evangelical Divinity School, Deerfield, Illinois, USA

Global Perspective Series

Leadership Training in the Hands of the Church

Langham
GLOBAL LIBRARY

Leadership Training in the Hands of the Church

Experiential Learning and Contextual Practices in North Africa and the Middle East

Joseph Nehemiah

© 2021 Joseph Nehemiah

Published 2021 by Langham Global Library
An imprint of Langham Publishing
www.langhampublishing.org

Langham Publishing and its imprints are a ministry of Langham Partnership

Langham Partnership
PO Box 296, Carlisle, Cumbria, CA3 9WZ, UK
www.langham.org

ISBNs:
978-1-83973-063-4 Print
978-1-83973-102-0 ePub
978-1-83973-103-7 Mobi
978-1-83973-104-4 PDF

British Library Cataloguing-in-Publication Data
A catalogue record for this book is available from the British Library.

ISBN: 978-1-83973-063-4

Cover & Book Design: projectluz.com

This book is dedicated to the courageous brothers and sisters
who serve Christ so faithfully in the Middle East and North Africa.
Know that when the chief Shepherd appears, you will
receive the unfading crown of glory. (1 Pet 5:4)

Contents

Acknowledgements

The seed for learning and teaching was planted during my childhood. My father was a professor of education and a teacher of teachers. It seems the desire to teach others was implanted in me at an early age.

My fascination with leadership came along a little later. As part of our church plant leadership team, the church planter handed me a book, *The Making of a Leader*, by Robert Clinton. Along with the book came an invitation to look at how God develops leaders and to apply this to my life and leadership. Looking back, I realize that was the beginning of my journey of learning how God forms leaders in his church.

Along the way, God has provided a number of leaders to teach me. Some of them taught me through formal means; most of them just lived their life of leadership and allowed me to come along for the ride.

I am indebted to Tom Hawkes, the church planter who gave me Clinton's book on leadership. Your simple request to work through this book together was the spark that ignited my passion to learn about the how of developing leaders. Thanks for your life, words and consistent model of a leader who develops other leaders. Most of all, thanks for being a friend who sticks closer than a brother.

I owe a deep level of gratitude to the leaders of God's church across the Arab world. God has used you to fan the flame of leadership development and grow it through my years in the region. You have faithfully sought God's glory and served his people in difficult circumstances and with precious few material resources. In persecution, pressures, betrayals and an ever-changing context, you have trusted God for what could not humanly be accomplished. Your love, joy, passion and vision for your people remind me of Nehemiah's heart as he led God's people. You pushed me and encouraged me to join you in developing leaders and materials that would help the saints you served. Your love for your culture and country provided needed correction to mine and others assumptions about what really benefits your fellow believers. Thank you for making this book possible. I trust your voices are found woven through its pages. For the honour to know you and share in the struggle of leadership, I thank you. I wish I could list your names here, but our heavenly Father knows each of you by name.

I would like to thank my doctoral mentor, Dr. Jim Plueddemann. As the flame of desire to train leaders grew, Dr. Plueddemann gave that flame direction and purpose. Your practical experience in education, missions and leadership was the combination I needed to transform my experience and studies into something useful and helpful to others. Thanks for accepting the invitation to be my supervisor. Thanks for your poignant and helpful comments and your encouragement to find ways to make my research useful to other practitioners.

I have been blessed with the support of my organization to pursue my studies. This allowance provided the time needed to research and write. We have been blessed in our time in the Arab world with so many faithful men and women to encourage us. Your support and prayers made the writing of this book possible.

I would like to express my deepest love and gratitude to my family. When we set out on this adventure called cross-cultural missions, we recognized it was a family enterprise. It has remained that, as you continue to sacrifice our being together as we serve alongside the church in the Arab world. Leadership begins in the home as does learning how to lead. Thanks for letting me test some of my leadership theories on you. A special shout out to my daughter who did some of the early editing of my manuscript. No doubt you gained some pleasure in correcting your father who corrected so many of your essays in school.

To my closest leadership confidant, my wife, I say thanks for walking with me during this journey. Your model of faithfulness and service to others is something I wish I could encapsulate into a leadership pill to give to young leaders. The wisdom, support, sounding board and insight you provide has helped me lead better, serve better and be better. Your love for our brothers and sisters in the region is apparent to many – you are a model of Christ-like servant leadership.

This book is certainly the product of many people's input into my life. I am amazed at God's goodness in providing the right people at the right time. This book is a testament to God's grace in helping me learn and grow. My final word of thanks is to God for the privilege to be part of His church in a different culture, for sustaining me and my family, and for providing leaders to build his church for his glory.

Introduction

Across the Middle East and North African (MENA) region, the number of believers is growing. This growth has accelerated since the events of the Arab Spring in 2011. This movement has produced numerous believers and seen the formation of many churches. God's work in the Arab world is truly amazing and a reason for thanks and praise.

This book is for the church in the Middle East and North Africa, a broad region made up of many ethnicities. I have been blessed to interact with many and want all readers to understand and appreciate the unique ethnic differences that exist in the region. But for briefness, I will use the term *Arab* to include all ethnicities and countries in the MENA. I understand that for many in the region, Arab is not how they identify themselves. I use the term Arab for two reasons. First is that the cultural studies I use, define the region as the Arab cluster. Second is the shared use of the Arabic language, even in different dialects, throughout North Africa and the Middle East.

God loves his church (Eph 5:25). He promised that he will build her and that the gates of hell will not have victory over her (Matt 16:18). Part of God's provision to build his church is to give her leaders. Throughout the history of God's relationship with his people, he has always given leaders to shepherd and guide. Of course, Christ is the head of the church. He has provided leaders to care for and shepherd God's people.[1]

It's a joy to hear of and see the many different ways God is fulfilling his promise in the Arab world. The church has one Lord and one faith (Eph 4:5–6), yet it looks different from place to place. In some places the church is led by a single leader. In other places it is led by a group of leaders serving together. In some places the church is a large group, in other places just a few people. Some groups have leaders who have walked with the Lord for many years. Others are being led by young believers who are still new to their faith. Some groups are learning about their faith; others have studied the Scriptures deeply.

Whatever the picture, God's promise and provision are the same. He promises to gather believers together into a church (Matt 16:18). He provides for his church by giving her pastors and shepherds to care for and lead the

---

1. Acts 14:21–23; 20:17, 28; Eph 4:11; 1 Tim 3:1–7; Titus 1:5, 7; 1 Pet 5:1, etc.

flock (Acts 14:23).[2] These shepherds or pastors[3] are called to serve, lead, and care for God's people. They have an important role in God's church. To fulfil this role, they need to be like Jesus, the Good Shepherd.

Throughout the history of God's relationship with his people, he has always given her leaders to shepherd and guide her. As God grows his church in the Arab world, the need for leaders is great and growing. The need is also for leaders who exhibit the character and knowledge found in the Scriptures.

The growth of the church in the region has been accompanied by an increase in the number of seminaries, training programmes, curriculums, and courses for training leaders. We thank God for these resources. Accompanying these resources are a myriad of options and approaches for developing leaders. Whether these approaches are from the Arab world, Asia, or the West, Arab leaders aren't always sure which programmes are actually effective.

Local leaders need to be able to evaluate whether these programmes, resources, and approaches contribute to effective training. For example, leaders must determine if a programme is simply a collection of informative lectures or will help produce the heart change Jesus talks about. In other words, will it produce true growth and transformation or just fill the mind with knowledge? How can leaders know which programme is appropriate for their church? If the programme is from another culture, how can they know if it will work in their culture? How can they decide which courses will be most helpful for their leaders? Do churches need to look outside to train potential leaders, or can they train them locally? These are just some of the questions to address in order to develop the godly leaders needed in the growing Arab church.

My interaction with believing leaders from a Muslim background (BMB) across the region sparked a desire to address these questions. Whether I was working with a small group or a larger number, I knew I needed to grow in my ability to teach and train in ways that are culturally suitable. As well, I have witnessed numerous programmes designed to teach and train believers and have been frustrated by what have seen. Some teachers were non-Arabs seeking to apply their programme with little or no cultural filter. Some by both Arabs and non-Arabs were lectures disguised as training.

---

2. Though different terms are used for those who serve and shepherd God's church like pastor or shepherd, the primary word used in the New Testament is elder. God provides us with lists of the characteristics he wants in those who shepherd his church (1 Tim 3:1–7; Titus 1:5–9; 1 Pet 5:1–10, etc.). To serve as under-shepherds of the Chief Shepherd (1 Pet 5:4), elders are to be examples of Christ to his flock (Heb 13:7).

3. The term "pastor" (قس) is not uniformly used among believers across the Arab world.

This frustration led me to read, to experiment, and to seek to learn from Arab believers. My personal desire was to discover whether the experiential adult learning principles that are prevalent in the West could be successfully used in the Arab world where I live and serve. If so, then what are the best ways to incorporate them into teaching and training? As I researched this question, I sought to validate my findings through interviews with BMB church leaders in the Arab world.

As I began this process, I was struck by the lack of literature on using experiential learning with Arab adults. Nonetheless my research and interviews showed that this type of learning does work, and there are fruitful ways to implement it in an Arab context. I also discovered the "what and how" of using culturally adjusted experiential learning. Despite the usefulness of this type of training, my research and interviews revealed an even better way. I saw that it is more effective to build into Arab leaders and help them imbibe the principles and practices to train their leaders.

Why do I believe this is a better way? My answer is related to the contextual milieu of the emerging Arab church. I will highlight just four issues that I think are pertinent to the topic of leadership development in this context.

1. The context of the Arab church includes issues related to security; lack of easy access to training programmes, both formal and informal; and a lack of indigenous theological and biblical resources. These are just a few of the challenges that prevent some leaders from being able to participate in training or traditional seminary programmes.

2. In different ways, much teaching and training in the region is ill-informed by educational or cultural principles that should shape how training is conducted. Some use Western methodologies of education and training that tend to be abstract, and they are conducted with little or no adaptation to the cultural context, which limits the fruitfulness of these programmes.

3. Arab-culture educational models rely heavily on memorization, and they tend to be teacher focused. These characteristics also limit the ability to provide effective training that produces godly leaders for the Arab church.

4. Training tends to be programme- or seminary-centric. I mean two things by this. First, much of the training is centred in the classroom and is lecture oriented. Second, seminaries or pre-determined

programmes have a fixed curriculum that we fit leaders into rather than fitting the curriculum or programme to the needs of the leaders.

In both recent and ancient examples in the church, we see an emphasis that tends toward the academic. We are not rejecting the important role seminaries have in the leadership development process. Instead we want to encourage church-centric training in partnership with seminaries and other programmes.

As the church matures, leaders need to continue to grow deeper in Christ for the long term. They need the power, wisdom, and sustaining grace to serve others. They need a deeper understanding of God's word. They grow weary as they seek to disciple believers and to care for the believers' myriad of physical and personal needs. Leaders need to grow in their ability to minister to the deep needs of new believers while sharing the gospel and seeing the church multiply. Where will long-term leaders find the support and teaching they need both personally and for the leaders they need to develop?

Addressing the Challenges

The needs and specific context of the growing church drive the purpose of this book. I seek to define an effective framework for the teaching and learning process in an Arab context that is biblically rooted and contextually and culturally appropriate. This framework will enable Arab BMB church leaders to design programmes to develop the shepherd-leaders they want to develop.[4] It will help them assess which teaching and training resources they decide will be most helpful in developing their leaders. This project seeks to put the development, teaching, and training of leaders into the hands of church leaders in the MENA region.

A number of approaches have been used to address the above challenges including the need to train local leaders in their context. Malcolm Webber summarizes three approaches used in leadership development by local churches.[5] One is using foreign curriculum, foreign teachers, and foreign funds. This approach replicates Western models and offers a degree. In general,

---

4. As noted above, the New Testament tends to use the term *elder* for those who lead the church. I will use the term *shepherd-leader* in this book. The terms are not interchangeable. Although every elder is a leader, not every leader is an elder. I think the term *shepherd-leader* best describes the type of servant heart we want to see in all leaders in the church.

5. Malcolm Webber writes about his experience with leadership development in China. Although the culture is different in some ways, the context of the Chinese church is similar to that of the Arab world. Malcolm Webber, "Leader Development: What Is Our Role?," 18 March 2008, ChinaSource.

importing foreign ideas and practices is not very effective. The second model is a "train the trainer" approach that is slightly more effective. But Webber says experience shows this approach is not deeply contextualized and that effectiveness is watered down with each subsequent training. It is a bit rigid as well and unable to be easily adapted to changes in the local situation. Both of these methods have been used extensively in the Arab region. The third model Webber suggests is what he calls the "build the designer" approach. Building the designer means putting the principles and tools for building a training programme in the hands of local church leaders. The "designers" are local church leaders, and this approach helps them build their own programme and curriculum.

Webber's is a long-term approach, but an effective one. He states, "Clearly, this method is considerably more difficult than the first two. *However, if successful, it will yield a leader development process that is truly indigenized and contextualized, and is entirely owned, designed, operated and funded by the national leaders, one that is capable of being sustained and multiplied; one that is entirely capable of being changed whenever necessary.*"[6]

I believe the "build the designer" approach to leadership development is the best way to develop effective, long-term, contextual training.[7] It builds into the lives of Arab leaders the ability to evaluate, design, and develop the curriculum, practices, teaching, and training they decide they need to develop their leaders. This approach takes a long-term view that builds up shepherd-leaders who in turn will support and lead the church.

A crucial step for building the designer is understanding the learning and cultural background of the potential leader. Understanding Arab culture is critical for producing effective teaching and training. But cultural insight alone is not enough. It is actually a means for understanding what I believe to be the essential factor in effective cross-cultural teaching and training: students' prior learning experiences. These experiences are the ways adults have been taught which influence their expectations of teaching. Understanding the leader's formative learning experiences is crucial for using culturally effective teaching and training, and knowledge of culture opens our eyes to understand students' previous learning experiences. Culture then guides us in determining what

---

6. Webber, "Leader Development," emphasis added.

7. The length of time to fully imbibe this paradigm will vary dependent on the leader's experience with this sort of approach. The reasons for this will become clearer as we examine educational and cultural issues. I am currently using this approach with different groups of believers. Though different in makeup, feedback affirms the long-term nature of this approach but also increased ownership of the process, making it more indigenous, fruitful, and sustainable.

elements comprise effective training and how to include these elements in training. Culture serves as a bridge to understanding students' prior learning as well as the types of training that will be effective.

Building the designer, the local leader, facilitates training by giving ownership to Arab leaders which allows them to conduct training locally as part of their church. They design and determine the process. This in turn makes it more contextualized and sustainable as we train toward our goal of rooting leaders deeply in Christ and his word.

What are the pieces of the building the designer framework that are educationally effective and culturally appropriate in our Arab context? That is the focus of this book.

What This Book Is About

This book offers a blue print of a biblical leadership development model that employs adult educational principles, a model that can be used by local leaders to design and build programmes to develop their leaders. The book also gives the tools to evaluate programmes, curriculum, and seminaries that leaders may want to include in their training. These principles are culturally and contextually appropriate for the church in the MENA region.

This book is not just for leaders; it is also from leaders. It is not just about providing principles but also practical application. As we progress through this book, we will glean the wisdom and practical experience from practitioners in the region. A significant part of this book is the result of my conversations with church leaders in the region. I spoke with thirty-six BMB leaders in the region to discover the answers to one question: "What were the most significant experiences that God provided that contributed to your formation as a leader?" Leaders provided almost three hundred and fifty comments to answer this question. A summary of their responses are found in the appendix. I have included their comments and insights throughout the book so we can benefit from their experience. Here is a short summary of some salient points from their replies.

Regional Leaders and Leadership

Leaders recognize the importance of training new leaders, and they framed their development as a part of discipleship. This discipleship includes a number of different elements. Whether they are planting a new church, teaching, leading their church, teaching children, or reaching out to others, leaders testify to God as the first and primary one who develops them. They share the many different ways the Holy Spirit developed them.

Leaders also identified the importance of fellow believers in the church for their development. They were taught the Scriptures by others. The church was used by God to confirm their call to ministry and showed the leaders what they lacked and areas in their life that they needed to develop.

God especially used mentors to encourage leaders as they served in ministry. These relationships involved studying together and walking together as trainer-disciple over a long time. Mentoring included the trainer teaching and modelling for the disciple what it means to live the Christian life. With the mentor, disciples learned from their mistakes, and they reflected with their mentor to grow from their trials. All this took place in the midst of ministry.

The BMB leaders view training as a critical part of becoming a leader. They value the importance of going deeper in learning, doing, and being like Christ. This training includes both formal and informal training. The leaders grew from informal teaching and training which included being involved in ministry. The leaders were shown how to do ministry. For example, they were shown what it takes to plant a new church, how to teach, how to handle conflict, and what it means to love and lead your family based on Scripture. They were supervised while they attempted to learn by doing.

Leaders benefitted from studying in formal programmes to learn the Bible and theology. Leaders grew by studying through a system that provided the assurance that they understand what is right. This assurance helped them to be certain of their knowledge and that what they believe is not just their personal feelings or thoughts. Leaders also participated in formal leadership training that helped to shape them. This character development also helped them grow as a leader.

We have much to learn from the experience of godly leaders shepherding the Arab church. As we will see, much of their wisdom confirms and informs the principles we will look at as we seek to build the designer.

Goals

For those of us who have the privilege to serve alongside Arab believers, I hope that this book will (1) inform our teaching and training efforts with those in the region; and (2) help us know how to build into the shepherd-leaders (designers) God is raising up in the Arab church. God gifts leaders with the character, knowledge, and ability to shepherd his church. Yet he also uses others to develop these characteristics and to help leaders grow. In the New Testament, we find teaching and principles to guide us on how to develop leaders. This is why the church throughout history has recognized the need to teach, train, and prepare those called to serve God's church. God has given us a role in the development of leaders for his church. If God has given us a role, we need to understand how we can fulfil this role in the best ways possible.

The audience for my research is the many BMB leaders in the region that I have the privilege of knowing and learning from. The material in this book has been translated into Arabic for their use. They are the designers discussed below.

As we begin our journey, remember that God is working to develop leaders for his church. He is using us in that process. You are the leader God is using to develop younger shepherd-leaders. You are the designer. You are the builder. This book is for you, the designer. It provides you with culturally tested training principles that you can use in your context. In order for these principles to be effective, they "need to be expressed in forms and cultural and religious language that can be understood and internalized in Arab countries."[8] This book defines a biblically rooted, contextually, and culturally appropriate framework for training leaders in your context.

The combination of culturally relevant educational principles with the practical experience of professors and local leaders are the ingredients that make up our recommended educational framework. These are the elements of the paradigm we will develop in this book. Our process will take us from foundational principles to learning from teachers and leaders to forming a culturally relevant paradigm for implementing training in your context. At each step we will define the pieces of our paradigm that you can use to form a practical model for training leaders in your churches.

The Pieces of Our Paradigm

In section 1, we define the scriptural foundations that will guide us as we develop our model. We begin with the Bible because that is where Arab leaders begin. They have a deep trust in the Bible as the source of life and wisdom. Using discipleship as our overarching paradigm, we look at biblical passages that help us define what we should teach and how we should conduct training. These include biblical categories we should focus on in training leaders. We also look at biblical methods for how we should develop leaders. Then we look at a few

---

8. Eugenia Samier, "The Ethics of Islamic Leadership: A Cross-Cultural Approach for Public Administration," *Administrative Culture* 14, no. 2 (2013): 204.

examples from church history of how the church has developed her shepherd-leaders. Finally, we look at the biblical goal of teaching that transforms the mind, heart, and actions of the learner. These biblical foundations anchor our practice in Scripture and guide the goals and methods of our teaching and training. The Bible must be the cornerstone of building the designer.

In section 2, we examine educational principles for learning that doesn't just inform the head but transforms the heart. There is a lot of research into learning and especially how adults learn. We look at principles from three leading educators: Benjamin Bloom, Malcolm Knowles, and David Kolb. Their principles include how adults learn, how learning happens, and the goals of learning. These educational principles provide helpful insights into how to achieve learning that transforms the mind, heart, and actions of the learner. Our desire is to apply these principles in ways that are appropriate to the Arab culture.

In section 3, we look at relevant cultural issues that shed light on where students come from, what our training goals for them should be, and how to reach those goals. Trying to apply educational principles without regard to culture will inhibit our goal of transformational learning. So we examine the prior learning situations of students in the Arab world. Then we study the cultural factors that influence education and leadership in the Arab world, including perspectives from the Arab world as well as recognized cross-cultural studies. We will see that educational principles can be successfully used in the Arab world when cultural factors are appreciated and accounted for in the learning process.

In section 4, I suggest a culturally appropriate ways to successfully use adult educational principles in an Arab context. This is where we coalesce what we have looked at in previous sections. Having sifted educational principles through the sieve of culture and context, we are ready to suggest a paradigm of what fruitful leadership training might look like in an Arab context. I will first draw on the experience of adult educators in the region. Universities in the Arab Gulf provide actual situations where our education principles are being used with Arab adult learners. Professors share reflections on their teaching experiences and provide suggestions for teaching that produces real change. Then I offer some guidance on how to implement our paradigm in an Arab context. To help facilitate use of these principles in our context, I will mention some key contextual elements to consider in implementing our build the designer framework. Finally, I will suggest an outline for how to design and deliver training. In this outline, I combine the pieces of biblical foundations, educational principles, and wisdom from leaders that you can use to design, develop, and deliver a training programme for your leaders.

Summary

The goal of this book is to put the knowledge and tools for developing leaders in your hands so that you can develop your leaders in your context. We want to build this knowledge into you, the designer. This includes principles to evaluate the many resources such as books, programmes, and courses that are available for training leaders.

The biblical and educational principles presented here have been successfully used in the Arab world. No matter the size of the church or the role of the leader, this book is designed to help you know how to develop leaders in your church to serve the people in your area. You are the designer.

This material is also helpful for those of us who serve alongside designers. We can learn more about those we teach and train and how to use experiential learning in culturally effective ways. It is possible for leaders to develop a deep and growing understanding of Christ and the Scriptures while remaining in their context. Deeply understanding both Christ and ministry context is vital for effectiveness in reaching and serving. I believe it is possible to see shepherds who possess the necessary skills, biblical character, and deep knowledge of Scripture needed to fruitfully serve the church in their context.

As the principles in this book are used in training leaders, our hope is that these leaders will more effectively serve as shepherds and be even more fruitful leaders of churches. God is growing his church in the region. I trust this book will help you as you develop shepherd-leaders in your congregation which is part of the growing church in the region.

Section I

Biblical Foundations

Leadership development is part of the overall discipleship process. As we will see, regional leaders overwhelmingly emphasize discipleship as how God develops leaders. In this section, we will take a brief look at how the Bible describes developing leaders as discipleship. We will first look at *what* areas we should focus on in developing leaders as part of the discipleship process. We will then examine *how* leadership development, or training shepherd-leaders, developed in the church from the time of Christ. Finally, we will study Psalm 119 which ties together what areas to develop and how to effectively develop these areas. This study should give us a good guide for how we should train leaders in our churches. We will fit our educational principles into this model.

Regional leaders understand that leadership development is part of discipleship, keeping the process of developing shepherd-leaders connected to its biblical roots. Therefore, regional leaders more readily accept teaching and training programmes that are rooted in the Scriptures. My experience training in the region confirms this commitment to scripturally based programmes as well as suspicion of programmes based on secular principles like business and social sciences.

Keeping our training rooted in the Scriptures connects us to the overarching theme of discipleship which is deep learning for real transformation. This biblical transformation is our goal in developing leaders. It aims at the heart, involves others, and is based on knowledge of God's word that leads to lives conformed to Christ and the Scriptures. Discipleship defines both the goal (what) and the process (how) of developing leaders. It is key to recognize this definition so that leadership development is included even in the early stages of discipleship.

What Regional Leaders Say

In my conversations with leaders, it was clear that discipleship is how God develops his people and especially leaders who shepherd his church. These leaders communicated that without discipleship, it is hard to be a fruitful Christian and almost impossible to be a Christian leader. Discipleship is an assumed activity of the Christian life. It is what the Lord did with his disciples and what he commanded us to do. The leaders strongly believe that discipleship of believers must happen. For them it is foundational to Christian faith and life.

The Goal of Discipleship

The Scriptures tell us that all believers are called to be conformed to the image of Christ (Rom 8:29). The Holy Spirit transforms us into this image as we gaze upon Christ (2 Cor 3:18). Following Christ by the Spirit is what produces in all believers the godly characteristics of Christ-likeness. This is true for elders and leaders as well.

To shepherd God's people, leaders need to strongly possess godly characteristics as well as other characteristics and abilities that are unique to shepherds of God's flock. To serve as under-shepherds of the Chief Shepherd (1 Pet 5:4), elders are to be examples of Christ to his flock (Heb 13:7). Leadership characteristics of Christ-likeness in heart, mind, and ability are described in Paul's letters to Timothy. These letters are known as the Pastoral Epistles. In these letters, Paul gives Timothy many practical points of advice to help him be an effective shepherd of God's people, the church (1 Tim 1:18–20; 3:15; 5:1, 17; 6:11; 2 Tim 1:13; 2:3, 22; 4:1–2; see also Titus 2:6–7). The Pastoral Epistles provide us with characteristics that God wants in the shepherd-leaders of his church (1 Tim 3:1–13; 4; Titus 1:6–9; etc.). God develops these characteristics fully and deeply in leaders through the process of discipleship.

Regional leaders state that discipleship happens when a more mature leader teaches someone younger in the faith. They emphasized that discipleship encompasses going deep into the word of God which should be done in a group. The focus of discipleship is knowing our Lord personally and deeply. It also focuses on helping leaders know themselves and understand their strengths and weaknesses, and it addresses and corrects behaviour that is not in line with the Bible. Discipleship is learning all that God wants to teach us and helps leaders be more rooted in their faith.

Discipleship provides the framework for developing leaders with the goal being conformity to Christ. First Timothy 4:14–16 gives us a helpful summary of this goal for leaders – *what* elements to focus on. The ministry of our Lord affirms the elements to focus on in training leaders. Using examples from our Lord, the apostle Paul, and the church in history, we see patterns for *how* to effectively develop leaders toward the goals Scripture gives us. Finally, Psalm 119 coalesces both the goal and means to lead leaders toward greater conformity to Christ and more effective shepherding and leadership in the church.

1

What We Train: Four Areas

The majority of this book focuses on *how* to effectively develop leadership programmes that produce fruitful leaders. But before doing this, we need to define *what* a fruitful leader looks like. The first area to glean from the Scriptures is the content of our training, or what areas we should focus on in developing leaders. A brief look at what Jesus and Paul focused on as they discipled leaders calls our attention to key elements of leadership development. We will use Paul's first letter to Timothy to identify four essential areas to be developed in a leader's life.

Paul's Four Training Areas

First, we will look at Paul's advice to Timothy. Timothy is a young pastor, and Paul is writing to him to teach him how to shepherd and lead the church. Both letters to Timothy include a wealth of wisdom for developing shepherd-leaders and shepherding God's flock. First Timothy 3:1–12 provides us with the characteristics that elders and deacons should have. In 1 Timothy 4, Paul gives practical pastoral advice to Timothy.

As we seek to develop a biblically based model of leadership training, we will use Paul's advice in 1 Timothy 4:11–16 to define four main areas of development that are vital to fruitful leadership in the church. These four areas provide us with categories for a model to develop shepherd-leaders. They are understanding the call to ministry (v. 14); the importance of knowledge and teaching (vv. 13, 16); the importance of the heart and character (v. 16; see also v. 12); and developing skills for ministry (v. 15).

Jesus's Training Example

Our Saviour modelled the leadership characteristics Paul describes and more, and his teaching is designed to develop these in his disciples. Jesus taught his disciples with authority (Matt 7:28–29). He focused on developing their character such as rejecting self-righteousness (Matt 6:1) and worry (6:25) and practicing humbleness (18:1–4; 20:25–28). He also gave them experiences to develop their ability to minister to people and shepherd them (Matt 17:15–20; Luke 9:1–6; 10:1–12, 17–20). Finally, Jesus helped his disciples understand their calling (Matt 28:18–20; John 15:16; 17:18; 21:15–19). Much of this development took place outside of formal teaching times. How Jesus trained his disciples is expanded in more detail in chapter 2. As we seek to follow Christ's model, our goal should be to see shepherd-leaders, "Grow in the grace and knowledge of our Lord and Savior Jesus Christ" (2 Pet 3:18).

What Regional Leaders Say about the Four Areas

The four areas from 1 Timothy 4:11–16 that we should focus on as we develop leaders are calling, teaching, character, and ministry skills. Calling is the initial step into ministry. Teaching, character, and ministry skills are the areas that called leaders need to develop. Below is a summary of how leaders in the region emphasized the importance of each of these areas.

Call

The leaders' discernment and understanding of their call from God is foundational to a proper start in ministry. Regional leaders recognize both an internal and external aspect to discerning and confirming a leadership call. One group was adamant that there must be a call, and that "God is the one who gives the call."[1] For these leaders, God's call is primary. Another group of leaders clearly stated that it is the church who confirms the call. The leaders agree that it is God who calls leaders, and he uses the church to recognize and confirm that call. Regional leaders affirm that a deep belief in their call is what helps them persevere during the hard times.

Teaching

Paul tells Timothy to, "devote yourself to the public reading of Scripture, to exhortation, and to teaching" (1 Tim 4:13), and to, "Keep a close watch on yourself and on the teaching" (v. 16). Regional leaders state that the word

---

1. Personal interviews for doctoral project, "A Contextual and Cultural Adult Education Model for Leadership Development in the Arab Middle East," 17 February 2018.

of God should be the primary subject and main focus of all teaching. Right teaching leads to right doctrine which is critical for the church. Leaders are responsible to correctly teach God's people as part of their care for them. Leaders will give an account for their teaching (Jas 3:1). If leaders do not rightly understand the word of God, they will lead others into error and spiritual harm. The church then has a critical role to determine right and wrong teaching.

True teaching isn't mainly about knowledge. One group of leaders pointed to the connection between teaching and holy living. They quoted Jesus saying, "Whoever has my commands and keeps them, he it is who loves me" (John 14:21). We can't love Christ if we don't know his commandments. Doctrinal knowledge is important to enable the leader to live a life worthy of our Saviour. This true teaching needs to be passed on to the shepherd-leader's flock so they too can grow in holiness.

Because right teaching is so important, it should be foundational in the life of leaders. Learning the Scriptures early in their faith created a hunger in the regional leaders to learn more about God's word and how to live the Christian life. Knowledge of the word provides a sure foundation when they come into contact with different teaching and helps them be able to discern right from wrong teaching. Knowledge of the word of God equips leaders to share the gospel more effectively and answer the questions of those who are investigating the Christian faith. It also gives them clarity when their old religion challenges some of the basic tenets of their new faith.

The key to growth in understanding both the doctrine and practice of the new faith of the BMB regional leaders was encountering someone to teach them either directly or as part of a study programme. Participation in formal or semi-formal study programmes helped them to systematize their knowledge. Having categories through which to understand biblical teaching helped them to better discern truth from error.

Character

Leaders that I spoke with expressed the importance of living out what we learn. The life of leaders must align with what the Bible teaches which means applying God's word to every area. Integrity is living by biblical principles and not compromising those principles. It is having faith in God and loving him and others. Character is formed through intimacy with God and manifested through leaders' relationships with others. The leaders believe that God develops godly character that is marked by truth, faith, and love and that this character is foundational for Christian leaders. One leader remarked that the integrity of leaders can be demonstrated by how they handle money and whether they serve in order to gain money. Integrity of character means doing what God's word says.

Skills for Ministry

Finally, leaders need to develop skills to be able to minister to and lead others. Ministry is about working with people. Leaders need to know how to wisely and effectively care for people, teach them, resolve conflicts, and plan. These are just a few of the many ministry skills leaders need to develop in order to effectively lead God's church. Learning these skills is not just for our personal growth but for the sake of those we serve.

Over a third of the answers regional leaders gave for how to develop ministry skills focus on training "on the job." This training consists of a leader recognizing potential leaders and challenging them with tasks to help them grow in their gifting and ability to minister. Leaders said they grew through on-the-job training or field work and by being challenged to take on more responsibility. When their leaders saw that they had been faithful in the small responsibilities given to them, they gave them more responsibility. Facing problems and challenges actually helped leaders grow in their passion to serve and ability to minister to others, develop others, and form teams. Exercising responsibility early in their faith developed their ministry skills.

Summary

Paul's advice to Timothy in 1 Timothy 4:11–16 defines four main areas of development that are vital to fruitful leadership in the church. These are the shepherd-leaders' calling, teaching, character, and skills. We see that Jesus focused on developing his disciples in these same areas. Paul points to the importance of understanding God's call to serve his church. Regional leaders affirm that clarification and assurance of a call are vital for leaders. A young leader's call should be confirmed by both internal motivation to serve and external recognition by others of their gifting. In addition to calling, Paul's instructions to Timothy give us three categories to focus on in developing leaders. Regional leaders confirm that it is critical for leaders to be developed in these three areas to be fruitful in ministry. So we will use these three categories to define what we want to include in our teaching and training.

Although these three categories are distinct, we see from leaders' comments that they are interconnected as well. Good *teaching* about God should lead to evidence of good *character* through right actions. Loving God and being motivated to serve him and others, both *character* traits, should create a desire to know more about God from his word through *teaching*. In order for leaders to develop *skills*, they need to know what to do through the *teaching* of God's word. Practicing the right thing, *skills*, also influences the *character* of our hearts to desire to serve others. Thus these three categories of training complement and confirm each other.

Helping leaders grow in their call, teaching, character, and ability to minister is the goal of our training. In the next two chapters, we will take a brief look at how leaders in the New Testament and the church trained leaders through discipleship in the context of community.

2

How We Train: Jesus, Paul, and Discipleship

In the previous chapter, we looked at the four areas in Paul's letter to Timothy that we should focus on in developing leaders: calling, teaching, character, and skills. We saw that Jesus focused on these areas with his disciples. So we too should focus on these areas in leadership development. We will now look briefly at *how* Jesus and Paul developed disciples in these areas. In the next chapter, we will examine how some leaders in church history followed their example. In later sections, we will look at the development process in detail.

Discipleship in the Midst of Life

Both Jesus and Paul developed leaders via the process of discipleship. Jesus did so primarily in the midst of the time he spent with his disciples. Paul too discipled a number of leaders in the midst of life as he travelled, preached, and planted churches.

At the end of 1 Timothy 4, Paul says that shepherd-leaders who focus on developing their doctrine, their character, and their skills become more Christ like and also cause others to become more Christ like: "Persist in this, for by so doing you will save both yourself and your hearers" (v. 16). This order is important because leaders can only lead others to the level they have reached. Before any leader disciples another person, they should first be discipled. Without discipleship, ministry and leadership are ineffective. Ministry is the natural outgrowth of discipleship. Discipleship and growth should be continuous in the life of a leader.

In order to help shepherd-leaders develop in these areas, training should happen in the midst of life. The character traits of a leader including love, forgiveness, and humility can be learned and developed, in part, by studying the Bible in a formal setting. Yet Christ-like character can't be developed only by study. It has to be lived out in our relationships with others as many of the "one another" verses in the New Testament indicate (Mark 9:50; Rom 12:10; Eph 4:32, etc.). Christ-like character must also be developed and evaluated in the midst of the pressures of life. For example, when others offend us, do we forgive or strike back? Do we love God and others more than ourselves? These behaviours can't primarily be developed in a formal setting but as the leader goes through life.

Both Jesus and Paul trained their disciples in the midst of life. They taught them as they were ministering to others. Jesus and Paul were role models who taught their disciples using real life ministry, reflecting on their ministry, and supporting the disciples as they ministered. Let's take a look first at how Jesus developed his disciples and then at how Paul did.

The Discipleship Relationships of Jesus

The preparation of leaders for the church began with Jesus. What he viewed as important and how he developed the first disciples should inform our methods. A number of good models examine the leadership practices of our Saviour. We can't look at all of them, but we will try to summarize some of the key practices identified in these models. Below we will look at how Jesus developed disciples via relationships, modelling, challenging, reflection, and support in the context of community.[1]

In the Gospel of Mark, we see that Jesus developed his disciples through relationships. Jesus chose "those whom he desired, and they came to him . . . that they might be with him" (Mark 3:13–14). Though relationships are important in any culture, the relational nature of Arab culture points to the effectiveness and necessity of developing others in the context of and through relationships.

Jesus combined informal relationship, which is more natural and organic, with more formal ways of relating with his disciples. In a way, he formalized their relationship by calling them apostles (Luke 6:13). This was not just an informal friendship, but a relationship with a purpose imbibed with a sense of importance and calling. He brought structure to their relationship through teaching times specific to them (Luke 9:18–22) and giving them ministry

---

1. I am indebted to Michael (first name only), "Mentoring in a Chinese Context," 28 October 2011, ChinaSource, for many of these principles of Jesus as mentor (Mark 3:13–15; Luke 6:12–13). The similarity of the Chinese context with the Middle East is helpful.

assignments (Luke 9:1–2). So Jesus's relationship with his disciples was organic and natural but formed the context of their calling and ministry. Training relationships need structure to help those being trained fulfil the purpose for which they are called. Thus Jesus modelled the importance of balancing relational and authoritative interactions between the trainer and trainee.

As Jesus spent time in relationship with his disciples, he modelled what he taught. For example, he both taught and showed them how to handle persecution, care for the poor, interact with sinners, handle money, and face governmental authorities as well as how religiosity differs from spirituality. Jesus's training of his disciples was life on life. We should also develop others in the context of life – family, work, trials, relationships, etc. – as much as possible.

Part of Jesus's formal relationship with his disciples included giving them specific ministry assignments. Jesus sent them out to minister, to preach, to care for the sick, and to cast out demons (Mark 6:7–13; Luke 9:1–6; 10:1–5). Growth involves practicing what we are learning, seeing our actions bear fruit, and facing challenges just like Jesus set before his disciples. They learned through doing and asking Jesus questions in the midst of their ministry assignments (Luke 9:49–50, 54–55). They also learned through their mistakes and Jesus's correction. Ministry assignments serve as tangible experience through which important teaching principles and character are learned.

When Jesus taught, corrected, and reflected with his disciples about their ministry assignments, he was supporting them. We see examples in his personal interactions with John (Mark 9:38–41) and Martha and Mary (Luke 10:38–42). When Peter did not rightly understand Jesus's call to the cross, Jesus rebuked him (Matt 16:21–23). But after Peter denied him, Jesus supported Peter by reaffirming his call (John 21:15–19). Martha was taught about faith in the midst of a challenge (John 11:17–27). Jesus addressed Thomas's doubt and affirmed his faith (John 20:26–29), supporting him in the midst of another challenge. Jesus also interacted with disciples in small groups like Peter, James, and John in various situations (Mark 9:2–8; 14:32–42).

Jesus supported his disciples by reflecting with them on life and ministry. For example, after the seventy-two returned from their ministry assignment (Luke 10:1–12), Jesus reflected with them about their experiences and offered important personal application (Luke 10:17–20). He also used questions that caused the disciples to reflect on their lives. For example, "If you love those who love you, what reward do you have? Do not even the tax collectors do the same?" (Matt 5:46). After Peter sank while walking on the water, Jesus had him reflect on the reason. "O you of little faith, why did you doubt?" Jesus asked

(Matt 14:28–31). Notice that Jesus supported Peter both by rescuing him (v. 31) and helping him learn from the event.

To summarize, Jesus taught via relationships. He formalized his relationships with the disciples he was training to lead and modelled life and ministry for them. He provided them with real-life ministry experiences. In the midst of challenges, he supported his disciples. He taught them by using reflective questions. After his resurrection, Jesus then commissioned his disciples to live out what he taught them (Matt 28:18–20). Jesus developed his disciples by addressing and engaging each man's heart, mind, and actions.

Jesus knew he would not remain on the earth to lead his church. That is why from the beginning our Lord called leaders to shepherd his church (John 21:15–17; Acts 20:28; 1 Peter 5:1–4). The New Testament makes it clear that it is the responsibility of the church to prepare leaders to shepherd her (Acts 20:28–30; 2 Tim 2:2). The pastor-teacher is called to equip the saints for the work of ministry that Christ has given each believer (Eph 4:11–12). As Paul modelled with Timothy, more knowledgeable and experienced leaders are responsible to help develop the character, teaching, and ministry skills of leaders who will then be able to help develop others. A shepherd-leader must be able to teach (1 Tim 3:2) and be one who is "rightly handling the word of truth" (2 Tim 2:15). This truth is the main tool of the trade.

Glimpses from Paul's Discipleship Relationships

We see from Paul's time with his fellow servants that he served as an example for them in both life and ministry. Paul had more than twenty co-laborers and over forty patrons of his work.[2] These co-laborers were involved with Paul in ministry to differing degrees. We find different lists of his co-laborers in his letters (Rom 16:1–5; Phil 4:2–3; Col 4:7–17) and in chapters sixteen through twenty in the book of Acts. Some are called companions (Acts 13:13), but most are called fellow workers or coworkers (Rom 16:3, 9; Col 1:7; 1 Thess 3:2; Phlm 1:1).

Paul no doubt interacted with these different co-laborers in different ways depending on their role and the amount of time they were together. We gain helpful insight into what Paul focused on and how he developed these co-laborers through his varied interactions with them. Paul reminds the overseers,

---

2. Robert Banks, *Paul's Idea of Community: The Early House Churches in Their Cultural Setting* (Peabody, MA: Hendrickson, 1994), 149–150, 163. See also Acts 15:40; 16:3; Rom 16:3, 6, 9, 12, 21; 1 Cor 3:9; 2 Cor 8:23; Phil 2:25; 4:3; Col 1:7; 1 Thess 1:2; 3:2; 2 Thess 1:1; Phlm 1, 24.

deacons, and saints in Philippi (Phil 1:1) that his interaction with them involved learning, receiving his teaching, hearing, and seeing him minister (Phil 4:9). Each of these words provides insight on *how* Paul developed these leaders. He calls them to practice what they have received from him through learning, hearing, and seeing him. The call to practice is to live (character) and do (skills) what they have learned.

We see this pattern of teaching and training repeated in Paul's second letter to Timothy (2 Tim 3:10–11). Here Paul states that Timothy has followed Paul's teaching and his "aim in life" (v. 10). Timothy has also observed Paul's faith in action through patience, love, steadfastness, persecution, and suffering (vv. 10–11). These varied means of interaction show that Paul clearly developed Timothy in the midst of life and ministry. He taught him but also demonstrated godly character in specific places like Antioch, Iconium, and Lystra (v. 11). Second Timothy 2:2 serves as a summary of Paul's methods where Paul reminds Timothy that just as Paul taught him along with others, Timothy should do the same. Paul modelled for Timothy how to train leaders. Paul trained Timothy in community, "in the presence of many witnesses" (2 Tim 2:2). Paul describes his relationship with Timothy as a father and son relationship (Phil 2:22).

Paul's practice of developing leaders in the midst of life and ministry consisted of modelling ministry for them, which is seen in his call to imitate him (1 Cor 4:15–17; 11:1; Phil 3:17; 4:9; 2 Thess 3:7–9). When he wrote his letters, Paul wasn't only offering teaching; he also offered his life as an example. His co-laborers were to learn from what he did and to teach through both instruction and modelling as he did.

Paul calls on Timothy to "continue in what you have learned" (2 Tim 3:14) and saw in him. For example, during Paul's three years with the church in Ephesus (Acts 20:31), he lived among the believers "the whole time" (20:18). He taught them "the whole counsel of God" (20:27). He instructed them everything that was "profitable" (20:20) and admonished them (20:31). But he also showed them his life (20:35) and a model to imitate. This passage provides a glimpse into how Paul ministered to, taught, and developed those in the Ephesian church.

Paul also developed leaders by taking them with him in ministry. Although it is hard to track all the comings and goings of his co-laborers, we see that they accompanied him as he ministered. Acts 20:4–6 tells us that Sopater along with at least six others accompanied Paul during his ministry in Macedonia. In 15:40, Paul chose Silas to be with him as he travelled "strengthening the churches" (15:41). Silas was also with Paul in prison (16:25–30). After the Jerusalem council (15:1–22), Paul took Timothy with him to deliver the apostles' decision to the churches, ministering to them as they went (16:1–5). Silas and Timothy were with Paul as he ministered in Berea (17:10–14). After leaving for Athens, Paul wanted them to join him as soon as possible (17:15), and they caught up with him in the ministry in Corinth (18:5). Paul always seemed to have one or more disciple with him as he ministered.

When Paul came to Corinth, he found Aquila who was a tentmaker like himself (Acts 18:1–4). While there, Paul "reasoned in the synagogue every Sabbath" (v. 4). Paul spent eighteen months there "teaching the word of God" (18:11). Acts 18 doesn't specifically mention that Aquila and his wife, Priscilla, were involved with Paul in ministry. Yet verse 18 says they went with him when he travelled to Antioch, so it seems they had become involved in ministry. By accompanying Paul, he could further develop them. This must have happened because in Romans 16:3–5, Paul greets his fellow workers Aquila and Priscilla who had a church in their house. It seems that Aquila progressed from being a fellow tentmaker to a disciple of Paul's ministry to finally leading a church along with Priscilla.

Paul had a myriad of disciples that joined him as he taught, evangelized, suffered and lived life. Above are just some examples of the different ways Paul called alongside and ministered with a diverse group of disciples.

Not only did Paul take disciples with him; he also sent them out to minister. Priscilla and Aquila discipled Apollos after Paul left for ministry in Galatia (Acts 18:26). We then see Apollos ministering in Corinth while Paul travels to Ephesus (19:1). Paul sent Tychicus to the church in Ephesus to minister there (2 Tim 4:12). Ephesians 6:21 tells us that Tychicus was a "faithful minister in the Lord." Paul was ministering with Titus in Crete, and then Paul left him there to "appoint elders in the churches" (Titus 1:5). Appointing elders is a big responsibility that Paul felt Titus was ready for. Epaphras was a faithful minister of the gospel in the church in Colossae (Col 1:7). Paul calls Epaphras a fellow worker who also ministered faithfully in Laodicea and Hierapolis (Col 4:12–13).

Paul's relationship with and development of Timothy gives us the clearest picture of Paul's method of developing ministers of the gospel. Paul developed his beloved son Timothy by modeling ministry while Timothy was with him. Paul also commissioned Timothy to minister to different churches in the region. Paul sent Epaphroditus to the church in Philippi (Phil 2:25) and was hoping to send Timothy as well (Phil 2:19–23). Paul sent Timothy to the church in Corinth to teach them (1 Cor 4:17). We see in Acts 19:22 that Paul sends Timothy and Erastus to Macedonia while Paul remains in Asia. Another time,

Paul remained in Athens while he sent Timothy to the Thessalonian church to exhort and encourage them (1 Thess 3:1–3).

Whether with him or separated, Paul developed Timothy with the heart of a father. Timothy was his beloved son (1 Cor 4:17) and his "true child in the faith" (1 Tim 1:2). Paul not only taught Timothy. He modelled faithfulness and how to endure suffering in front of him. Paul took Timothy with him as he traveled and ministered. He then sent Timothy to a number of different churches to do the same. Finally, Paul supported Timothy with practical ministry advice on difficult issues as Timothy pastored the Ephesian church (1 Tim 1:3–7). We find more detailed illustrations of Paul's advice in his two letters to Timothy. We can conclude that Paul's interaction with Timothy is representative of the quality of Paul's interaction with his many co-laborers, although certainly not to the same degree with each person. Paul developed leaders in the midst of life while doing ministry.

What Regional Leaders Say about Mentoring

Leaders I spoke with clearly communicated that ministry is about people. God uses leaders to help us develop so that we will be able to minister to others. Discipleship happens in the context of the church and in the midst of living with and serving others. The discipleship and training relationships of these regional leaders mirror the priorities of teaching, modelling, providing ministry challenges, reflecting on experiences, and supporting that we see in the leadership training methods of Jesus and Paul.

The discipleship model assumes that a more mature leader will disciple a younger leader. The discipler, perhaps better called a mentor, helps the growing leader learn how to live out their biblical faith with others. The role of the mentor is a salient theme in many of the leaders' comments. Mentors are key in helping shepherd-leaders make sense of events in their lives and guiding them in applying what they have been taught in real-life ministry situations.

Because ministry is about people, the church is an incubator for leadership development. Regional leaders recognize that growth and development come through interaction with others. These others include believers and unbelievers, those who treat us well and those who don't. As young leaders come in contact with others, they feel the need to learn. When they experience conflict, their mentors should ask them to relate Scripture to the situation. When young leaders see needs, mentors should ask them how they can draw on Scripture to provide biblical help and counselling to the struggling brother or sister.

Having a good mentor was identified by the regional leaders as crucial to making ministry experiences useful for growth. But equally important are mentors who not only teach but also model how to live out God's word. Mentors should be a living testimony to what a life of godliness looks like. The lives that mentors live in front of young leaders challenge the values and thinking of these developing leaders. They also challenge and encourage developing leaders to aspire to something greater than they currently are.

Summary

We see from the practices of Jesus and Paul that preparing leaders to care for God's church should take place in the context of community because community enables building close mentoring relationship. Training should also take place in the midst of life and ministry with the mentor serving as the model for both. Life is the place where ministry challenges happened, and we saw how Jesus and Paul took time to reflect on ministry challenges as they happened. We also saw how Jesus and Paul supported their disciples by encouraging them and spurring them on in growth and development. Jesus and Paul provide us with tangible examples of how to develop the qualities that Scripture requires for leaders in the church. This is *how* we develop leaders.

A shepherd-leader's calling, character, skills, and teaching are *what* we focus on in developing leaders. These elements should be developed and tested in the midst of life and in the context of community. Only here can we put into practice what we are learning so that it is not simply informational. It is in the midst of the church that we discover if we are really living out the words of our Saviour. It is through relationships, observing and imitating role-models, practice, reflection, and support that we grow in Christ-like character. It is as we practice ministry that we develop our ability to minister and serve others in fruitful ways, and that our calling is affirmed. Godly mentors serving as role models who also support us and reflect with us are critical to our fruitful growth as shepherd-leaders.

In the next chapter, we will see how the four leadership training areas of calling, teaching, character, and skills were developed after the New Testament era in the early church and beyond. We will also see the role community played in developing leaders in the church as she grew throughout her history.

3

Leader Development in Church History

As we walk through this book, we have the blessing of being able to learn from the wisdom and experience of leaders in the region. We have seen, and will see, what they say about leadership development and how God develops them and guides them as they develop other leaders.

We now have the opportunity to learn from our "older" brothers in the faith, those from church history who experienced God's blessing as they taught, trained, and modelled godly leadership. Looking at the historical church provides us with real-life, practical models of how to develop leaders. The historical church also offers us some helpful direction on how to apply these models. Some of the leaders we will look at including Clement and Origen of Alexandria, Egypt, and Augustine of Hippo, Algeria developed leaders in the North Africa church.

As the post-apostolic church began to prepare new leaders, they focused on personal conversion, character, and right teaching. In regards to right teaching, the *Didache*, a collection of teaching from around AD 70 says, "Welcome whoever comes and teaches all the aforementioned things to you; but if a teacher himself turns aside and teaches another didache (teaching) which undermines the aforesaid teachings, do not listen to him."[1] Those who would lead God's church must also exhibit Christ-like character. "Appoint for yourselves bishops and deacons worthy of the Lord, men who are unassuming and not greedy . . . true and approved."[2] This passage seems to indicate some

---

1. *Didache* 11:1–2. Quoted in J. B. Lightfoot, *The Apostolic Fathers* (Grand Rapids, MI: Baker, 1991), 155.

2. *Didache* 15:1. Quoted in Lightfoot, *Apostolic Fathers*, 157.

way to test or approve these leaders, yet whether there was a formal system to develop leaders is not clear.

"In summary, the earliest equipment for Christian leadership – over and above the basic conversion experience and knowledge common to all – was charismatic gifting, practical experience at lower levels of responsibility, and the personal guidance and instruction of men of God who were either in the front lines of Christian service, such as bishops, or were specially set apart for the task of giving instruction in leadership."[3] The areas of leadership development we have looked at are found throughout this passage. "Charismatic gifting" points to calling. "Practical experience" highlights the importance of experiencing challenges to develop ministry skills. "Personal guidance" by others points us to the role of mentors in the process. No doubt this guidance included the leader's personal character. We see as well their role in instruction or teaching. From its earliest stages, the church put into practice directives and guidance from the Scriptures.

Clement of Alexandria

The Catechetical school of Alexandria in Egypt was a place of scholarship committed to teaching the sciences and the philosophy of the day along with the biblical principles.[4] Despite this academic emphasis, the school provided practical training in godliness. Clement, one of the early leaders of the school and a brilliant theologian, recognized the practical aspect of instruction.

> The Instructor being practical, not theoretical, His aim is thus to improve the soul, not to teach, and to train it up to a virtuous, not to an intellectual life. Although this same word is didactic, but not in the present instance. For the word which, in matters of doctrine, explains and reveals, is that whose province it is to teach. But our Educators being practical, first exhorts to the attainment of right dispositions and character, and then persuades us to the energetic practice of our duties.[5]

---

3. Harold Rowdon, "Theological Education in Historical Perspective," *Vox Evangelica* 7 (1971): 76.

4. Some say the school was started by the apostle Mark in the first century. Others say it was started in the second century. What we know for sure is that it was the earliest and largest school of Christian learning in the early church. See Thomas Oden, *How Africa Shaped the Christian Mind* (Downers Grove, IL: InterVarsity, 2007) and Michael Kruger, *Christianity at the Crossroads* (London: SPCK, 2017).

5. Clement of Alexandria, *Paedagogus*, 1.1.

According to Oliver, "The early church could not offer a better example of an intellectual Christian than Clement. He insisted that the goal of Christian education is 'practical, not theoretical and its aim is to improve the soul, not to teach, and to train it up to a virtuous, not an intellectual, life' (*Paed.* 1.1.1.4–1.1.2.1)."[6] Oliver goes on, "Clement maintained a threefold process for acquiring knowledge: study (leads to) knowledge (leads to) action. He reserved Biblical interpretation for the Christian intellectual, purely out of concern for misunderstanding."[7] Clement combined the cognitive with the practical. In his mind they no doubt reinforced each other.

Origen of Alexandria

Origen, who succeeded Clement, communicated to his students not only scholarship, but also godly character. "In the case of Origen, at least, it is clear that the force of his Christian character, the strength of his devotion to Christ, and the rigours of his personal standards of behaviour formed an important part of the training."[8] To quote Rowdon again, "Origen transformed his disciples still more by his personal influence than by his scholarship. He was not a lecturer who merely appeared from time to time before an audience; he was a master and tutor who lived constantly with his disciples."[9] Origen modelled biblically effective teaching and training. He sought to facilitate or lead his students in learning, not just to provide information. According to Oliver,

> Origen did not want to add knowledge to his students, but to "teach them to answer by themselves the questions that arose in the process of learning one or another discipline" (Behr, Louth & Conomos 2003:53). He was highly student oriented and he aimed to preserve unity amongst his classes, based on mutual respect and friendship. He therefore knew his students well. He saw the most important task as teaching the love of God (Barrett 2011:42). Origen rather wanted to be a lifelong mentor than to be a teacher (cf. Green 2004:112). The way in which he conducted

---

6. Willem Oliver, "The Heads of the Catechetical School in Alexandria," *Verbum Eccles* 36, no. 1 (2015): 6.

7. Oliver, "Heads of the Catechetical School," 6.

8. Rowdon, "Theological Education," 76.

9. Rowdon, 76.

his personal spiritual life was a good example to his students and it attracted them.[10]

The Alexandria Catechetical school, although academic in nature, was focused on the development of practical ministry skills and godly behaviour. How was this achieved? Clearly it happened through teaching and instruction. But the practice of personal interaction, at least by Origen, served as great a teaching tool as the lecture hall. Origen, who learned from Clement, lived with his disciples and while doing so, served as an instructor, a model, and a support.

Augustine of Hippo

In the fourth and fifth centuries, Augustine's leadership in the church and monastery-type living were greenhouses for leadership development.

> During Augustine's tenure as bishop, the number of clergy in North Africa was large and the clerical offices were well developed. At the council of Carthage in 411, the catholic bishops alone numbered 268. Most towns had their own bishop, and some like Hippo, even had presbyters and deacons serving in the church. According to Victor de Vita, there were around five hundred clergy in Carthage at the time of the Vandal conquest in 439.[11]

Augustine's development of such a significant number of leaders included personal involvement with his disciples in day to day living. He not only taught them but interacted with them on practical life issues. "This intimate personal association of the bishop with his clergy provided a source of inspiration and direction to untried clergy. The epitome of such training is to be found in the group of clergy which Augustine of Hippo gathered around him in the early fifth century."[12] Augustine's commitment to carrying out the teaching of God's word and holy living in the midst of community was one of the secrets of his success. Augustine developed leaders through teaching, personal mentoring, modelling, and sending out disciples to serve in the church.[13]

Augustine's mentoring included a "daily Scripture reading programme as well as the opportunities for the men to hear Augustine preach and teach" and

---

10. Oliver, "Heads of the Catechetical School," 8.

11. Edward Smither, *Augustine as Mentor: A Model for Preparing Spiritual Leaders* (Nashville, TN: B & H Academic, 2009), 125.

12. Rowdon, "Theological Education," 75.

13. Smither, *Augustine.*

"how to interpret the Scriptures and teach them to others."[14] Finally, he sent them out to churches to serve. Possidius wrote that "they prepared brothers for the priesthood and then advanced them to other churches."[15] Again we see the combination of teaching, modelling, and practical experience in the development of shepherd-leaders.

Medieval Universities and the Reformation

In the Dark and Middle Ages, the preparation of shepherd-leaders began to be separated from the church and church leaders. The movement away from the church began with a rise of persecution that pushed the training of ministers to monasteries. "The Church of these 'Dark Ages' found itself faced with two enormous tasks: In such circumstances, it is hardly surprising that Christian instruction and training found refuge in the seclusion and relative safety of the monasteries."[16]

The rise of the medieval universities as centres of learning accentuated the separation of preparation of church leaders from the church and its leaders. This was a movement away from the model described in 2 Timothy 2:2. The medieval university aimed to produce mastery of the whole field of learning, with theology considered to be the Queen of the Sciences. Unfortunately, since the whole course might extend for up to seventeen years and included not only disputation but also lecturing, this training became less and less related to the work of the ministry and more and more the route to a life of academic scholarship.[17]

The university would maintain its importance in ministerial preparation for centuries. But the dawning of the Reformation age saw a reuniting of both the academic and practical aspects of training and a renewed connection between the academy and the church in preparation of shepherd-leaders. The best example of this reuniting was John Calvin's Academy in Geneva. "The Academy was integrated with, and under the authority of, the church of Geneva, which would bring the students under the Word, sacraments and discipline."[18] The involvement of pastors with students was a crucial

---

14. Smither, *Augustine*, 151.

15. Possidius, quoted in Smither, *Augustine*, 255.

16. Rowdon, "Theological Education," 77.

17. Rowdon, 77.

18. Thomas Hawkes, *Pious Pastors: Calvin's Theology of Sanctification and the Genevan Academy* (Milton Keynes, UK: Paternoster, 2016), 231.

ingredient in the preparation of pastors. "The students were closely mentored and supervised by the Company of Pastors, who worked to produce not only skilled but godly pastors. . . . The professors of the Academy served as models of holiness."[19]

This connection between the church and the academy allowed for on the job training. "The idea that much can be learned during the course of a curacy maintained the emphasis on 'learning on the job' which is as old as the Church."[20] The return to involvement of the church and the academy in leadership training flowed outward to countries impacted by the Reformation. In England, J. B. Lightfoot, known for his excellent scholarship, modelled his teaching for his students through interaction with them. "During the nineteenth century, several diocesan colleges were established. . . . Bishop Lightfoot, for example, gathered graduate ordinands around him at Durham."[21] Academics was accompanied by personal interaction between the ordinands and clergy.

John Wesley

Another successful example of training servants in both knowledge and skill is John Wesley's training of preachers. "At least 802 lay and ordained leaders served under John Wesley's oversight from the early days of the movement in 1743 until his death in 1791. There were 541 active leaders under Wesley's direction at the time of his passing."[22] They were men trained on the job. But Wesley was keenly aware of their need for "mental stimulation and practical guidance."[23] According to Rowdon, "Wesley insisted that his preachers should combine dedicated study with dedicated itinerant preaching."[24] Wesley's success in developing leaders included development in holiness, theology, and ministry skills.[25]

As Christianity grew in the United States, different denominations were formed. Each denomination wanted a college that would teach their distinctive theology. "From the seventeenth century well into the nineteenth, Protestant

---

19. Hawkes, *Pious Pastors*, 231.

20. Rowdon, "Theological Education," 83.

21. Rowdon, 83.

22. Mark Gorveatte, *Lead Like John Wesley: Help for Today's Ministry Servants* (Indianapolis, IN: Wesleyan, 2016), 14.

23. Rowdon, "Theological Education," 85.

24. Rowdon, 85.

25. Jordan Vale, "The Healthy Pastor: A Holistic Approach to Pastoral Training," (MReligion diss., Reformed Theological Seminary, 2014).

denominations founded most of the colleges in North America; and in the early nineteenth century, these denominations . . . began to establish separate theological schools for the training of ministers."[26] With the move toward universities, and thus the movement away from connection to the local church as the major training ground for pastoral ministry, the focus became more and more on academic knowledge. This has significantly shaped how the Western church looks at developing shepherd-leaders and is the model that the West has largely exported to the growing church around the world. Remnants of this model are what we seek to address in the remainder of our study.

Summary

This brief overview of history provides some examples of the role the church plays in developing leaders. In the early life of the church, training shepherd-leaders included practical, personal, and intellectual aspects offered in the context of relationships. Later, the centrality of the church was marginalized in pastoral preparation as a more academic-oriented approach was adopted. Most modern seminaries are the legacy of this process.

Maintaining the seminary as the centre of the leadership development process won't allow us to develop the shepherd-leaders needed. Timothy Webber summarizes what many in theological education are coming to realize. "The result [of seminary education] may be better sermon preparation and delivery, yet those trained outside the seminary were found to be leading churches that were 'vital, alive, growing and clear about purpose, mission and organization.'"[27] This does not mean that seminaries have no role in preparing leaders. It does point to the fact that where seminary education happens in isolation from the church, the preparation of shepherd-leaders is often stunted and incomplete.

How can the training of leaders reflect the best practices of our Saviour, the early church, and the church throughout history? How can the seminary "be a place where serious theological study occurs, in the best tradition of Christian scholarship"?[28] It happens when the seminary's mission is to "serve

---

26. Timothy Weber, "The Seminaries and the Churches: Looking for New Relationships," *Theological Education* 44, no. 1 (2008): 66.

27. Weber, "Seminaries," 81. See also Carl Dudley and David Roozen, *Faith Communities Today: A Report on Religion in the United States Today* (Hartford, CT: Hartford Institute for Religion Research, Hartford Seminary, 2001).

28. Cornelius Venema, "Mid-American Reformed Seminary: An Academy with a Vocational Aim," *Mid-American Journal of Theology* 13 (2002): 14.

the churches by preparing her students for the ministry."[29] The seminary's role in training shepherd-leaders should be within the context of the body-life of the church. This is the type of training we find modelled by Christ and Paul, the early church, in Alexandria, and by Augustine, Calvin, Wesley, and others. This is a framework that includes scholarship, practice, character formation, and a direct connection between learning and practice in the context of the church.

We saw in 1 Timothy 4:11–16 four essential areas to focus on in developing shepherd-leaders. We have also seen how Jesus and Paul developed their leaders. These examples of what we train leaders and how we train leaders are affirmed by the practices and experience of regional leaders. In the next chapter, we will look at how Psalm 119 combines both what and how we teach and train leaders in God's word.

---

29. Venema, "Mid-American Reformed Seminary," 14.

4

Biblical Teaching for Transformation: Psalm 119

Whole-Hearted Interaction with and Response to God's Word

We saw in the previous section that our goal as believers is to "grow in the grace and knowledge of our Lord and Saviour Jesus Christ" (2 Pet 3:18) so that we are more and more conformed to the image of Christ (Rom 8:29). The Scriptures tell us what this looks like. In 1 Timothy 4:11–16, Paul draws our focus to four specific areas that are critical to the success of shepherd-leaders. As we look at a transformational model for development and deep learning in the lives of shepherd-leaders, we see that transformation must take place at the level of the heart. As we will see, the biblical definition of the heart includes the mind, the affections, and the will.

This chapter serves to connect the biblical roots of developing and providing effective training with the practical steps we will define to accomplish our purpose. Our focus on Psalm 119 echoes the importance of the mind, heart, and action in Paul's instruction to Timothy. It is a clear reminder of the goals of our leadership training or what we are trying to achieve.

At the same time, Psalm 119 informs how we should approach the development process. Its varied and recurrent pictures of interaction with God's word call us to examine the content and methods of our training. The psalmist describes interaction with God's word that involves the mind, heart, and actions. He reminds us that our teaching and training should be a full-orbed approach that addresses the entire learner. The method of the psalmist should be our method – teaching the word of God by addressing the mind, heart, and actions (method/how) to produce transformation of the mind, heart, and actions of the learner (purpose/what).

The Biblical Heart

Jesus emphasized the primacy of the heart in the Christian life. In Matthew 12:34–35, Jesus states, "For out of the abundance of the heart the mouth speaks. The good person out of his good treasure brings forth good, and the evil person out of his evil treasure brings forth evil." Our desires, our thoughts, and our actions all flow from our heart.

The father in Proverbs 4:20–23 tells his son to "be attentive to my words" (v. 20) and to "keep them within your heart" (v. 21). Then he tells his son in verse 23 to, "Keep your heart with all vigilance, for from it flow the springs of life." It is the heart that is the target of teaching and training because our thoughts, our emotions, and our actions flow from the heart.

If we want to see leaders who think like Jesus and love like Jesus and live like Jesus, our teaching and training must focus on the transformation of the heart. So we will look at Psalm 119 as a scriptural foundation for both the goal and the means of teaching and training that produces deep or transformational learning. The psalm serves as a clear model of biblical learning. It also keeps our principles and practices rooted in the Scriptures as we prepare to look at educational principles.

Psalm 119: A Model of Instruction

Psalm 119 is referred to as a Torah psalm.[1] Along with Psalms 1 and 19, Psalm 119 provides a number of different references to God's word.[2] This multifaceted expression of God's word or Torah in Psalm 119 sets God's word as the goal of one's learning.

These varied facets of God's word provide varied benefits or blessings to the psalmist. God's word is life (Ps 119:40), comfort (v. 50), riches (v. 14), wisdom (v. 98), and understanding (v. 104). It keeps the psalmist from shame (v. 6) and sin (v. 11), brings blessings (v. 45), and makes him sing (v. 54). The multifaceted terminology expressed by the fullness of God's revelation expresses the richness of God's salvation. This includes the total transformation of the

1. James Luther Mays, "The Place of the Torah-Psalms in the Psalter," *Journal of Biblical Literature* 106, no. 1 (1987): 3–12.

2. God's word in Hebrew is called law (*tôrâh*), promise (*'imrah*), rulings (*mishpâṭ*), statutes (*chôq*), testimonies (*'êdâh, 'êdûth*), commandments (*mits-vaw'*), precepts (*piqqûd*), word (*dâbâr*), and way (*derek*). Francis Brown, S. R. Driver, and Charles A. Briggs, *Hebrew and English Lexicon, Unabridged*, Electronic Database, Biblesoft, Inc., 2006; Benjamin Sargent, "The Dead Letter? Psalm 119 and the Spirituality of the Bible in the Local Church," *Evangelical Quarterly* 81, no. 2 (2009): 104. Taken together, this cluster of nouns comprises the fullness of what is meant by the word of God.

believer. God's word is to be interacted with and imbibed by our entire person that is made up of intellect, emotion, and will. It is when the totality of our person interacts with God's word that true transformation of the totality of our person takes place. This is real change. Psalm 119 is a practical how-to guide for a full-orbed interaction with God's word to teach and train shepherd-leaders. It instructs us how to interact with, understand, and apply God's word. This interaction with God's word is personal.[3]

I am using Psalm 119 as a model for instruction for the following reasons:

1. Scripture as Foundation – First and importantly, Psalm 119 anchors us in Scripture as we develop principles and seek to delineate a practical how-to for training and developing shepherd-leaders. My experience working with regional leaders is that they are biblically focused and committed to principles and practices based on the Scriptures.

2. Biblical and Educational Categories – The three dimensions of the heart in Psalm 119 correspond with our three training areas in 1 Timothy 4:11–16. As we will see, they also align with effective educational principles, for example Bloom's three dimensions of learning.[4]

3. The Context of Psalm 119 – The psalm's context of persecution and trials fits with the context of the leaders we seek to develop.

4. Full-Hearted Interaction with God's Word – The psalm highlights the critical priority of the heart that both interacts with and is transformed by God's word. It highlights the areas of our heart that are to be transformed in teaching and training. The psalm also shows a full-hearted way to interact with God's word in order to produce heart transformation. This must be the goal of training. Understanding this paradigm is important.

5. Biblical Truth is Personal to the Believer – Understanding how the reader was intended to interact with the psalm provides Western teachers with insight into how Arabs interact with truth. In contrast

---

3. "However the psalmist's primary treatment of the sacred text is fundamentally existential, continuously viewed, from the perspective of the individual who stands in dynamic relation to the text." Sargent, "Dead Letter," 106.

4. B. Bloom, M. Englehart, E. Furst, W. Hill, and D. Krathwohl, *Taxonomy of Educational Objectives: The Classification of Educational Goals. Handbook I: Cognitive Domain* (New York: Longmans, 1956).

to the Western "objective," abstract, and theoretical approach to truth, Arabs view truth as part of a person or connected to the person who imparts the truth. Truth is more personal in the Arab world, and this is the perspective of the psalm.

The Context of Psalm 119

The context of Psalm 119 is similar to that of the shepherd-leaders serving in the Arab region. Psalm 119 reveals God's word as the support, comfort, joy, and sweetness of life. The psalmist is in need of all of these and more because he lives in the midst of persecution and affliction. "The statements concerning persecution and oppression (vv. 61, 78, 84, 110, etc.) are to be taken quite seriously. . . . It is only if we understand them as being at the root of the poet's utterances that we can apprehend the strength and the comfort which God's word and his law impart to the life of the poet."[5]

> The poet is a young man, who finds himself in a situation which is clearly described: he is derided, oppressed, persecuted, and that by those who despise the divine word (for apostasy encompasses him round about), and more particularly by a government hostile to the true religion (Psalm 119:23, Psalm 119:46, Psalm 119:161). He is lying in bonds (Psalm 119:61, cf. Psalm 119:83), expecting death (Psalm 119:109). . . . and in the midst of it God's word is his comfort and his wisdom, but he also yearns for help, and earnestly prays for it. The whole Psalm is a prayer for steadfastness in the midst of an ungodly, degenerate race, and in the midst of great trouble.[6]

Support by and reflection on the Torah help the young man learn from his trials and challenges. The result is not just keeping God's word, but such delight that, "The word proceeding from the mouth of God is now more precious to him than the greatest earthly riches."[7] Joy in this certain, all-encompassing word has upheld the poet in his affliction (Ps 119:92). "He who has been persecuted and cast down as it were to death, owes his reviving to it (Ps 119:93). This is

---

5. Artur Weiser, *The Psalms: A Commentary*, The Old Testament Library (Louisville, KY: Westminster John Knox, 1962), 740.

6. C. F. Keil and Franz Delitzsch, *Commentary on the Old Testament* (Grand Rapids, MI: Eerdmans, 1971), 243–44.

7. Keil and Delitzsch, *Commentary*, Psalm 119, StudyLight.org.

past experience."[8] The law being his delight is what upholds him and supports him in the midst of his affliction. The outcome is that he never forgets (deep learning) God's precepts, for they have been his delight and have given him life.

This psalm speaks deeply to the context of shepherd-leaders in the Arab world. Psalm 119 describes the importance and priority of the word in directing, motivating, comforting, and teaching God's people. It speaks to these priorities in the midst of persecution, hardship, and danger, the context of shepherd-leaders in the region. The vocabulary of how to interact with God's word to be able to stand, learn, and be strengthened by God's word is instructive. Psalm 119 provides a model of how God's word transforms the thinking, affections, and actions of his servants in the midst of persecution.

Full-Hearted Interaction with God's Word

The Spirit of God uses the word of God to transform us. As we expose a leader to God's word, we seek to see transformation of the entire person. The Scriptures are directed to the entire person – the heart – and it calls on the entire person to interact with it in order to be changed. This means that the mind, the will, and the emotions should be engaged in interacting with God's word so that they will be transformed through this interaction. Psalm 119 provides a model of both the means and the effects of engaging with God's word.

When we interact with God's word with the whole of our being, we experience multiple blessings including but not limited to support, comfort, and strength in the midst of the most strenuous circumstances. The fire of trials of life create the hunger for Christ and develop Christ-likeness, both of which are the goals of our instruction and training.

Psalm 119 is a lengthy and multi-faceted treatise on the efficacy of God's word for life. But its format is designed to help the hearer memorize what the psalm teaches.[9] Each section begins with a successive letter of the Hebrew alphabet which helps the reader memorize God's word. The format also provides direction for how believers are to interact in ways that increasingly incorporates it into their lives. Further, Psalm 119 repeats the prevalent biblical call to meditate on God's word (Josh 1:8; Ps 119:15, 23; etc.). Psalm 119 calls for interaction with God's word that includes the mind, the heart, and the will because this tri-partite interaction produces transformation of the heart.

---

8. Keil and Delitzsch, *Commentary*, Psalm 119, StudyLight.org.
9. Charles Spurgeon, *The Treasury of David* (Pasadena, TX: Pilgrim, 1983), 356.

The Mind

The Old Testament ties the mind or intellect to the heart. It is the heart that most often is aligned with what we would think of as intellectual activities. For example, Proverbs 23:12 tells readers to, "Apply your heart to instruction." In Jeremiah we read that one promise of the new covenant is "a heart to know that I am the LORD" (Jer 24:7). There is a cognitive aspect of the heart whereby we know or understand a proposition.

Part of the biblical definition of transformation is for the mind to learn. Psalm 119 encourages the reader to imitate the psalmist in learning and understanding God's word. Verse 7 says the psalmist's goal is to "learn your righteous rules." In verses 26, 124, and 171, he asks God to "teach me your statutes." In verse 11 he says, "I have stored up your word in my heart." Verse 144 illustrates the importance of learning God's word: "Your testimonies are righteous forever; give me understanding *that I may live*." A further illustration of the importance of learning is that the words for being taught (*lāmad*) and understanding (*bîn*) are used in 25 of the psalm's 176 verses.[10]

There is no doubt that the teaching process is critical to the transformation process. The psalmist recognizes the agency of God and appeals to him to instruct him (Ps 119:125, 135). It is God who teaches us (John 14:26; 16:13). He shines the light of knowledge into our heart (2 Cor 4:6). He writes his law on our hearts (Jer 31:33). God takes the information of his word and begins to apply it to transform our hearts which produces ever deeper understanding.

This understanding is not detached knowledge of information or a merely intellectual grasp of the content of God's word. For the Hebrew mind, the activity of understanding consists of "directing the soul toward something which it can receive into itself."[11] Truth isn't something external to the person; it is something personal to be imbibed. This is also the Middle Eastern view of truth.[12] When the word of God, or any truth, is presented to us, we only understand it when we internalize it. The agency might be the cognitive activities of instruction by another or memorization which is expressed in Psalm 119 as not forgetting. Whatever the means, externally received truth needs to be imbibed into the heart. The Holy Spirit is the Teacher, and Scripture

---

10. Ps 119:12, 18, 26, 29, 31, 33, 34, 64, 66, 68, 73 (twice), 95, 98, 99, 100, 104, 108, 117, 124, 125, 128, 135, 144 and 171. Psalm 119 also affirms the importance of memorization for heart transformation.

11. Johannes Pedersen, *Israel, Its Life and Culture, I–IV* (London: Oxford University Press, 1964), 109.

12. Geert Hofstede, *Cultures and Organizations: Software of the Mind* (New York: McGraw Hill, 2010), 51.

calls us to take the necessary steps to learn and to transfer the truth he teaches us into our hearts.

An important link between instruction and transformation is the activity of meditation (Ps 119:15, 23, 27, 48, 78, 97, 99, 148). The meaning is to meditate, muse, or consider.[13] This musing or reflecting on God's word can be done individually or with another person. A teacher or mentor can help us reflect deeply on what we have learned. Reflection and meditation are more steps that move learning from detached truth to transformational reality, in keeping with the Hebrew understanding of learning.

Meditation is the process of God's word becoming part of our being. It is not something external but occupies our thoughts, our time, and our attention. An example is found in Psalm 119:15 where the psalmist says, "I will meditate on your precepts and fix my eyes on your ways." The psalmist becomes occupied with God's word and God's ways. Even in the midst of opposition, he meditates on God's statutes (v. 23) instead of focusing on the opposition. In verse 78, meditation on God's precepts is the psalmist's response when people have "wronged me with falsehood." In fact, meditation on God's law consumes him the entire day (v. 97). The psalmist is so occupied by God's promises that he even loses sleep so that he can meditate on them (v. 148). Meditation is a key step in truly understanding God's word and is part of the process of deep learning.

Finally meditating on God's word, or the truth to be taught, so that it begins to take centre stage in our thinking is crucial in the transformative process. We need to teach for this kind of understanding, which is what the psalmist seeks. In our teaching, we need to encourage shepherd-leaders to consider, cling go, regard, observe, and keep God's word always before them because doing so leads to understanding, open eyes, and wisdom. These are cognitive results of instruction.

The Emotions

Psalm 119 also addresses the emotions, mainly love (ʾā·haḇ) and (my) delight (ša·ʿă·šu·ʿāy). "Firstly, the text of scripture is primarily an object of desire and love."[14] The psalmist gives us the example of delighting in God's law (vv. 16, 70, 77); inclining our heart to God's testimonies (v. 36); loving his commandments (v. 48); longing for him to fulfil his promise (v. 82); and rejoicing in God's word

---

13. Sargent, "Dead Letter."
14. Sargent, "Dead Letter," 107.

(v. 162). The psalmist's emotional response to God's word shows how deep the penetration of God's word can be into an individual's heart. Love and delight in God's word serve to drive it deeply into our heart so that it becomes hidden or stored there (v. 11). This penetration is a great contrast to surface learning or merely an external assent to God's word.

The psalmist expresses even more emotions using word pictures. He has tasted God's word and found it to be "sweeter than honey" (Ps 119:103). He treasures God's word more than "thousands of gold and silver pieces" (v. 72). The psalmist longs for God's word (v. 40), even opens his mouth and pants for it like a thirsty deer (v. 131), to the point that his soul is consumed with longing (v. 20). His response to testimonies about God in his word is so great that the psalmist calls them "the joy of my heart" (v. 111).

The depth of penetration of God's word into the psalmist's heart produces physical actions to express it. For example, love for God's word causes him to lift up his hands (v. 48). Love motivates the psalmist to seek after God in his word "with my whole heart" (v. 10), to seek after, literally to beat a path to God's word (v. 94) and to cling or hold fast to it (v. 31). It is not enough simply to memorize or to know God's word. An important part of the transformation process is for our emotions to be changed to desire and delight in God's word and his ways.

Our teaching should create a love and desire for God and his truth. It should penetrate the heart and impact the emotions of the learner. The proper teaching of God's word should create a visceral response so that students love and long for more of what is taught. We want them to consider what they learn to be sweet, even if it is a hard truth. Ultimately, we want students to value what is taught more than earthly treasure (Ps 119:72). If they value God's word, they will hide or store it in their heart and see it as essential for living their life. Good teaching creates a desire, a longing that motivates students to beat a path to learning. Good teaching motivates students to cling to or hold fast to what is taught. Merely intellectual assent will not move a person. True transformation happens when the learner's emotions, value system, and motivations are changed, which can be seen in the learner's actions.

The Will

Psalm 119 includes the importance of the will and resultant actions in biblical transformation. What we understand and delight in produces our actions. The opening verses of Psalm 119 say that blessing comes to those "who walk in the law of the LORD" (v. 1) and "keep his testimonies" (v. 2). We are to diligently keep God's statutes (vv. 4–5, 8–9, 17, 34, 44, 57, 88, 100). In verses 59–60, the psalmist chooses to "turn my feet" toward God's testimonies and "hasten" to keep God's word. This is an example of exercising his will in relation to God's word. Another is that the psalmist has chosen God's way and sets God's rules in front of him (v. 30). In verse 32, he models a strong will by running in the way of God's commandments.

By choosing to learn and understand God's word and to follow his commands, the psalmist is enabled and emboldened to speak of God's testimonies before even powerful kings without being put to shame (Ps 119:46). He describes his firm choice to obey God by saying, "I *incline my heart* to perform your statutes *forever*, to the end" (v. 112). Because of what the Lord has taught him, the psalmist is determined to stay away from evil and obey the Lord (vv. 101–102). Because he has chosen to trust the Lord and rely on his word, the psalmist is enabled to endure mistreatment and suffering (vv. 50–51, 92, 109–10). Even when he is weak and despised by others, when he is in trouble and anguish, the psalmist choses to cling to what he knows to be true and calls to the Lord to save him (vv. 141–146). The psalmist shows us that the word of God changes the will and that the result of a changed will is changes in action. Like a good mentor, he teaches by living what he believes (v. 79).

Biblical Truth Is Personal to the Believer

Biblical teaching should bring about growth and transformation in a person's thinking. It should impact emotions and turn affections toward Christ. Finally, biblical teaching should result in changed actions. "The biblical understanding of the heart encompasses the mind, the will and the emotions."[15] It is the entire being affected by God's word that brings true transformation. The Hebrew way of thinking is to see our being in its entirety, and, "When man remembers God, he lets his being and his actions be determined by him."[16] That which is received into the soul must influence the character of the whole.[17]

Truth in the biblical sense is not something that is external to the believer. "What we call objective, that is to say inactive, theoretical thinking, without further implications, does not exist in the case of the Israelite."[18] Otto Piper

---

15. Robert Saucy, *Minding the Heart: The Way of Spiritual Transformation* (Grand Rapids, MI: Kregel, 2013), Kindle location 605.

16. Pedersen, *Israel*, 106.

17. Pedersen, *Israel*.

18. Pedersen, 106.

explains, "For the Hebrews, 'to know' does not simply mean to be aware of the existence or nature of a particular object. Knowledge implies also the awareness of the specific relationship in which the individual stands with that object, or of the significance the object has for him."[19] Westermann points out that the text is understood in Psalm 119 as a "living entity," rather than a passive object. This may contribute to an understanding of how it can have such a variety of effects upon the individual. The psalmist highlights these multiple effects through words like longing, seeking, treasuring and exalting.[20] This multi-faceted interaction with God's word also includes bodily activities involving the mouth (v. 43), tongue (v. 172), lips (v. 13), eyes (vv. 15, 136), hands (v. 48), and feet (v. 101). According to Whybray, "the use of these organs is intended to express a sense of the completeness of the individual's response to the text."[21] It is clear that God intends us to interact with his word with all of our being. As well, it is God's intention that God's word reaches and transforms all of who we are.

Summary

The psalmist of Psalm 119 reminds us of the essence of Christian education and that transformation is the work of God in us. The psalmist asks of God, "Open my eyes, that I may behold wondrous things out of your law" (v. 18), and, "Make me understand the way of your precepts" (v. 27). He appeals to God, "Lead me in the path of your commandments, for I delight in it. Incline my heart to your testimonies, and not to selfish gain!" (vv. 35–36). It is God's love and mercy that gives the psalmist comfort and life (vv. 76–77). The psalmist knows that only God can truly uphold and support him (vv. 116–117, and that only God's gracious love opens the path to life and freedom from oppression (vv. 132–135). The psalmist knows that God is the ultimate teacher (vv. 33–34, 64, 66, 125, etc). It is God's word and God's presence that give life, protection, and salvation to the troubled psalmist who is persecuted and lives in the midst of a perverse generation.

The word of God is the golden thread of Psalm 119. God beautifully weaves this thread into the entire fabric of our being through interaction with his

19. Otto Piper, *Knowledge*, IDB, 3, 43, 10, trans. Aslaug Moller (London: Oxford University Press, 1973), 43.

20. Claus Westermann, *The Psalms: Structure, Content, and Message* (Minneapolis, MN: Augsburg, 1980).

21. Richard Whybray, "Psalm 119: Profile of a Psalmist," in *Wisdom, You Are My Sister*, ed. Michael L. Barré, *CBQ Monograph Series* 29 (Washington, DC: CBAA, 1997), 31.

word. Psalm 119 provides us with a picture of transformational teaching and deep learning that is absorbed into the entire life of the learner and changes actions. Like the psalmist, we are to sing about, hope in, stand in awe, rejoice in, love, long for, meditate on, incline our heart, and guard our way with God's word. God's word transforms our hearts, including what we think, what we feel, and what we do. This is the purpose of God's word, which also provides us with models of this transformation, like the psalmist.

Psalm 119 also serves as a mirror to help us reflect on our teaching. The different words used on how to interact with God's word form a multi-faceted approach to learning that includes the entirety of our being. As we study Psalm 119, we see how our teaching methods and outcomes compare to the methods in the psalm and outcomes in the psalmist. As we reflect on the psalm, some questions we might ask ourselves are the following: Does our teaching create a longing to learn? Have we presented truth theoretically or in a way that is personal for the learners? Is their heart more inclined toward the Lord? Do our students stand in awe of God and his word more after we teach? Do they find comfort in God and his word? Are they growing in their understanding of God's word? Do they know how to apply God's word in their life and ministry? These and similar questions inform and help us evaluate the methods and outcomes of our teaching and training.

Psalm 119 provides us with the goal of biblical teaching. But it also guides how we should teach. It provides divine wisdom on the process of real heart change which is the goal of our training. It shows us that transformational training includes material and activities that addresses the whole of our being, which aligns with Paul's instruction to Timothy to focus on his doctrine (thinking), his character (emotions), and his ministry skills (doing). Interaction with God's word should produce deep transformation of the heart. As we think about how to develop leaders in our church, we should ensure that our teaching and training addresses the entirety of the leaders we train and promotes their heart transformation.

I have found that using Psalm 119 as an introduction to the leadership process sets the tone for teaching and training by rooting what we do in Scripture. The context of the psalmist also helps students see the value and purpose of the training, which they comprehend in more pronounced ways when I give them time to work through the psalm or sections of the psalm. I direct them to ferret out verses that focus on cognitive, affective, and active interaction with God's word. We also look at how the psalmist's thinking, feeling, and doing are changed by this interaction. This process of self-discovery helps to implant the idea that the goal of our training is transformation of all three aspects of our being. The psalm's alignment with the categories in 1 Timothy 4:11–16 further cements the importance of our purpose and the methods we will use.

As we move our focus in the remainder of our study to practical principles, Psalm 119 will help us hold together the pieces of the leadership development process by connecting the priority of Scripture with the goals and methods of developing fruitful shepherd-leaders. Psalm 119 is at the heart of our discussion.

5

Summary: What and How We Train

Because God loves his church, he provides her with shepherds to lead and care for her. These leaders are called elders in the New Testament. Besides elders, many others lead the church in different ways. This is why leadership development is key to a healthy church. We recognize that it is God who sovereignly develops shepherd-leaders to serve his church. Yet we also have a role in that process which should motivate us to seek how best to do this important task.

As we saw with our Lord, developing shepherd-leaders is part of discipleship. The experience of regional leaders affirms the practice of our Lord. Keeping leadership development as a part of discipleship is imperative because it roots the process of developing shepherd-leaders in Scripture and the biblical discipleship paradigm. Although there are some issues that are particular to leaders and shepherds, how we grow and the areas of growth are the same for all believers. Training rooted in discipleship is aimed at the heart, involves others, and includes knowledge of God's word that leads to lives conformed to Christ. These areas are what Paul focused on in his leadership training.

In 1 Timothy 4:11–16, Paul calls Timothy to focus on four areas that are essential to fruitful leadership in the church. These areas are the understanding of calling to ministry (v. 14) and our three areas of discipleship: developing skills for ministry (v. 15), growing in Christ-like character (vv. 12, 16), and deepening understanding of God's word to be better able to teach others (v. 16). Thus Paul provides us with a model containing clear categories for developing shepherd-leaders that should guide our planning as we develop courses, practical experiences, reflection, training, and other exercises to develop leaders.

Keeping these areas in balance contributes to a healthy church. An overemphasis on knowledge comes at the expense of being able to minister to people and defines Christian faith as what we know instead of a faith that bears fruit that honours God and blesses others. Also, there are plenty of examples across the world of church leaders who have charismatic personalities and are gifted in many areas, but who leave a trail of battered souls in the wake of their ministry. Further, we can all think of examples of moral failures by church leaders. These issues are why we need shepherd-leaders who more and more reflect the image of our Saviour in their life and ministry. Finally, practice that is not grounded in Scripture fails to bear fruit that remains. Although godly character is primary to godly leadership, it is not enough to simply be a good person. Those we serve have deep questions that we need to answer and deep needs we need to be able to address. Scripture is the source we must draw on to address these questions and needs.

The Arab church faces these issues as well. Holding onto the scriptural emphasis to develop all three areas will result in developing whole-hearted leaders who lead fruitful ministry for the glory of our God.

Our ultimate desire is to have local leaders determine what their leaders need to be able to shepherd God's church in their context. Yet some development areas are shared by all shepherd-leaders. They must have a deep knowledge of the Bible including understanding the both Old and New Testaments, what the Bible teaches about the Godhead, the individual members, and their work; salvation by grace and faith; living the Christian life; and more. They must have strong ministry skills including how to teach and preach; how to pray and lead prayer; how to lead a small group; how to shepherd God's people and minister to their needs; how to make and maintain peace; how to develop leaders; how to react biblically to persecution; and how to evangelize, among others. They must have and be growing in Christ-like character traits such as a love for God and others including enemies; patience and endurance; honesty and integrity; humility and a servant's heart; faith and courage in the face of trials, and more. These are far from exhaustive lists, and though many needs are common to all leaders in all places, local knowledge and personal evaluation will serve to define training needs in particular contexts.

The Scriptures, the church throughout history, and the wisdom of regional leaders affirm the importance of these areas in the lives of fruitful shepherd-leaders. A brief overview shows us that through much of her history, the church played a central role in developing those who have led and served her. However over time, the church was slowly marginalized as leadership development shifted toward a more seminary-centred academic approach that tends to isolate leadership preparation from the church. This model still directly and indirectly influences the practices that are used in the region. But understanding this tendency should not set the church and seminary in opposition. Both have an important role to play. Instead, it should encourage us to a more church-centred approach.

Romans 8:29 tells us that the goal of the Christian life is "to be conformed to the image" of our Saviour. This means a complete transformation of our heart that includes the way we think, feel, and act. Psalm 119 provides focused and repeated affirmation that real transformation includes our thinking, our emotions, and our will, and this kind of transformation should be the goal of our teaching and training. Psalm 119 also highlights the importance of addressing each of these areas of our heart. How to develop teaching and training to achieve this goal is the focus of the remainder of the book.

We will now turn our attention to investigating educational and cultural principles that need to be understood and appropriated to reach this goal in the MENA region. It is crucial for us to learn these principles in order to understand which teaching and training practices are appropriate to our context and how best to use them. In the next section, we will look at some educational principles that provide practical guidance that will help us transform what we've learned from Psalm 119, 1 Timothy 4:11–16, and other biblical passages into practical, effective teaching and training programmes for developing leaders.

Section II

Adult Education Principles

Adult Education in Deuteronomy 6 – Bloom, Kolb, and Knowles

Our goal is seeing leaders developed in the church in the Arab world. The three parts of this goal are adult leaders, the church, and the Arab world. Before we look at cultural and contextual issues for the church in the Arab world, we want to understand the nature of the adult leaders to be developed. Answering questions like how do they learn, what are their needs, what motivates them to learn, what are their goals in learning, and what is the teacher's role will help our teaching and training be more fruitful. It is important to address these and other questions about adult learners because the more we understand them and effective principles for teaching and training them, the better we will be able to adapt these principles to the context and culture of the Arab world.

Who Are Adult Learners?

Seeking to keep our paradigm tethered to Scripture, we will briefly look at an adult learning situation in Deuteronomy. Deuteronomy 6:6–9 provides well-known principles for teaching children (pedagogy) in the context of life. Parents are to continually teach their children God's commandments, when they rise up, lie down, and go out (v. 7). Deuteronomy 6:20 continues this theme of teaching, but shifts from a more passive, one-way path of instruction from parents to children to children asking questions about the meaning of the commandments. They know the commandments, signifying that they have heard and memorized them. They now desire to know what they mean, why they are important, and how to live them out.[1] The answer is provided via a reminder of the story of how God fulfilled his promise to his people followed by the rationale for the commandments – so that they might experience "good always" and that the Lord "might preserve us alive, as we are to this day." Finally is the call to obey God's commandments (Deut 6:21–25).

Although we don't know the age of the child in Deuteronomy 6:20–25, the inquiry as to the meaning of the commandments points to an older or mature child. So this passage is a good picture of adult education. Adult learners want to know why, so their teacher should respond to their inquiries like the parent, by explaining how the commandments benefit them and why they should obey. Adults want to learn information that is relevant to their life and how to apply or live out the information being taught. Deuteronomy 6 hints at the difference between teaching children and teaching adults. Deuteronomy 6:6–9 is downloading information for children to learn and memorize. In Deuteronomy 6:20–25, the goal is the application of learning for the specific purpose of preserving their life (24). This is a more advanced form of learning that is more suited to older children and adults.

The focus of our training for transformation is adult learners, and the passage from Deuteronomy points to something we instinctively know: adults learn differently than children. When we think about how we learned in school and how we learn now, we can see the differences. A number of education professors have researched and defined principles of learning that are unique to adults. As we look at training adults, we will use some of the principles gained from this research. Three educators have made significant contributions to explaining the learning process: Benjamin Bloom, David Kolb, and Malcolm Knowles. Below is a short summary of their theories. We will look at each in more detail in the following chapters in this section.

Bloom and his colleagues focused on three domains of learning – cognitive, affective, and psychomotor. These are popularly known as thinking, feeling, and doing, or head, heart, and hands. They align with the deep learning we saw in Psalm 119. These three domains also correspond with the three shepherd-leader development areas of knowledge, character, and skills in 1 Timothy 4:11–16 that we looked at in section 1. Understanding Bloom's three domains

---

1. Peter Craig, *The Book of Deuteronomy, International Commentary on the Old Testament* (Grand Rapids, MI: Eerdmans, 1976), 174.

will help us move beyond learning in the cognitive domain, which for many of us is the primary focus in education, into affective domain of values and beliefs and the reflexive training of the psychomotor domain.

Kolb's experiential learning theory (ELT) consists of four steps that occur in the process of learning, which is called the learning cycle. Learning styles derived from these four steps describe different ways that people learn. Our focus will not be on learning styles. Instead, we will emphasize the importance of including the four steps of the learning cycle as part of an effective adult learning model. The elements of reflection and experimentation that describe how we process information will be especially important in forming our paradigm.

A look at the adult learning theories of Malcolm Knowles will help us define the learner we seek to teach and train. His theories describe the differences between how adults and children learn. These principles will help us better understand our students and thus enable us to develop more effective learning that is transformative.

Finally, we will coalesce what we learn from Bloom, Kolb, and Knowles. Their theories overlap in some ways but also complement each other in forming an adult education model. Understanding their principles will contribute to our ability to apply them in our Arab context. There is limited but growing work on the application of these adult educational principles in the Arab world, including some analysis of Bloom's learning domains and quite a bit of literature on the validity of Kolb's learning styles, which I will touch on in the chapter on Kolb's theory. We will use the relevant principles from each professor's theory and discuss some practical applications of these principles for our context.

6

Benjamin Bloom: Learning Taxonomy

We saw from Psalm 119 that learning God's word should affect our entire being – our thinking, our emotions, and our actions. In the same way, our training should address the entire being of those we teach because deep learning produces transformation. These three areas have been described as learning domains by Benjamin Bloom and his colleagues.[1] Understanding Bloom's three domains of learning will help us move the learning process toward the goal of biblical transformation and will also help us as we partner with leaders in their own development process.

Bloom defines three categories or domains of learning: cognitive (thinking), affective (feeling), and sensory or psychomotor (doing). Each domain contains levels of learning from basic or lower-order to more advanced and mature or higher-order learning and through which learners should progress. For example in the cognitive domain, learning should move from the lower-order memorization of facts to the higher-orders of analyzing, evaluating, and applying the facts to real-life situations. Higher-order processes build upon the lower-order processes, so lower-order processes must be mastered before higher-order processes can be achieved.[2] According to Bloom, deep learning occurs when students advance to the highest levels in each domain. Therefore, learning activities should address and promote progress in all three domains.

---

1. Benjamin Bloom was an educational psychologist who worked with others in the 1950s to develop a paradigm for classifying educational objectives. His goal was to describe objectives that define what mastery of a subject looks like. His taxonomy is still used quite extensively in education, and explanations of it can easily be found on the internet.

2. B. Bloom, M. Englehart, E. Furst, W. Hill, and D. Krathwohl, *Taxonomy of Educational Objectives: The Classification of Educational Goals. Handbook I: Cognitive Domain* (New York: Longmans, 1956), 18–19.

The Cognitive Domain

The cognitive domain is the informational aspect of learning. In the cognitive domain, learning moves from lower-order memorization to understanding and using the information. Movement continues as learners progress to the higher-level thinking skills of analyzing information, discerning patterns, and making judgments about the value of the information. The highest order is the ability to use all of the previous skills to come up with new ideas or solutions to complex problems. Below is a summary of each stage.[3]

1. Remembering – Being able to recall previous learned information.

2. Understanding – Being able to comprehend the meaning of the information.

3. Applying – Being able to use the information in a new situation.

4. Analyzing – Be able to break down the information into its parts.

5. Synthesizing – Being able to take parts from different ideas and relate them together to form new information.

6. Evaluating – Being able to make judgements and determine the value of the information.

7. Creating – Being able to put parts together to form a whole, with emphasis on creating a new meaning or structure.

For example, suppose we are teaching about forgiveness. For the first level, we could have students memorize Matthew 18:21–22 which tells us to forgive our brother "seventy times seventy." After learning what this verse means, for the next level, we have them explain its meaning in their own words, like in a mentoring discussion or an essay question. In the third level, we would ask students to apply this verse to different situations in their lives were others have sinned against them.

For the analysis level, we want to help students break down forgiveness into its parts including saying, "I forgive you" but also praying for ourselves and those who have sinned against us and choosing to forgive them. The goal here is to look at forgiveness from all angles. Synthesis is putting all of the parts back together to see the big, and radical, picture of what Jesus is teaching. For the level of evaluation, we want students to judge the value of Jesus's teaching on forgiveness, which should include the parable he tells afterward and evaluating

---

3. "Bloom's Taxonomy of Learning Domains," 12 January 2015, http://www.nwlink.com/~donclark/hrd/bloom.html#intro.

how they practice forgiveness in light of the truth of what Jesus is teaching (Matt 18:23–30). The highest level, creating, could involve helping the students take all they have learned and use it to see how much is required of Jesus to continually forgive us.

Our goal is to move beyond the simple, but important, step of memorizing verses about a particular subject. We want our students to know what the Bible says about life, but we want them to do more than acquire biblical data. We want them to understand the meaning of what they learn, to be able to explain it to others, and to apply it to real life situations. We want them to meditate on what the Bible says which includes looking at each part as well as the whole, exploring how one passage relates to others, seeing the truth of God's words in their lives and the lives of others, and taking his truth deeply inside of them as part of their being. Whether what we are teaching is forgiveness, experiencing the peace of God in the midst of trials, seeing how God's Spirit uses his word to make us more like Christ, or other subjects, we want the truths we teach to become part of our students' lives.

The Affective Domain

The affective domain involves attitudes toward learning, engagement in the process, and willingness to assess and even change values and beliefs. It is the value we place on what we have learned. Effective teaching engages our emotions and motivates us to respond to what we have learned. Movement from lower-order to higher-order levels is movement from merely receiving information to engaging with information and ideas and determining if they are valuable or useful. At the highest levels, the levels of deep learning, students organize the information to determine those that have the highest priorities and internalize the information or ideas so that it becomes their own, changing their values and beliefs accordingly. Below is a summary of each stage.[4]

1. Receiving Phenomena – Being willing to pay attention to and receive new information or instructions.

2. Responding to Phenomena – Actively participating or responding to the information or instruction presented.

3. Valuing – Determining the worth or value of the information, from simple acceptance to more complex commitment.

---

4. "Bloom's Taxonomy: The Affective Domain," 12 January 2015, http://www.nwlink.com/~donclark/hrd/Bloom/affective_domain.html.

4. Organizing – Ranking information according to importance and being willing to transform values into priorities.

5. Internalizing Values – Adapting the values and making them your own. Believing the information.

In our example of teaching forgiveness, the goal is to help students see the value of forgiving others, to make forgiving a priority, and to internalize the desire or internal motivation to forgive others as Jesus has forgiven us. The first step toward being internally motivated is being willing to listen to the teaching. We know that sitting and listening is a long way from being self-motivated to do something, but it is a necessary first step. Our next challenge is engaging students in a discussion about forgiveness and encouraging them to actively participate. We want them to ask questions about the teaching or express their opinion because these are signs that they are in some way motivated to learn about forgiveness.

The next level is helping students to see the value of forgiving others and encouraging them to be willing to accept that we should forgive. They don't just agree with it mentally, but are deeply convinced and believe that it is imperative that they practice forgiveness. The final level is when our students internalize the truth and make it their own. They are internally motivated to forgive, even if it is difficult, and demonstrate this internalization by actively forgiving others who sin against them.

Our goal is for leaders to reach the highest level of affective learning, to be internally motivated to seek God, love and long for more of his word, obey him, serve others, and teach them to desire and do the same. Leaders often do not have others who are telling them what they should and should not do or who are exhorting and encouraging them. By God's grace, they need to develop the internal desire to live like Christ even when it is difficult or will cost them personally. It isn't enough to understand what forgiveness is and why we need to forgive others. We need to be motivated to actually forgive our brother or sister even up to seventy times seventy, which is especially important in ministry in the church.

The Psychomotor Domain

Although Bloom's psychomotor domain primarily applies to learning mechanical skills like operating machinery or building houses, we can glean principles for learning ministry skills such as teaching, evangelizing, leading a small group from this domain. Psychomotor or sensory development moves from lower-order observation to higher-order ability to execute complex actions and adapt skills to different situations.[5]

Psychomotor learning starts with low-level observation of someone else doing the activity, for example preaching. Learners then progress to being ready to do the activity and then imitating another's actions while being guided, such as preaching in their church. Then students move to being able to do the activity on their own, perhaps haltingly rather than slowly in our preaching example, and then being able to do the activity with increased skill. The higher-order skills are attained when the student is able to adapt what they have learned to different situations, for example preaching in different churches. Mastery is the ability to create new ways of doing the activity, for example using different styles of preaching to reach different groups of people. Below is a summary of each stage.[6]

1. Perception – Learning how to do something by watching another.

2. Readiness – Being ready to act or do.

3. Guides Response – Imitating the actions one has seen with supervision.

4. Mechanism – Doing something on one's own, yet slowly.

5. Complex Overt Response – Being able to do something with skill, precision, and speed.

6. Adaptation – Being able to adapt skills to different situations.

7. Origination – Being able to invent or create new movements or skills. Creativity.

Many people learn best by watching someone else and then trying to do the action themselves. We can adapt our example of forgiving others to the ministry skill of resolving conflict. As the teacher-trainer, we can have our students "observe our actions" by explaining the steps we take when helping others resolve conflict such as praying for them, teaching them about forgiveness, challenging them to forgive, etc. When students fully understand how to resolve conflicts, we will want to give them an opportunity to try while we are next to them to guide them. We may let them be the one who teaches about forgiveness.

---

5. Elizabeth Simpson, *The Classification of Educational Objectives in the Psychomotor Domain: The Psychomotor Domain* (Urbana: University of Illinois, 1966), 31.

6. "Bloom's Taxonomy: The Psychomotor Domain," 12 January 2015, http://www.nwlink. com/~donclark/hrd/Bloom/psychomotor_domain.html.

If students are involved in a conflict, we can walk with them through the conflict, providing advice along the way for bringing about resolution. Or we may want to bring students to the next level by letting them figure out how to resolve a minor dispute on their own. They will of course struggle in doing this, but after they return from helping to resolve a conflict, we can discuss how they learned from their experience. As they practice the skill with different kinds and levels of conflict and gain more experience, they should move to the level of being able to resolve conflicts more easily and be able to teach and counsel others without having to think a lot about what they need to do. Finally, they should be able to think of creative solutions to really difficult conflicts based on their knowledge, skill, and experience.

We can apply the principles of Bloom's psychomotor skills to teaching many ministry skills including preaching, teaching, leading small groups, and evangelism. In fact, these are the steps we should follow when involving shepherd-leaders in ministry in a mentoring relationship: observation first with a discussion of the activity after so the learners understand how and why certain actions were performed. Then practice in a safe environment under supervision or with the mentor followed by independent action in a situation that will promote slow learning. Shepherd-leaders can then be encouraged to progress by doing different and more difficult ministry, reflecting with a mentor and being guided by wise advice until they gain mastery in the skills of life and ministry.

Summary of Bloom's Taxonomy

Bloom's three domains of learning are each unique, but they are also interconnected. For example, it is important to know and understand what the Bible says about forgiveness. But what good is it if we know what we should do, but aren't motivated to do it? And if we know what we should do and have the desire to do it, what good is it if we don't have the skills to do it? All three learning domains need to be developed in order for deep learning to occur.

Bloom's three learning domains complement and confirm each other and can be used in combination to help adult shepherd-leaders grow in knowledge, motivation, and ministry skills. A good example is teaching. Learning a skill like teaching involves understanding the actions that are involved (cognitive). However, reading books about how to teach (cognitive) doesn't mean a learner knows how to teach. The learner must actually teach and in the process learn what to do and what not to do (psychomotor/sensory). To keep trying to learn this difficult skill, the learner must be motivated and view teaching as a valuable activity and high priority (affective). Practicing the skill, particularly when confronted with students' questions, should also motivate the learner to go deeper into God's word, and the challenges of teaching should encourage them to learn how to improve their teaching and internalize the truth of God's promises to enable.

Our goal is deep, transformational learning described in Psalm 119. However, many educational models do not progress to this level. Bloom's taxonomy provides insight into the learning levels students should achieve and how they should progress to reach the higher levels where deep, life-transforming learning occurs. This being true, then our teaching-training processes should address each of these domains in order to produce real change in learners. In keeping with our goal to applying what we learn in an Arab setting, we will look at how these three domains have been part of the growing process of leaders from the Arab world.

What Regional Leaders Say about Bloom's Taxonomy

Regional leaders asserted over and over that real learning moves beyond the cognitive. For them, real learning is doing what one knows. They affirmed that higher order learning is necessary for a leader to be fruitful.

The regional leaders emphasized that leadership development fits within the biblical paradigm of discipleship, and they equated discipleship with deep learning. Discipleship is full-orbed learning that affects the mind, the heart, and the actions of leaders. Discipleship should involve true change in the life of believers as they grow deeper and more mature in the Lord in every area of life. This description fits with our understanding of Psalm 119 as a model of involving all of our being in interacting with God and his word. This transformation is the goal of discipleship.

A key component of discipleship is learning God's word. The regional leaders interviewed stated repeatedly that knowing God's word involves much more than just head knowledge. It includes a depth of understanding that enables the leader to discern true from false teaching. Discipleship should result in living out what one knows, applying it to one's life, being able to accurately handle the Scriptures.

Regional leaders believe that discipleship includes growing in the ability to minister to others. It involves learning the Scriptures in personal study and from others that includes both knowing and obeying the Scriptures. Discipleship is transferring that knowledge to others, teaching them to know and live out their faith. It is so internalizing God's truth that the results are living it out in service to others.

Discipleship encompasses Bloom's three domains of learning. The regional leaders' concept of teaching was primarily cognitive. They valued the importance of learning the Scriptures and the doctrines that derive from the Bible. Yet their understanding of teaching goes beyond simple, lower-order cognitive knowledge. It reaches to Bloom's higher-order cognitive categories of synthesis and evaluation.

For the leaders interviewed, good teaching leads to good practice, the necessary outcome. If young leaders do not know the right thing to do, then they won't be able to do it. Teaching includes training on how to live and minister, including developing skills, not just knowledge. Teaching should lead to doing.

The regional leaders' emphasis on a "heart to serve" relates to Bloom's affective domain. The heart to serve is a desire to serve that is devoid of personal motives. Leaders value deeply serving others, and they stated that the desire to serve should not come from external motivations like money, rewards, or praise from others. The desire to serve, to learn, to develop, and to grow should be internal. Regional leaders believe an inner motivation to serve, despite the lack of external encouragements or the presence of discouraging challenges, is a sign of God's calling and development of a young leader.

A common theme among regional leaders was the importance of experience, or doing, in the learning process. Being able to do is part of deep or real learning. This reflects Bloom's psychomotor domain. Regional leaders recognize the need for shepherd-leaders to have skills or abilities to be able to shepherd God's flock. The development of skills should be for the purpose of ministering to and benefiting others. Skills are abilities that are developed and refined through practice. Since they are for the benefit of others, they are developed through interaction with and ministering to others. Proper development of skills contributes to fruitful leadership.

Because regional leaders connect knowing and doing, they understand that knowing and doing reinforce each other. True knowledge is doing what we know, which they described as obedience to God's word. They also understand that doing strengthens what we know. Both knowing and doing are necessary for developing Christ-likeness.

Summary

Bloom's three domains of learning affirm what we saw in Psalm 119. In each of these domains, learning should move from simple education to higher-level thinking skills, adjustments in values and beliefs to match the truth of God's word, and skill mastery. For true life transformation, learners must reach higher-level learning in all of the domains: cognitive, affective, and psychomotor, or thinking, feeling, and doing.

Regional leaders testify that their development as leaders included learning each of these areas. In different ways, leaders value the importance of knowing, feeling, and doing as part of their development as leaders, and they naturally experienced all three in their development process. They also understand how each of these domains complements and completes the other. Developing teaching and training in the context of discipleship will lead us toward producing deep learning in young leaders' thinking, feeling, and doing.

7

Malcolm Knowles: Adult Learning Theory

The way we were educated in primary and secondary school tends to be the default model most teachers use when we teach adults. As young children we were told to go to school, told what to learn, and told that what we were learning would help us in the future. This isn't a bad system. But as we saw in Deuteronomy 6, there are differences between how children and adults learn. Yet many of us use teaching approaches with adults that were used with us in primary and secondary school. Because our focus is the teaching and training of adult shepherd-leaders, understanding how adults learn will guide us to be more effective in this endeavour.

Malcolm Knowles was a professor of adult education.[1] He highlighted differences in how adults learn, andragogy, from how children learn, pedagogy. He says that as education moves from childhood forward, it becomes "progressively regressive."[2] This means that as the student gets older, pedagogical teaching methods become less and less effective because the maturing child naturally adapts an adult learning posture. Thus, pedagogical principles need to morph into andragogic principles as the learner matures.

Adult learning differs from teaching children in some important ways. Malcolm Knowles was a pioneer in developing the theory of adult learning – andragogy. Understanding his principles will help us better understand the adult learners we work with, teach and train. In 1980, Knowles proposed four

---

1. Malcolm Knowles, *The Modern Practice of Adult Education* (Cambridge, NJ: Englewood Cliffs, 1988).

2. Malcolm Knowles, *The Adult Learner: A Neglected Species* (Houston, TX: Gulf, 1973).

points and added a fifth in 1984.[3] His principles about the adult learner are the following:

1. The adult learner is an independent, self-directed learner (as opposed to dependent).

2. The adult brings experience as a resource to the learning experience (as opposed to a child who has little or no life experience).

3. The tasks of life and work determine the adult's readiness to learn (as opposed to a child preparing for life).

4. Adult learning is problem-centred (as opposed to subject centred), thus more immediate in application.

5. Motivation for the adult learner is internal (as opposed to external). Adults are motivated by their need to know.

A brief explanation of the five principles will help us relate them to the educational context in the Arab world.

Independent

Adult learners are independent, self-directed learners, rather than dependent like children. Adult learners are able, and desire, to provide input and direction to their learning process, including both the goals and the means of the learning process. This independence does not negate the role of the teacher. Instead of the teacher taking full responsibility for the learning process, teachers encourage and nurture movement toward self-directed learning. The lives of adults and the challenges they face motivate them to learn. The teacher should understand these challenges and use them to define what the student needs to learn. Instead of forcing a completely fixed-curriculum, adult learning is more beneficial when adults have input into what they study. This independence also includes how they learn. "Even in learning situations in which the learning content is prescribed, sharing control over the learning strategies is believed to make learning more effective."[4]

This approach is different than the way almost all of us were taught in elementary and secondary schools. When we learned as children, the teacher

---

3. Malcolm Knowles, Elwood F. Holton, III, and Richard A. Swanson, *The Adult Learner: The Definitive Classic in Adult Education and Human Resource Development* (San Diego, CA: Elsevier Butterworth Heinemann, 2005).

4. Knowles, Holton, and Swanson, *Adult Learner*, 183.

alone determined what we were to learn. They directed the learning process. They did not seek our input into what we learned nor how we learned. For children, this is okay. They don't know what they need to learn. Adults are different. They still need a teacher, but they are more able to be involved in defining what they learn and what methods might be most helpful in how they learn.

Involving adults in determining what they need to learn gives them ownership in the learning process. This ownership challenges the model of professors as mere answer-givers and students as passive-receptors. But when adult learners have ownership of their own learning, they are motivated to learn. This motivation is internal, not external, and independence correlates with the fifth principle on motivation.

Experienced

Adult learners enter an educational situation with a great deal of life experience. As we will see in Kolb's learning cycle in the next chapter, experience is a valuable resource to the learning process – adults bring a wealth of experience with them. The prior experiences of adult learners have the potential to be both a building block and a stumbling block in the learning process. Experience is a building block when it is a "rich resource for learning."[5] It is a stumbling block when it "creates biases that can inhibit or shape new learning."[6] According to Knowles, "On the one hand, experience can aid in learning new knowledge if the new knowledge is presented in such a way that it can be related to existing knowledge and mental models. On the other hand, those same mental models can become giant barriers to new learning when the new learning challenges them."[7]

Adults enter the learning process already having experimented and drawn some conclusions from that experience. For example, they may have shared in a certain ministry activity that wasn't successful. So they may have incorrectly concluded that this ministry activity is not helpful or that they aren't able to do it successfully. This previous experience provides wisdom to build on. Yet it could also inhibit learners from trying again with an open mind. Knowles recognizes the value of experiential learning in utilizing experience. "Experiential learning approaches have the dual benefit of appealing to the adult learner's experience

---

5. Knowles, Holton, and Swanson, *Adult Learner*, 189.

6. Knowles, Holton, and Swanson, 194.

7. Malcolm Knowles, *The Adult Learner*, 7th ed. (New York: Taylor and Francis, 2014), 178.

base as well as increasing the likelihood of performance change after training."[8] Performance change, or change in what we do, is deep learning.

Adult learners bring an inventory of experience to the learning process. These experiences are an important part of learning. Their understanding of God, the church, people, leadership, teaching, how change happens, and many other issues related to shepherding God's people are based on their cumulative experience.

Being aware of the experience of learners helps the teacher build upon what adult learners already know. It also provides insight into how learners may view the subject we are teaching. What handles can we, and they, grab onto to facilitate learning? What experiences can be used as referents as we design teaching or training? What touch points can be referred to as we reflect on current experiences and explore the reasons why they were or were not successful? This is the value of understanding prior experiences.

Just as experiences can serve as building blocks to learning, they can also be stumbling blocks. The cumulative experience of learners may tell them that the way they do things is sufficient. Or previous experience may inhibit change and growth either by demotivating learners to seek change or not allowing them to see what change and growth look like. Experience may tell learners that something has already been tried and didn't work. They may have concluded from their experience that change is painful and not worth the effort. These are all inhibitors to learning.

Whether experience is something we can build upon to facilitate growth, or could be an inhibitor to growth, the teacher-trainer needs to be aware of the previous experience and its impact on learning. This is where evaluation of learners is helpful. Interaction with learners prior to training/teaching (1) provides the teacher-trainer with valuable insights that can help in the learning process; (2) helps learners understand how God has been working in their life to prepare them to take the next step; and (3) identifies possible hurdles to growth and learning they will need to overcome. Prior interaction also gives learners a voice and ownership in the learning process.[9] Understanding the experiences that adults bring to learning is invaluable.

---

8. Knowles, Holton, and Swanson, *Adult Learner*, 199.
9. Knowles, Holton, and Swanson, 193.

Tasks of Life Oriented

The tasks of life and work determine readiness to learn in adult learners, as opposed to children who are preparing for life. Adults are ready to learn when they perceive a need to know or do something in order to perform more effectively in some aspect of their life, for example personal, vocational, family, or societal. Also, "[adults] learn best when new information is presented in real-life context. As a result, the experiential approach to learning has become firmly rooted in adult learning practice."[10]

Adults are ready to learn when they have a need, which generally arises as they assume new roles. For example, the movement from being single to being engaged creates the need to learn about marriage. Or a young leader may move from discipling youth to leading a small group. This new role should create questions about how to lead a small group, what to teach them, etc. At this point, the young leader is ready to learn.

If a need is not present, then learning will not be as effective. This has implications for seminary-based learning that is constricted to a specific time-frame. Not all of the learning will correlate to the need of the student, which will lessen the depth of learning and weaken the transformational impact on the learner's life. So Knowles urges that the "timing of learning experiences . . . coincide with the learners' developmental tasks."[11]

I have experienced this challenge when training leaders. As we discussed the importance of their relationship with God to enable them to withstand the pressures of ministry, the older leaders' eyes and ears were wide open. The younger leaders understood the importance of this concept, but they had not yet experienced the pressures of ministry that create desperation for God's filling. So they did not value the learning as much, and the benefit for them was less.

Adults are motivated to learn when they realize a gap in their knowledge or experience that hinders them from advancing socially, professionally, or personally. When they see a discrepancy between where they are and where they want to be, they are motivated to learn. The situation creates in them a need to know. This need to know helps to overcome the gaps between the learners' current developmental needs and the learning experience being offered. We sometimes teach things that students are not ready to learn and do not need to know. For example, teaching how to run a meeting when students are junior people who will not be asked to run a meeting for a good while.

---

10. Knowles, Holton, and Swanson, *Adult Learner*, 197.
11. Knowles, *Modern Practice*, 47.

This need to know helps to increase the effectiveness of learning experiences when there is incongruence between the learner's developmental need and the learning experience being offered. Therefore, learning experiences should be aligned with developmental needs or "induced" through creating the need to know in the learner.

Evaluation of learners can help here. Adult learners may be able to recognize some of their own gaps. For example, they may realize that in order to teach others, they will need to study the Bible more deeply. They may understand that to lead others, they have to learn to be more patient and forgiving. They may realize that their character does not measure up to the characteristics listed in 1 Timothy and Titus. It is at these moments that learners are motivated to learn.

This evaluation of learning should be "organized around life categories" of the learners.[12] Learners have needs not just in ministry, but also in their personal character, family life, vocation if they are bi-vocational, etc. As learners see their need, they develop a willingness to learn from others and an inward desire to grow and learn. These are a teachable people open to deep, transformative learning. Understanding the life categories that potential leaders are involved in will help us form and time our training according to their life challenges.

We are not always able to perfectly match training to need. But Knowles says that "there are ways to induce readiness."[13] When it is necessary to present teaching that doesn't coincide directly to the tasks of learners, we can create scenarios that show the need to learn for a future situation. For example, we want to address the importance of being able to lead others in the midst of opposition. Young leaders may agree theoretically, but they may not have experienced opposition as a leader. We can induce readiness to learn by having these young leaders think of a time when someone opposed their opinion. Or we could use a case study or perhaps have experienced leaders share testimonies of when they became angry in the midst of opposition and describe the negative affect this had on their leadership. Or they could share how they successfully led others who opposed them. All of these are ways to replicate, in some way, the life stage where knowledge, skill, or a character trait is needed.

In summary, adults learn as they are involved in life. They learn to address issues that they face in the midst of their different roles, and they want to connect what they learn to their roles and responsibilities. Understanding these roles and responsibilities helps the teacher-trainer identify the needs of

---

12. Knowles, Holton, and Swanson, *Adult Learner*, 44.
13. Knowles, Holton, and Swanson, 67.

learners and relate what we are teaching to their life. Here we see the advantage of conducting training as close to the context as possible.

Problem Centred

Adult learning is problem centred, as opposed to the subject-centred learning of children, and thus more immediate in application. Because adults are motivated to learn by needs in their life, their learning is problem focused or task centred. For adults, learning is about developing competencies. They want to apply what they have learned as quickly as possible to the real-life challenges they face. So learning activities need to be clearly relevant to their needs. When developing learning challenges for adult learners, we should ask ourselves questions like: Will it help them become more competent in the area they choose to study? Will it help them solve a problem that they are facing?

Pedagogy, teaching children, tends to be content based, which means it focuses on learning a subject regardless of its connection to the student's life or needs. Children's education is largely teacher centred: students gather information but there is very little practical application of the material. This is due to the delayed nature of learning for children. Most of what they learn will be used at a later date or to achieve a delayed purpose. For example, students in high school study so they can pass a test but won't use the information until they graduate and get a job.

This doesn't mean that teaching content is wrong, but adult learning is different. Adults learn best when they can use the content to address their problems. Andragogy, teaching adults, should be problem based. As we train adult leaders, we should capitalize their desire to connect what they learn to what they want to do. Doing what one learns is also an important part of the learning process because it reinforces and solidifies the learning. Teaching adults in this way leads to deep learning. This is real learning that produces real change.

Because adult readiness to learn is increased when there is practical use or application of the material, we as trainers should incorporate active learning activities in our training programme. "Deep learning and 'doing' travel together. Doing in itself isn't enough. Faculty must connect activity to the abstract conceptions that make sense of it."[14] Being aware of the problems facing learners helps us connect our training to their life challenges.

---

14. James Rhem, "Deep/Surface Approaches to Learning: An Introduction," *The National Teaching & Learning Forum* 5, no. 1 (1995): 4.

Motivated

The above four factors contribute to the motivation of adult learners. Motivation for the adult learner is internal, as opposed to the external that children require. Adults are motivated by their need to know. "The most potent motivators for adults are internal ones – for example, quality of life, satisfaction, and self-esteem. Said differently, the learning that adults value the most will be that which has personal value to them."[15] When adults are learning something that helps them address important issues or challenges to them, then they are motivated to learn. When they are hungry to learn, teaching will be effective. "Deep approaches, learning for understanding, are integrative processes. The more fully new concepts can be connected with students' prior experience and existing knowledge, the more likely it is they will be impatient with inert facts and eager to achieve their own syntheses."[16] Our teaching needs to capitalize on the need to know.

The best situation is when "the learners discover for themselves the gaps between where they are now and where they want to be."[17] We as trainers need to explain or better yet help learners understand what will be taught, why it is important, and how teaching and training will be conducted. Explaining the why of learning helps create the need to know in adult learners.

Summary of Knowles

Adults are not chiefly motivated by content-based learning that has little or no relevance to their life. Instead, learning that connects to their past experience, provides solutions for their current problems, and helps them achieve their future goals motivates them to learn. Connecting learning to life categories and showing how learning will help address problems and challenges increases their motivation to learn.

For example, we see this motivation when leaders finally learn how to address an issue they have been struggling with. This connection creates in them a desire to learn more skills needed for fruitful ministry. Deep learning that is transformative and affects the thinking, feeling, and actions of the

---

15. Knowles, Holton, and Swanson, *Adult Learner*, 200.

16. Eeva-Lissa Kronqvist, "Alfa Course in Oulu: Organization Development and Innovative Project Work," in *Management in Education: An International Teaching Project for Strengthening MA Programmes in Education*, ed. Dietmar Waterkamp (Berlin: Waxmann, 2000), 21.

17. Knowles, Holton, and Swanson, *Adult Learner*, 65.

learner also creates a hunger for more and sets the adult learner on the path of life-long learning, a critical trait in the life of a growing leader.

What Regional Leaders Say about Knowles' Adult Learning Principles

Conversations with leaders in the region affirm that adult learning principles were successful in helping them develop as leaders. Below are some short statements that relate Knowles' principles to their descriptions of how they learned and what they think is important in training leaders.

1. Adult learners are self-directed

Regional leaders understand this principle and connect it to the importance of leaders recognizing their call. Part of this call includes being self-motivated and self-directed in developing themselves and growing, including being responsible for their spiritual and ministerial development. They are also responsible for their behaviour. They need to watch themselves to ensure that they are walking with the Lord and living out his word. Finally, leaders need to constantly seek to grow in their abilities and skills. They can only lead others as far as they have travelled. So they must be self-motivated in developing their life with the Lord and with others. If leaders are called, they should be self-directed, which is a sign of leadership. When we see self-direction in leaders, we should note that it is a sign that they are called to be a leader.

2. Adults bring experience as a resource to the learning process

Regional leaders gained experience in ministry as they grew. They were willing to attempt new ministries. They would try new ways to minister. As they grew, their experience grew. They recognized the importance of experience in helping them learn the character and skills needed to be a fruitful servant in God's church. As well, leaders had experience gained prior to coming to Christ. All this experience was valuable for their learning.

Leaders from the region affirm that ministry experience and challenges are an important part of their development as a leader, and they value its inclusion as they develop other leaders. Trials and mistakes help leaders grow and learn the wisdom and skills they needed for ministry. These experiences are a source of wisdom about how to interact with people and how to respond to certain situations. Life experience, trials, and mistakes are valuable elements of the development of leaders and should be a part of the overall process of training shepherd-leaders.

Mentors are key in helping make sense of events in leaders' lives and guiding shepherd-leaders toward life-application of what they have been taught. One specific and important way a mentor uses the experience of young leaders is to help them recognize God's hand in their life. Leaders testified again and again of God's sovereign hand helping them, providing for them, protecting them, teaching them, and leading them.

Knowles tells us that adults bring experience to the learning process. As believers we recognize God as the one who determines and shapes the experiences of his children, and God is the one who provides shepherd-leaders for his church. The truth of God's sovereign work in developing leaders should cause us to pay close attention to the experiences leaders bring to the development process. We should recognize these experiences and build on them.

3. The tasks of life and work determine readiness to learn

The church and community are two of the spheres of life where shepherd-leaders serve. As young leaders assume increasing responsibilities in shepherding and serving those in the church, they develop not only their gifts and abilities but a heart of faithfulness. They also serve members of their community and reach out to them. Young leaders should be stretched and challenged to help them grow as shepherd-leaders in the various roles in which they serve.

There is a connection between learning in life categories and learning that is problem centred (principle 4). Regional leaders shared that they learn as they minister. As they served in ministry, they encountered challenges that caused them to seek help from a more mature believer to teach them. The challenges created a desire to learn, which in turn made the learning transformative in their life. This is the deep learning that is the goal of our training.

4. Adult learning should be problem-centred

Learning in life categories (principle 3) creates a readiness, a need, to learn. It is in the midst of life that we encounter problems and challenges. Leaders in the region connect learning with doing. Much of the need for teaching arises from problems or issues leaders face.

Many leaders talked about having ministry thrown on them. These situations created in them the need to learn and grow. For example, one young leader was asked to disciple new believers even though she was a young believer herself. As she discipled new believers, she would return to her leader with a desire to learn how to respond to questions the new believers had and how to help them in their struggles with sin. Another leader described how he was thrown into ministry from the very beginning of his faith. The weight of responsibility pushed him to learn. He believes that the pace of learning was too fast, but he had no choice. Serving in the midst of the tasks of life caused this young leader to confront many challenges and problems.

Whether they were given ministry or thrown into ministry, leaders encountered challenges that caused them to wrestle with how to do ministry and forced them to apply what they knew in order to address the issues. Challenges included taking on increasing responsibility. Leaders learned from both their successes and mistakes. As they struggled with growing responsibility, their passion to find solutions to their challenges grew, and they developed new skills to meet these challenges.

5. The motivation of adult learners is internal

Fruitful leaders in the region recognize the reality of internal motivation and the need for young leaders to have some ownership in their learning process. Leaders in the region appreciate the importance of being motivated to learn and serve not from outside, but internally. If young leaders lack this personal desire, they will serve the desires of their flesh. They will shrink back when challenges arise in their ministry. They must have a sense of responsibility and drive to help through the hard times.

Internal motivation is related to the idea of calling mentioned above. A leader's call is not based on external rewards, nor only on the opinions of others. It is a deep desire to serve and grow as a leader an internal desire which aligns with Knowles' fifth principle.

Summary

Knowles' principles point out the importance of getting to know the leaders we want to develop and observing them as they interact with others in the church. It is also helpful to take time to evaluate and assess the needs of each. Assessment helps us understand their experience and to discover both what they need to learn and what we can build upon to make training more effective. Understanding the young leader helps us determine both the content and method of training we will use.

1. One of the most important principles Knowles delineated is the role that experience plays in the adult learning process. Experience is a valuable resource that should be fully utilized in the training process. So we should discover and understand the experiences leaders already have and build upon them in the training process.

2. The learners' work and life categories including personal, family, society, and church life should be used, as much as is realistic, to define when and what type of training is offered. Because involvement in ministry is a key part of developing leaders, teaching and training should happen while learners are involved in ministry in the church. A more mature leader should seek to involve them in the normal life of the church as quickly as possible and deploy them as they recognize their maturity and gifts. This ministry responsibility also serves to develop their gifts and abilities as they minister.

3. Training will be valued and thus more effective if we provide adult learners with opportunities to use what they are learning to solve problems or challenges. These opportunities should include ministry challenges where learners can practice and develop their gifts and skills, such as serving in the community, outreach, and providing shepherding and support to people in the church. Encountering challenges and problems motivates young leaders to seek answers, learn, and grow in wisdom and know-how. We should also help young leaders apply what they are learning to their own real-life experiences.

4. Fruitful leaders need to be both life-long learners and self-directed leaders.[18] To promote growth toward these character traits, teacher-trainers should utilize the tendencies toward self-direction and internal motivation to learn that adult learners already have. Trainers and mentor don't have to release the entire learning process to learners, but they should involve the learners in the learning process

---

18. Gerald Grow describes the movement from dependent receiver to the goal of self-directed learner. Grow, addressing this issue, postulates four stages and corresponding teaching styles: Stage 1: dependent student/authority, coach/teacher; Stage 2: interested student/motivator, guide/teacher; Stage 3: involved student/facilitator teacher; and, Stage 4: self-directed student /consultant, delegator teacher. Gerald O. Grow, "Teaching Learners to be Self-Directed," *Adult Educators Quarterly* 41, no. 3 (Spring, 1991): 125–49. Quoted in Knowles, Holton, and Swanson, *Adult Learner*, 201.

to recognize their abilities and communicate that they share in the responsibility for their development.

Knowles' principles on adult learners direct us to make training practical, related to life, and usable for addressing the ministry challenges leaders face. When we understand the nature of the adult learner in general and their experience and needs in particular, we can more effectively teach and train them to be fruitful servant-leaders.

8

David Kolb: Experiential Learning Cycle

David Kolb was an educator who recognized the importance of experience in learning and saw the relationship between doing and learning. "Learning is the process whereby knowledge is created through the transformation of experience."[1] Kolb also understood that people perceive and process information differently.

Four Stages of Learning

From his observations and study, Kolb developed a model describing the role of experience in learning. Because experience is a valuable part of learning, Kolb's model is called experiential learning theory (ELT). "The ELT model portrays two dialectically related modes of grasping experience – Concrete Experience (CE) and Abstract Conceptualization (AC) – and two dialectically related modes of transforming experience – Reflective Observation (RO) and Active Experimentation (AE)."[2] Each of these modes represent four stages in learning that together compose a learning cycle. Kolb states that effective learning happens when the learner progresses through each of these four stages. Different people begin the learning process at different stages in the learning cycle. These are the learning styles that many of us are familiar with. Whatever one's learning style, Kolb believes that learners must pass through each stage for real learning to happen.

---

1. David Kolb, *Experiential Learning: Experiences as the Source of Learning and Development* (Englewood Cliffs, NJ: Prentice Hall, 1984), 41.

2. Kolb, *Experiential Learning*, 41.

Kolb's learning cycle describes what happens in the learning process. According to his four-stage learning cycle, immediate or concrete experiences are the basis for observation and reflection. Reflections are assimilated and distilled into abstract concepts from which new implications for action can be drawn. These implications can be actively tested and serve as guides in creating new experiences.[3]

Concrete experience and abstract experimentation are two different ways we perceive and grasp information. Some people start from experience and then learn from there. Others start with a theory or idea and then learn from there. Reflective observation and active experimentation are two ways that people process information. Some people like to think about what they have done. Others like to try out a new idea before thinking about it. Both of these ways of processing information are important to helping people learn. Without them, deep learning doesn't happen.

Concrete Experience

The first stage in the learning cycle is concrete experience. This simply means that all of us encounter different experiences in our life. Whether we are trying to fix our car, teach a lesson, cook a meal, talk to our boss, or make peace between family members, our lives are full of experiences. Kolb says that experiences are a valuable part of how we learn and are the foundation upon which we build. For church leaders, these experiences might include leading a meeting, sharing the good news with a friend, preaching a sermon, resolving conflict, and many other activities.

Experiences can be both positive and negative. We may have succeeded in preaching a sermon, and we can learn from this positive experience. Or we may have struggled to lead a meeting. Maybe people in the meeting didn't listen, and we weren't able to make any decisions. But we also learn from negative experiences like these. Whether positive or negative, experience is a valuable for learning.

Reflective Observation

How do we learn from experiences? Kolb says that reflective observation is the second step in the learning cycle, meaning that we learn by thinking about or

---

3. David Kolb, *Experiential Learning Theory: Previous Research and New Directions* (Cleveland, OH: Case Western University, 1999), 3.

reflecting on what happened. For example, we ask ourselves why something worked. If we didn't do well, we think about the reasons why we weren't able to succeed. Reflecting on what we did, both successes and struggles, makes experience useful in helping us learn. You can probably think of important lessons you learned from your failures. Sometimes failure can deeply impress us about what not to do. Whether we succeed or fail, the experience won't help us learn if we don't take time to reflect on the reasons why we failed or succeeded. We can do this reflection by ourselves or with others.

Abstract Conceptualization

After we reflect on our experiences, we draw conclusions. Kolb calls this abstract conceptualization, meaning that we form ideas about things we should or shouldn't do. We conclude that some things are good and others not. Or we conclude that some ways of doing something work, while others don't. Then we generate new ideas about how we should do something. We may keep some things and change others as we begin to form a new way of doing something.

In our example above about leading a meeting, we may conclude that the meeting wasn't a success because people didn't have a chance to share their opinion. Maybe only one person talked the whole time. So we form an idea about what we will change the next time we meet. We decide that we will have twenty minutes for questions and discussion. We don't know if this will actually work, but it is an idea formed after reflecting on our previous meeting.

Active Experimentation

This brings us to the final stage of the learning cycle, active experimentation, which means actively trying out our idea. We won't know if our new idea will work until we use it. So we actively test our idea to see if it is practical and will bring the results we are hoping for. Active experimentation is important for deep, transformational learning because it moves learning from being theoretical to being practical and real. This is higher-order learning that Bloom talked about, learning that brings about real change.

The Repeating Learning Cycle

After the active experimentation stage, we have new concrete experience to learn from, and the learning cycle repeats. Our hope is that this repetition is an upward spiral of learning more and better ways of doing something. In our meeting example, after giving people twenty minutes for questions and discussion, we find that people are more involved and committed to the group. Yet we also discover that opening up the meeting for discussion means we have less time for planning. So we will have to reflect on this new experience and create some new ideas on how to balance discussion and planning. We will try these, keep what works, and not use what doesn't work.

Kolb's ELT points us to the interaction between content and experience whereby each transforms the other.[4] Content or information informs how we do something, and we can learn new ways of performing tasks. What we do transforms what we know, which aligns with the biblical model of learning we looked at previously. As we saw, effective learning is comprised of thinking, feeling, and doing. These inform and transform each other in producing deep learning. Kolb's ELT helps us understand how experience and information, doing and thinking, interact in the learning process.

Summary of Kolb

For deep learning to occur, each of the four steps in the learning cycle needs to be included. Learners do perceive and process information in different ways. These are learning styles. But our interest is the relationship between experience and learning. Regardless of a person's learning style, deep learning includes experience, reflection, conceptualization or formulation of new ideas, and experimentation or testing of new ideas. These steps should be part of any model for teaching and training adults in an Arab context.[5]

The underlying principle of ELT is the importance of experience to the learning process. Kolb rightly identifies the steps involved in learning and the

---

4. See also Malcolm Knowles, Elwood F. Holton, III, and Richard A. Swanson, *The Adult Learner: The Definitive Classic in Adult Education and Human Resource Development* (San Diego, CA: Elsevier Butterworth Heinemann, 2005), 197.

5. Studies show that cultural differences also impact learning styles, although the effect varies depending on education level. Simy Joy and David A. Kolb, "Are There Cultural Differences in Learning Style?" *International Journal of Intercultural Relations* 33 (2009): 83–84. However, their study indicated that large sample sizes would better represent the Middle Eastern cluster. Other studies seem to indicate that "students from diverse cultural backgrounds, countries, and schooling systems with fundamentally different pedagogical bases have remarkably similar learning profiles based on Soloman-Felder ILS." I. A. Zualkernan, J. Allert, and G. Z. Qadah, "A Cross-Cultural Comparison of Learning Styles: The AUS-UMD Experience," paper presented at the Second International Conference on Innovations in Information Technology, Dubai, UAE, 16–18 September 2005, 7–8. Though there may be a tendency toward the active learning style, studies seem to point to the fact that all four learning styles are present among Middle Eastern learners and should be taken into consideration in teaching and training approaches.

interaction between experience, reflection, thinking, and doing in the learning process. Kolb shows us how people, including adults, learn.

We recognize that for adult learners, experience provides the basis for learning. Adults enter the learning cycle with experience. This does not mean that they are restricted to one type of learning style. It does recognize, as we will see below, that adults have an inventory of experience that they bring to the learning process. Most adults have reflected on these experiences and found them helpful or not helpful to solve their problem or address their challenge.

We who train and mentor leaders should include reflection in our teaching. As young leaders face problems or challenges in their life and ministry, effective teaching-training should lead them to reflect on their experiences, which should challenge their concepts of what will or will not work. New concepts can be introduced and experimentation to test these new ideas encouraged which should lead to the development of new practices.

When training leaders, it is very important that we include time for both reflection and experimentation in our teaching and training because helping young leaders think about their experiences helps them learn from their experiences. Whether the experience was positive or negative, reflecting is crucial, and facilitating reflection is one of the major roles we play as mentor, teacher, or trainer. Asking good questions can help young leaders process what happened and benefit from the experience.

We also need to make active experimentation a part of our teaching and training. Young leaders need to have the opportunity to try new ministries and new ways of doing ministry. Our role as mentor is to provide them with these opportunities. We need to support and encourage them, reminding them that they are learning and may not do it perfectly the first time. We need to give them the freedom to fail. By providing both the opportunity and the support to actively experiment, we help young leaders learn concrete lessons. This aligns with what we see in Psalm 119 and Bloom's principles of higher-order learning.

Fruitful teaching and training of adults will process through the four stages of Kolb's learning cycle. Experience is both a source of knowledge and an example of how knowledge is used to solve problems. Concrete experience is the basis for observation and reflection, which is also a source of knowledge. As adults find the knowledge to be helpful in addressing their need, they gain knowledge and grow. This is deep learning.

Asking good questions helps to facilitate the learning process. An example of questions we can use with leaders to help them learn from their experiences follow.

1. Concrete Experience – Describe a specific situation where you had an experience that relates to our lesson (whatever training or teaching topic you are presenting). Describe briefly the situation, what you did and how you felt.

2. Reflective Observation – Why did this situation have the outcome it did? What caused the situation to happen in the first place? What responses from yourself and others worked in this situation? Why was this effective? What did not work? Why?

3. Abstract Conceptualization – What lessons can you draw from this specific experience that could apply more generally? Given both your reflections and the information you have learned in this lesson, what would you do in this situation if it happened again? What general guidelines or principles would you create for handling this situation in the future?

4. Active Experimentation – What opportunities might you seek that would give you a chance to apply what you have learned in this lesson? How could you test the lessons, guidelines and principles you developed in step three?[6]

What Regional Leaders Say about Kolb's Learning Cycle

The elements in Kolb's learning theory are well represented in the elements that regional leaders said God used to develop them. Experience and reflection are an important part of their growth. Helping growing leaders reflect facilitates their learning from experience. Giving the growing leader the freedom and support to experiment and try new ideas is important. As well, leaders identified the importance of making and learning from mistakes. All steps in the cycle can be seen in the responses from the leaders. The activity of a mentor was identified as important to make the steps fruitful in producing deep learning.

Experience

Leaders from the region affirm that ministry experience and challenges are an important part of their development as a leader. They also value its inclusion

---

6. These questions are taken from Susan Komives, *Leadership for a Better World: Understanding the Social Change Model of Leadership Development* (San Francisco: Jossey-Bass, 2009), 438.

as they develop other leaders. Experience happens naturally as adult learners apply what they learn to real-life problems. Leaders benefit much from both positive and negative experiences. Two types of experiences are trials and mistakes, both of which helped regional leaders grow and learn the wisdom and skills needed for ministry. For example, they gained wisdom about how to interact with people and how to respond to certain situations. They learned ministry skills and how to lead by attempting ministry as they were growing.

Reflection

What makes experience useful is the presence of someone to help leaders learn from their experience. Kolb's step of reflective observation tells us that concrete experiences are most beneficial when we reflect on them. This happens best when done with someone who is more experienced. Regional leaders highlighted the need to have a more experienced leader help them reflect on and learn from their experiences. Reflection on life experience, trials, and mistakes with a mentor should be a part of the overall process of training shepherd-leaders.

Regional leaders also connected the importance of reflection to growing leaders' relationship with God. As leaders relate with God in prayer and reading the Bible, they should reflect on their life and ministry. They should evaluate their life in light of God's word and ask God to show them where they fall short and to conform them more and more to Christ. As they face challenges and opportunities in ministry, they should evaluate them in light of God's word. This reflective consideration of life and ministry should come through observing God's actions in his Scriptures.

Experimentation

Mentors should not only help young leaders benefit from their mistakes, they should also provide freedom and safety for young leaders to try new ways to minister. Regional leaders shared that being thrown into ministry, even when they didn't understand what they were doing, helped them learn. They communicated their struggles, but also told of how these struggles helped them learn, which corresponds to Kolb's stage of active experimentation. Mentors should provide freedom to experiment by giving young leaders permission to try something new.

Summary

Kolb describes how when we learn, we pass through each step of the learning cycle. Most of the time we are not aware that this is what we are doing. How learners process information, the steps of reflection and experimentation, is especially relevant to our focus on developing leaders in an Arab context. The reasons why will become apparent when we look at educational practices in an Arab context.

"For Kolb learning is . . . the interaction between content and experience, whereby each transforms each other."[7] Helping students process content and experience encourages learning. This processing happens through reflection and experimentation. So it is vital that we include ways for students to reflect on their experiences. We also need to offer students opportunities to experiment and test out what they are learning, and we should encourage and support them as they experiment. Both of these steps help learners more deeply absorb what is being taught.

---

7. Knowles, Holton, and Swanson, *Adult Learner*, 197.

9

Summary of Bloom, Kolb, and Knowles

Adults bring a number of resources to the learning process. In most cases, adults come to teaching and training because they want to, not because they have to. This is why we must explain why the teaching or training is important and how it is relevant to life. Adults focus on solving problems and accomplishing tasks, and they want to know what difference learning will make in their life and ministry. In other words, adults are motivated to learn in order to address the problems or challenges they are facing, and they desire to apply what they learn to the areas of life where they live and work.

Synthesizing Bloom, Kolb, and Knowles

The learning paradigms of Bloom, Kolb, and Knowles help us address these crucial questions and form learning that is truly transformational. Their paradigms complement each other and reinforce important ideas for deep learning. Coalescing principles from these three educators will guide us toward an effective teaching-training model.

Bloom summarizes the movement from lower order to higher order learning (deep learning) in our thinking, feeling, and doing. The goal of high-level learning in Bloom's taxonomy is achieved through Kolb's learning cycle. Knowles and Kolb highlight the important role that previous experience plays for adult learners. In showing us what happens when a person learns, Kolb shows us the role experience plays in the learning process. In turn, experience, reflection, and experimentation produce new ways of thinking, feeling, and doing.

This learning is applied to life tasks: "Adults seem to learn best when new information is presented in real-life context."[1] Kolb's cycle describes how new ideas and actions are produced in the life of the learner. Knowles summarizes the main ideas of adult learning. "The parallels between moderate views of constructivism and andragogy are rather striking. Both stress ownership of the learning process by learners, experiential learning, and problem-solving approaches to learning."[2] This is how deep learning occurs in adults.

Above is a small indication of how these principles mesh together to form a basis for an adult education model. As we work toward forming our model for the Arab world, we will focus on the following principles from Bloom, Kolb, and Knowles:

1. Bloom – Learning encompasses the domains of knowing (cognitive), feeling (affective), and doing (psychomotor or sensing). Deep learning is achieved when learners move to the highest levels in each domain.

2. Kolb – To achieve deep learning, learners must pass through each of the four steps of the learning cycle. Specific to our approach, teaching and training needs to include reflection and experimentation.[3]

3. Knowles – Adult learners are to some extent self-directed and internally motivated to learn. Their experience is a valuable resource to the learning process. Teaching and training should take place, as much as possible, within the work and life categories of the learners. Finally, adult learners want to use what they learn to solve problems or challenges they are facing.

Here is how we will use these principles in forming our teaching-training model.

1. We will use Knowles to understand the nature and needs of adult learners, which will inform the teaching and training process.

2. Kolb's steps of experience, reflection and experimentation will inform the actual teaching process.

---

1. Knowles, Holton, and Swanson, *Adult Learner*, 197.

2. Knowles, Holton, and Swanson, 193.

3. All four steps of the learning cycle are relevant to our goal. As we will see later, the need for reflection and experimentation is uniquely relevant to forming fruitful teaching and training in our Arab context.

3. Using these two principles will help us produce deep learning that Bloom tells us transforms our thinking, feeling, and doing. Bloom's principles will inform the goals of our teaching.

4. Combining principles from each educator provides us with a process whereby we (1) understand adult learners which (2) informs the use of experiential learning that (3) produces deep learning.

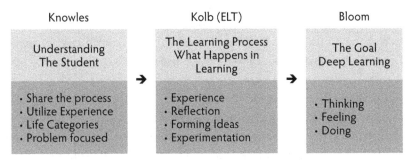

Knowles	Kolb (ELT)	Bloom
Understanding The Student	The Learning Process What Happens in Learning	The Goal Deep Learning
• Share the process • Utilize Experience • Life Categories • Problem focused	• Experience • Reflection • Forming Ideas • Experimentation	• Thinking • Feeling • Doing

Understand the Adult Learner (Knowles) to Effectively Use Experiential Learning (Kolb) to Produce Deep Learning (Bloom)

This is how principles from these three educators contribute to deep learning or true transformation that Psalm 119 describes.

The Teacher-Trainer Role

How might we use these adult education principles to help us think about designing and offering training that produces true transformation in the leaders we want to develop? Below are some practical suggestions about how to make these principles a part of our training process.

Our role as trainers begins with understanding learners in front of us. As Knowles points out, they bring an inventory of experience to the learning process. We need to explore these experiences so we can weave them into our training and teaching. Second, we need to discover the problems or challenges that motivate these adults to learn. Then we should help them apply what they learn to these challenges, which makes learning practical. Third, we should encourage learners toward self-discovery of solutions, but also support them in the midst of learning and help them identify mistakes and learn from them. Appreciation of these principles helps learners value what they learn, motivates them to learn, and produces deep learning the adult learners will apply to their life.

As we seek to create a process for deep learning, our teaching and training needs to involve Bloom's three domains. We need to consider what young leaders need to know and how we will help them gain this information. Will we use lectures, testimonies, readings, etc.? We should take time to think about how to motivate and encourage leaders to use what they learn. To do this, we might help them identify a need in their community and how they can serve to meet that need. From our assessment of learners, we should show them areas where they need to grow and also encourage them in areas where we see them growing. Finally, we need to determine what young leaders need to know how to do. What skills do they need to gain for ministry? Answering these questions helps us think about how to use practical ministry assignments to help them gain ministry skills.

Our role is also to provide students time and support to reflect on their learning both individually and with others. This reflection should serve to challenge their mental models or the way they view life.[4] We will need to provide them with opportunities for active experimentation, including the freedom to fail and to learn from their experimentation. This is the support that mentors and teacher-trainers offer learners. As learners actively experiment and apply new knowledge and abilities to real-life problems, they experience growth (deep learning) in their life, which in turn motivates them to continue to grow. This process causes learners to deeply value what is taught which serves as a further motivation for learning. Bloom states that this internal motivation is the goal of affective learning.

The experience adults bring to the learning process includes challenges, trials, and relational issues that growing leaders encounter in the midst of life. We can use these as "case studies" in our training. Because we believe that God is responsible for developing leaders, we are confident that these experiences and challenges are from God. Discussing how to apply the principles they have learned contributes to their growth. Learning in this context will achieve deep learning as learners attach what they learn to a real-life experience.

Summary

Adult learners have unique needs and approaches to learning. Understanding adult learners is a first step in forming effective teaching and training activities. These learning activities need to include experiential learning. Special care

---

4. Martin Tessmer and Rita Richey, "The Role of Context in Learning and Instructional Design," *Educational Technology Research and Development* 45, no. 2 (1997): 21.

should be taken to include reflection and experimentation in this process. Following these steps contributes to deep learning that transforms the learner.

To help us effectively apply these important learning principles in our context, we need to understand the culture and educational experiences of the learners. These will inform what learning activities we introduce and how to introduce them in ways that are amenable to the learners. In the next section, we will take the next step toward our goal by looking at the educational and cultural influences that have shaped adult learners in the Arab world.

Section III

MENA Cultural Foundations

As we turn to think about how to apply educational principles in ways that are culturally relevant, May Al-Dabbagh and Christine Assaad provide some helpful insight. "The common practice is to import programmes wholesale with the assumption that they are globally relevant or to 'culturally immerse' leadership trainers visiting the Arab world for a few days."[1] The effectiveness of this training is questionable. Mishal Kanoo, a Dubai based CEO, calls it a "mishmash of both systems."[2] We would be wise to take these caveats seriously.

In this section, we will examine educational and cultural factors that influence how we apply the educational principles from the previous section in meaningful ways. We can't assume that our Western educational principles will transfer directly to an Arab adult education context. We will need to sift these learning principles through the sieve of the educational and cultural background of our students.

Here are some questions to help us examine our teaching assumptions. Are reflection and active experimentation effective in Arab education, and if

---

1. May Al-Dabbagh and Christine Assaad, *Taking Stock and Looking Forward: Leadership Development in the Arab World* (Abu Dhabi: NYU Institute, Abu Dhabi, 2010), 14.

2. Bernard Zen-Rufinen and Serif Kaynar, *Business Leadership in the Arab World* (Dubai: Korn/Ferry Institute, 2011), 30.

so, how do we use them? How do we manage the tension between the teacher as the focus of learning and the students as self-directed learners? How do we create learning that is problem centred and not subject centred? How do we create deep learning that affects not just the mind, but also the affections and actions of the learners? Answering these and other questions will move us toward effective application of the principles we have gathered from Bloom, Kolb, and Knowles.

In this section we will examine (1) the previous educational experience of adult Arab learners, including how they were taught in primary and secondary school and to a lesser in adult situations; and (2) the cultural factors that determine how these adults learn. This examination will inform how we should introduce educational principles in ways that are acceptable to the learners.

10

Understanding Education in the MENA Region

I remember teaching a class with leaders from the Arab church on how to design and deliver courses that utilize adult learning principles to produce deep, transformative learning. The first part of the course was the theory behind these principles. The class included lecture, discussion, a short case study, and analysis of a Scripture text. The students were attentive and inquisitive.

But as I transitioned to having the students begin to design a course, having them doing more than listen, I noticed a real drop in commitment to the class. They appreciated my desire to make the class practical. But they were not familiar with nor sure that asking them to think through and apply the principles we discussed was the best way to learn. I could tell that they thought, in some way, what we were doing wasn't real learning and shouldn't be taken as seriously as lectures, even lectures that include discussion.

I addressed this thinking by using a study of Psalm 119 and having the students compare their prior learning experiences with deep, transformative learning principles. They all agreed that their prior learning included memorization, taking a test, and then forgetting the information. Despite our interchange, it was a struggle to help them value experiential learning as real learning and to see the need to use this kind of teaching.

In this section, we will seek to address issues affecting the kinds of cross-cultural learning that my example illustrates. Why do students not consider certain learning activities as important as lectures? Does culture affect the fruitfulness of using learning activities? If yes, how? How can we successfully introduce different kinds of learning activities into the learning process? What learning activities work, and which ones do not in the Arab context?

Addressing these and other questions will help us to better understand our students and enable us to tailor the learning process to achieve deep learning.

Connecting Adult Learning Principles to Arab Education

The wisdom of two Arab professors provides us a glimpse into the challenge that lies before us. Abeer Mahrous, a commerce professor at Cairo University, reminds us of the differences between Western and Middle Eastern educational practices. She says, "there are still sharp contrasts between the teaching and learning styles of the Middle Eastern and Western countries."[1] This implies that curriculum and teaching methods of Western universities will need adaptation before being employed in the Middle East.[2] Although we intuitively know this, we often fail to fully appreciate these differences when we try to implement Western learning principles in a Middle Eastern setting. Why is this? What is it that we need to understand about the curriculum and teaching methods?

Yusuf Sidani, a professor of leadership and business at the American University in Beirut, and his colleague Jon Thornberry offer keen insight into the learning process in the Arab Middle East.

> Since throughout his childhood and schooling he was made to submit to strong authority figures, he will be most comfortable in a group with a Zaim or strong leader at the top. The uniformity of the group means that the conformity he has been trained to expect will be more likely. Despite his intelligence, he will be suspicious of innovation and would prefer to keep things as they are, following the knowledge and experience of more senior persons.[3]

Because of the strong influence of childhood schooling, "it is difficult to introduce change, not just in schools, but to lead the student or students into new and effective educational methods."[4]

The above statements naturally raise the question of whether the adult education principles we looked at in the previous section that were developed in the West can be applied in the Arab Middle East. Will we be able to successfully

---

1. Abber A. Mahrous, "A Cross-Cultural Investigation of Students' Perceptions of the Effectiveness of Pedagogical Tools, The Middle East, the United Kingdom, and the United States," *Journal of Study in International Education* 14, no. 3 (2010): 292.

2. Mahrous, "Cross-Cultural Investigation."

3. Yusuf Sidani and Jon Thornberry, "The Current Arab Work Ethic: Antecedents, Implications, and Potential Remedies," *Journal of Business Ethics* 91 (2009): 128.

4. Sidani and Thornberry, "Current Arab Work Ethic," 42.

apply these principles if we use them in a different culture with students who have different primary and secondary school experiences? I believe the answer is yes. More than this, I believe we must find a way to make them work. The insight of Sidani and Thornberry is important for us. "Using these methods is more likely to produce critical thinking, reasoning and problem solving that are important parts of real learning."[5]

In order to understand if these educational principles are transferrable and how they can be used, we will examine two primary factors that will determine their success.

1. The students' prior learning experiences, including family, culture, and formal and informal ways of learning.

2. The influence of culture on students and on the educational process.

In exploring these issues, we will look at how culture influences both the students and their education by reviewing cultural studies conducted by researchers from inside and outside the Arab world. We will then use these findings to sift our adult learning principles to discover which ones can be applied in the Arab context. More importantly, we will look at how to successfully introduce these principles in our teaching and training.

Prior Learning Experiences

We saw in section 2 the importance of understanding adult learners. To understand Arab adult learners, we often begin with culture, thinking it is the most important factor to understand when introducing experiential learning. Certainly appreciating cultural influences on learning is crucial. But I believe that understanding prior learning experiences is the first step toward effectively using experiential learning in an Arab context, and others. Prior learning experiences are even more important today as students, despite being from the same culture, are being educated in increasingly diverse settings including government schools, Western-sponsored schools, religious schools, foreign schools, and English-language schools, some taught by Westerners, others taught by local teachers. This diversity makes understanding experiences of prior learning critical to our teaching and training.

A simple caveat before we look at our students' prior learning experiences. Prior learning does not just affect our students. It affects those of us who are involved in teaching and training. Our natural way of teaching will reflect the

5. Sidani and Thornberry, 41.

way we were taught. We need to be aware of this. Whether we are from the East or the West, we naturally default to the way we have been taught. So we need to be aware of not only our students' prior learning, but ours as well.

First we will examine prior learning experiences. Then we will look at the cultural factors behind these practices. Although prior learning experiences are impacted by the influences of family, culture, and informal ways of learning such as stories or sayings, we will focus mainly on the ways students were taught in their primary and secondary schools. Here we will find both positive practices that we can build on and negative practices that will need to be addressed. These school experiences will be the most common for the learners we train.

G. W. Hitt concludes from his observation of teaching physics in Kuwait and the UAE that it is prior pedagogy, more than culture, that impedes students from benefitting from new andragogic practices.[6] In my experience also, understanding prior learning is the critical factor to successfully introducing experiential learning. However, intertwined with this is a grasp of the cultural factors that shape the prior learning context because cultural factors help explain why teaching in schools is the way it is. It also provides insight into what students expect in the classroom and what "real learning" or "good teaching" looks like to them. "Both the learner's previous experiences and the context in which the learning is to take place influence the learner's preferences for long-term behavior of learning style."[7] Finally, culture informs us how and at what rate we can introduce change, in our case new experiential learning activities, in ways that will be acceptable to our learners. We will look more closely at culture in the next chapter.

The majority of adult learners in the Arab region have been taught in the context of Arab cultural patterns throughout their elementary and high school years. These patterns of teaching have been reinforced by professors during their college years. As we will see, these past educational experiences strongly influence the expectations of adult learners. As students become adult learners, their cultural-pedagogical background determines their expectations of what real learning looks like. "The context in which individuals learn, work and live has an important influence on creating and modifying the individual's

---

6. G. W. Hitt, "Secondary Implementation of Interactive Engagement Teaching Techniques: Choices and Challenges in a Gulf Arab Context," *Physics Review Special Topics: Physical Education Research* 10, no. 2 (2014): 1–20.

7. Roman Egger and Christian Maurer, eds, "Proceedings of the International Student Conference," ISCONTOUR 2013 (Norderstedt: Books on Demand, 2013), 183.

expectations and learning, management strategies and styles. Religion, ideology and social patterns, for example, Socratic, Confucian, Islamic, etc. have to be considered for a successful understanding of different cultural configurations and their evolution."[8] Our view of what encompasses real learning influences how we learn.

Shapers of the Learner's Prior Learning Experience

Below are some elements common to the educational background of many MENA regional students.

Influence of Islam

Islam has had a profound impact on how education is understood and practiced in the region. Islamic pedagogy is modelled on the way Muhammed taught his followers,[9] and Islamic schools were the primary means of education prior to the colonial period. "For Muslim societies, there is a clear division between the role of school for religious education and the role of school for modern development."[10] Both types of education exist across the region.

"The Koranic school, with lessons in Arabic by a teacher of religion [*maallam, Fikh*], is an essential part of the upbringing of a Muslim child. All children are exposed to Koranic recitation, and many progress to higher religious studies."[11] It is not just Qur'anic knowledge or ethics that are translated to the student. For school-aged children, the Qur'an is taught by memorization.[12]

Memorization

Memorization of the Qur'an is the primary purpose of Islamic schools.[13] Memorization is equated with knowing, despite the fact that students often cannot explain what they can recite. Although memorization is seen as the chief

---

8. Caroline Valiente, "Are Students Using the 'Wrong' Style of Learning?" *Active Learning in Higher Education* 9, no. 1 (2008): 74.

9. Helen Boyle, "Memorization and Learning in Islamic Schools," *Comparative Education Review* 50, no. 3 (2006): 478–495.

10. Abdeljalil Akkari, "Education in the Middle East and North Africa: The Current Situation and Future Challenges," *International Education Journal* 5, no. 2 (2004): 145.

11. Akkari, "Education," 145.

12. Boyle, "Memorization and Learning."

13. Boyle.

way of knowing the Qur'an, this does not necessarily mean that memorization is how all subjects should be taught.[14] Nonetheless, the Islamic primary method of learning has been transferred to secondary schools and universities, and memorization has become the primary means of teaching across the region.[15]

Memorization does have value as part of the overall learning process. Information cannot be used if it cannot be recalled. Students do graduate with good memories. Memorization is one of the ways we come to know information and make it available for use. We saw this in the example of the psalmist's interacting with God's word in Psalm 119. Memorizing is the first level of learning of Bloom's cognitive domain. However, the dangers are remaining at the first level of learning and viewing this level as true learning.

Despite the value of memorization in the learning process, by itself it is unable to bring about the real change or deep learning that is our goal in adult education. However, the reinforcement, year after year, of memorization as the way to succeed educationally has many ramifications for the learning and teaching processes.

National Testing

One of the negative ramifications of memorization-based learning is the connection between memorization and test-taking. "Many forces conspire to undermine the quality of higher education and to reduce learning to a process of memorization. The Koranic style teaching has been combined with the colonial system's emphasis on examinations. British policies of nationalized testing further reinforced this trend."[16] Richards goes on, "It is sometimes argued that modern Egyptian education more closely resembles traditional Qur'anic kuttab (where boys committed the Qur'an to memory) than is often appreciated."[17] Memorizing information in order to pass national tests is the educational experience of the majority of adult learners and has formed their view of what education should look like.

Memorization as the primary means of learning has more negative impacts. The greatest danger is that it creates a passivity in the learning process.

---

14. Boyle, 491.

15. Hitt, "Secondary Implementation"; Bernard Zen-Rufinen and Serif Kaynar, *Business Leadership in the Arab World* (Dubai: Korn/Ferry Institute, 2011).

16. Alan Richards, "Higher Education in Egypt," Washington, DC: World Bank Policy Research Working Paper, 1992, 13.

17. Richards, "Higher Education," 13.

Rather than actively engaging with information and using it to solve problems, students are conditioned to merely gather and memorize information so they can pass a test. "National examinations harmonize equitable access to higher education, but may also lead to 'teaching to the test' and even 'manipulation' of the results."[18] All of this short circuits the goal that learning is for growth.

Teacher-Centred Passive Learning

Memorization for test-taking is not about growth and change but simply about accumulating and regurgitating information in the form the professor requires. In this situation, the teacher becomes simply an answer giver and students become passive recipients. Although students might be able to repeat and recite words and sentences, they don't necessarily understand the meaning or principles behind those words.[19]

The classroom is highly teacher-centred because teachers are the ones who possess the answers that students need to know. Learning is a one-way transfer of information from the teacher to the passive students. When the teacher is the sole focus in the class, the students have little if any opportunity to apply what is taught to different situations. These practices are counter to effective adult learning that addresses the entire person, is reflective and experiential, includes past experience, and grants input into learning goals and means.

The teacher-centred approach can have positive impacts. The teacher's presence provides stability for the students. Also, Arabs view truth as personal, which is different than the Western view of truth as abstract and separated from the teacher. Students in the region see the wise teachers sharing their practical wisdom for life, which can help to connect students more personally with professors.

The teacher also provides structure to the learning process, and a prescriptive or defined learning process can be helpful in guiding adult learners. They want to know what they are doing and goals of learning. This structure and clarity will likely cause students to be involved in the learning process and aligns with one of Knowles' adult learning principles.

---

18. Ahmed Galad, *The Road Not Traveled: Education Reform in the Middle East and North Africa* (Washington, DC: World Bank, 2008), 124.

19. Nancy Sonleitner and Maher Khelifa, "Western-Educated Faculty Challenges in a Gulf Classroom," *Learning and Teaching in Higher Education: Gulf Perspectives* 2, no. 1 (2005): 1–21.

What Prior Learning Tells Us about Our Students

As stated above, not every student shares the same previous learning experiences. There are some exceptional teachers who provide care for their students and use interactive teaching practices including discussions with them and hands-on experiments. This diversity shows the importance of understanding the prior learning experiences of each student so that the learning situation is appropriate to individual needs.

Memorization as the primary method of learning prevents students from making meaning out of the information they receive.[20] As we saw in section 2, adults need to apply what they learn to real life situations. Memorization does not serve to connect the information to life in any meaningful way and even inhibits application. In many ways, memorization suppresses creativity, especially when one has been trained in this method of learning year after year,[21] because the highly structured classroom and studying contexts leave little room for creativity or critical thinking. Student are neither encouraged toward nor even allowed to engage in creative thinking, analysis, and problem solving.[22]

There are also cultural reasons why memorization is counter-productive to deep learning. Arab culture is a practical culture. As we will see in the next chapter, Arab culture is a concrete, high-context culture. Learners, especially adult learners, want to apply what they learn, which is a positive in light of Knowles' adult education principles. But the memorization model works against their cultural desires.

Despite the negative influences, memorization and other prior learning experiences in the Arab world can serve as building blocks to create a positive learning environment. These positive attributes can be successfully included as part of our active teaching and training approach for adults. We will look more at how in subsequent chapters.

Summary

Adult learners in the MENA region have been conditioned by their prior learning experiences, and these experiences influence what they expect in the classroom. This prior learning can be a barrier to introducing effective

---

20. Patricia M. Richardson, "Possible Influences of Arabic-Islamic Culture on the Reflective Practices Proposed for an Education Degree at the Higher Colleges of Technology in the United Arab Emirates," *International Journal of Educational Development* 24, no. 4 (2004): 429–436.

21. Sonleitner and Khelifa, "Western-Educated Faculty."

22. Galad, *Road Not Traveled.*

adult learning practices because the teacher-centred, passive memorization model of learning for passing tests needs to be overcome. However, positive aspects from prior experiences can be included and built upon when teaching adults. The holistic nature of learners tells us that they are amenable to adult learning practices. The collective culture and the concrete, praxis-oriented nature of the learners are all traits that align well with experiential learning. But prior learning experiences must be understood if we are to successfully utilize ELT practices.

As stated above, learning principles and practices are rooted in culture. Therefore, understanding the culture that forms and influences prior learning will help us as we seek to understand our students learning experiences in primary and secondary schools. We turn now to the cultural issues that shape these experiences in the Arab context.

11

Arab Cultural Factors That Influence Learning

To better understand our students' prior learning experiences and their expectations of what learning ought to look like, we need to understand the cultural elements that contribute to their learning experiences. For most of us it is easy to see how someone else is influenced by their culture. It is harder to recognize how our culture influences us. We also need to remember that cultural descriptions are generalizations about a group of people. They will differ from country to country and from person to person.

Cultural norms and practices are what undergird prior learning. People in different cultures do in fact learn in different ways.[1] "There are verifiably different cognitive processes in various regions of the world that affect how information is logically structured and perceived. Some people are serial learners and learn sequentially; others are trained as holistic learners."[2] Cultural psychologist Geert Hofstede says, "Our cognitive development is determined by the demands of the environment in which we grew up. . . . Cognitive abilities are rooted in the total patterns of a society."[3] To say it simply, learning contexts are culturally determined.

---

1. See Richard Nisbett, "Culture and Systems of Thought: Holistic Versus Analytic Cognition," *Psychological Review* 108, no. 2 (2001): 291–310; Marlene Enns, "'Now I Know in Part': Holistic and Analytic Reasoning and Their Contribution to Fuller Knowing in Theological Education," *Evangelical Review of Theology* 29, no. 3 (2005): 251–69; Valiente, "Are Students Using the 'Wrong' Style?," 73–91.

2. Timothy Tenant, *Theology in the Context of World Christianity* (Grand Rapids, MI: Zondervan, 2009), Kindle location 7709.

3. Geert Hofstede, "Cultural Differences in Teaching and Learning," *International Journal of Intercultural Relations* 10, no. 3 (1986): 307.

Understanding the cultural influences on the prior learning of our students will help us address negative aspects of learning and build on positive aspects. "The analysis of the learning process in different cultures highlights that both a learner's previous experience and the context in which learning takes place significantly condition the development of their preferred styles as a long-term structured behaviour, and their chosen learning strategies as a tactical response."[4] Discerning the underlying cultural influences on learning is no doubt difficult. Nonetheless it is crucial to our goal of meeting students where they are and leading them toward deep learning.

Cultural Influences on Learning

Our focus is the Arab world. By this I mean countries in the Middle East and North Africa whose chief language is Arabic. The Arabic language and the religion of Islam are significant unifiers that group sixteen Arab countries together culturally.[5] Jehad Al-Omani also adds a shared history as a cultural unifier.[6] Arab culture is highly collectivist, family, and tribally oriented. These collectivist societies are ruled by strong but consultative leaders. The result is an Islamic and Bedouin-based culture that is highly religious.

Islam governs all areas of life and therefore provides the structure for society. Najm Najm states, "The Arab culture seems to be most influenced by two main dimensions which are: (1) the religious dimension (or faith) and (2) family and tribal relationships."[7] These cultural traits are shared across the Arab Middle East. However they are not absolute to each person and differ from one country to another. Sidani says, "When one compares the existing Arab value system and compares it to professed Islamic values, one sees areas of commonality and areas of discrepancy. One finds commonalities in terms of the significance of the family and the importance of social bonds; one also sees discrepancies in the current character of Arab educational contexts and work values and orientations."[8]

Let's take a look at the cultural elements that shape the Arab learning situation.

---

4. Valiente, "Are Students Using the 'Wrong' Style?," 75.

5. Jehad Al-Omani, *Understanding the Arab Culture: A Practical Cross-Cultural Guide to Working in the Arab World*, 2nd ed. (Oxford, UK: How to Books, 2008).

6. Al-Omani, *Understanding the Arab Culture*.

7. Najm Najm, "Arab Culture Dimensions in the International and Arab Models," *American Journal of Business, Economics and Management* 3, no. 6 (2015): 426.

8. Sidani and Thornberry, "Current Arab Work Ethic," 38.

Islamic Culture

When referring to the Arab world and culture, we speak primarily about an Islamic culture.[9] Islam is considered to be the factor that shapes culture within Islamic countries and within Arab countries in particular.[10] Although there are historical and large Christian populations, particularly in Egypt and Lebanon, Islam comprises approximately 93 percent of the population of North Africa and the Middle East.[11] Across the region, the degree of orthodoxy and adherence to Islam varies.[12] Even so, the impact of the Islamic religion is pervasive in Arab culture and permeates a large part of life in the region. Islam is a way of life. It is a "system of belief and law that governs both spiritual and material conditions."[13] According to Samier, "It provides Muslims with detailed guidelines on how to conduct and manage their personal and professional affairs."[14] Arabic language, social life, and traditions are all rooted in Islam which is considered to be a complete way of life.[15]

Bedouin Culture

The other major component of Arab culture is the Bedouin background of the region. Prior to the coming of Islam, the Arab peninsula was inhabited by Bedouins,[16] and their culture was the predominant way of life during the rise of Muhammed. It was also the culture for those who succeeded him and endures in the region until today. Bedouins are tribal people who live in community and are ruled by a sheikh. Though the Arab region is now quite urbanized, the Bedouin culture remains imbedded in Arab thinking. "We have a tribal

9. Najm, "Arab Culture Dimensions."

10. Sidani and Thornberry, "Current Arab Work Ethic."

11. Drew DeSilver and David Masci, "World's Muslim Population More Widespread than You Might Think," 31 January 2017. Pew Research Center.

12. Hayat Kabasakal and Muzaffer Bodur, "Arabic Cluster: A Bridge between East and West," *Journal of World Business* 37, no. 1 (2002): 40–54.

13. Beverly Metcalf and Tony Murfin, "Leadership, Social Development and Political Economy in the Middle East: An Introduction," in *The Ethics of Islamic Leadership: A Cross-Cultural Approach for Public Administration*, ed. Beverly Metcalf and Tony Murfin (Cheltenham, UK: Edward Elgar, 2011), 10. See also Beverly Metcalf and Fouad Mimouni, *Leadership Development in the Middle East* (Cheltenham, UK: Edward Elgar, 2011).

14. Samier, "Ethics of Islamic Leadership," 194.

15. Bader Yousef Obeidat, "Toward Better Understanding of Arabian Culture: Implications based on Hofstede's Cultural Model," *European Journal of Social Sciences* 28, no. 4 (January 2012): 517. See also Najm, "Arab Culture Dimensions," 423.

16. Yasin Khalif Sarayrah, "Servant-Leadership in the Bedouin-Arab Culture," *Global Virtue Ethics Review* 5, no. 3 (2004): 58–79.

culture," says Ibrahim Dabdoub. "People always need a tribal chief in the Arab world." He goes on, "An important task of the sheikh is to care for the daily needs of the tribe."[17]

Arab culture is a collectivistic culture that places a strong emphasis on the family and the tribe. Both the family and the tribe are led by a strong father figure or tribal leader. The leader provides for and protects his people in return for unquestioned loyalty. The family or tribe is committed to preserving itself, the in-group. Members strongly desire stability that prevents disruption of this structure, and exceptions to this structure are seen as threatening.

The sheikh rules the people through a consultative system known as *shura*.[18] The leader interacts with and consults tribal members on decisions, yet upon making a decision, he is expected to be obeyed. *Shura* is defined as "the process of extensive discussion of an issue from all its aspects and dimensions, selection of the best given views on that issue and testing of those views to make sure that the best interests of the community are realized."[19] This cultural practice is part of both Islamic and Bedouin culture. According to the Qur'an, God emphasized the importance of *shura* by telling the Prophet, "And when you have come to a decision, place your trust in God alone."[20] A tribal sheikh cannot rule for a long time unless there is a consensus among the tribe regarding this matter. According to Tayeb, the importance of the tribal "in group" is emphasized by reinforcing "consultation, obedience to seniors, loyalty, face-to-face interaction and networks of personal connections."[21]

When Islam came to the Arab peninsula in the seventh century, it imbibed the tribal nature of community.[22] The Islamic religion and Bedouin tribalism are deeply woven into the Arab culture. "Al Wardi . . . claims that Muslims have Bedouin hearts while they speak with an Islamic tongue."[23] According to Najm, "Studies have shown interest in identifying the dimensions of the

---

17. Ibrahim Dabdoub, quoted in Farida Saidi, "A Study of Current Leadership Styles in the North African Church" (PhD diss., Fuller Seminary, 2011), 286.

18. Sarayrah, "Servant-Leadership in the Bedouin-Arab Culture," 67.

19. Ahmad Abul-Faris, *The Political System of Islam* (Amman: Library of the Modern Message, 1980), 79.

20. *Al-Qur'an: A Contemporary Translation*, trans. Ahmed Ali (Princeton, NJ: Princeton University Press, 1993), 68.

21. Monir Tayeb, *International Human Resource Management: A Multinational Company Perspective* (Oxford, UK: Oxford University Press, 2005), 76, quoted in Metcalf and Mimouni, *Leadership Development*, 76.

22. Darwish Almoharby, "Clarifying Islamic Perspectives on Leadership," *Education, Business and Society: Contemporary Middle Eastern Issues* 6, no. 3/4 (2013): 149.

23. Samier, "Ethics of Islamic Leadership," 190.

Arab culture in accordance with the teachings of Islam and traditions of Arab communities."[24] An understanding of the two threads of the Islamic religion and the Bedouin culture are important to understanding the culture of the Arab world as they affect all of life.

This influence includes leadership in other areas of society.[25] What distinguishes Islamic leadership from other theories of leadership is that it is "a social exchange"[26] with "a shared influence"[27] where leaders, while working for "the collective well-being of the society,"[28] seek advice and insights from followers through *shura* (consultation).[29] Leaders consult with their followers.[30]

Islam, along with tribal traditions and their collectivistic culture, are important factors that shape educational beliefs and practices in the Arab world. The importance of community, a strong leader, consultation, loyalty, and care are some of the relevant cultural factors that determine what happens in the learning process.

Honour and Shame

A key cultural descriptor of Arab society is honour and shame. Sania Hamady says that "Arab society is a shame-based society."[31] Arab culture can be described as an honour and shame culture rather than a guilt culture. Honour and shame are seen as external to a person, while guilt is internal. Roland Muller explains, "In order for shame-based cultures to work, shame and honor are usually attached to something greater than the individual. Honor is almost always placed on a group. This can be the immediate family, the extended tribe."[32] The honour or shame people feel is related to their "face" in respect to their

24. Najm, "Arab Culture Dimensions," 425.

25. Saidi, "Study of Current Leadership Styles."

26. Issa Rafik Beekun and Jamal Badawi, *Leadership: An Islamic Perspective* (Beltsville, MD: Amana, 1999), 7.

27. Abbas Ali, "Islamic Perspectives on Leadership: A Model," *International Journal of Islamic and Middle Eastern Finance and Management* 2, no. 2 (2009): 163.

28. Ali Mohammed Mir, "Leadership in Islam," *Journal of Leadership Studies* 4, no. 3 (2010): 69.

29. Samier, "Ethics of Islamic Leadership."

30. Ali, "Islamic Perspectives."

31. Quoted in Roland Muller, "Honor and Shame in a Middle Eastern Setting," Nabataea. net (2000), from Sania Hamady, *Temperament and Character of the Arabs* (New York: Twayne Publishers, 1960).

32. Muller, "Honor and Shame."

group, usually their family. "Social control in Arab society is based largely on shaming; hence it depends on primary and close groups."[33]

Muller states that "Arabs usually demand a high degree of conformity from those who are near to them. This conformity brings honor and social prestige and a secure place in society."[34] We see in Muller's statement ideas of community, stability, and status. Jackson Wu says, "A honor-shame perspective has at least three distinguishing emphases. These cultures particularly stress tradition, relationship and hierarchy. These three factors shape a person's social status or 'face.'"[35]

Honour and shame work through and can be seen in tradition, relationships, and hierarchy. These match up with three cultural factors we will look at in this chapter. "Tradition" speaks to the idea of stability and order. "[Honor-shame] cultures characteristically prefer constancy, uniformity, order and balance."[36] "Relationships" describe the community or group orientation of Arab culture. The idea of "hierarchy" points to the way people of different rank interact with each other, which points to the cultural factor of power-distance. All three of these cultural factors describe the outworking of honour and shame in societies. The idea of honour and shame undergirds these cultural factors and should be understood in our cultural evaluation of learning. We will mention below the influence of honour and shame as we examine adult ELT practices.

Arab-Originated Studies of Arab Culture

Arab-originated studies on culture support the reality that religion is an important factor shaping Arab culture. Arab models also affirm the influence of family and tribal orientation and a high degree of collectivism. Zaneb Salem and Syed Agil affirm the priority of religion, *shura* (collectivism), and authority as key factors in Arab culture.[37] Using terminology we will define below, both international and Arab studies point to a communal orientation that includes a strong leader and *shura*-style, or team- and humane-oriented interaction of the group. Al-Omani affirms the collectivistic and high power distance

---

33. Hamady, *Temperament and Character of the Arabs*, 34–35.

34. Muller, "Honor and Shame."

35. Jackson Wu, *Reading Romans with Eastern Eyes: Honor and Shame in Paul's Message and Mission* (Downers Grove, IL: IVP Academic, 2019), 13.

36. Wu, *Reading Romans with Eastern Eyes*, 16.

37. Zaneb Salem and Syed Agil, "The Effects of Islamic Management Ethics on Organizational Commitment of Employees in Libyan Public Banks," *Australian Journal of Basic and Applied Sciences* 6, no. 7 (2012): 267.

characteristics of the Arab culture.[38] Najm rightly makes the connection between Islam's belief in God as the absolute determiner of our fate and the high uncertainty avoidance in the Arab world.[39]

International Studies of Arab Culture

Below we will look at two well-known studies on global culture including the MENA region. These two studies are Geert Hofstede's *Cultural Dimensions* and the Global Leadership and Organizational Behavior Effectiveness (GLOBE) Leadership Study. These studies and others provide helpful handles for understanding culture and the cultural factors that shape adult education in our context. We will focus on Hofstede's research, but the GLOBE report uses the same, albeit expanded, cultural categories and applies them to leadership. Finally, we will look at Edwin Hall's description of high-context cultures and how his work helps us better understand the high-context nature of Arabic culture and communication.

From these studies we will identify six cultural dimensions that are most relevant to developing effective adult education models in the Arab region. We have already looked at two of them – the Islamic religion and Bedouin social structures and practices. Four additional dimensions flow from these two. They are (1) group and family collectivism, (2) power distance (PDI), (3) uncertainty avoidance (UAI), and (4) high or low context communication. Each will be explained below.

According to Hofstede's findings for the three cultural dimensions of collectivism, power distance, and uncertainty avoidance, the Arabic cluster rates high on group and family collectivism and power distance. It rates in the middle range for uncertainty avoidance. The GLOBE report affirms Hofstede's findings in the dimensions of power distance, collectivism, and uncertainty avoidance.[40] Arab studies attest to these findings as well. The last dimension, high or low context, influences how knowledge is communicated and received.

Hofstede's Cultural Dimensions Study

Geert Hofstede conducted one of the most comprehensive studies of how values in the workplace are influenced by culture. He analyzed a large database

---

38. Al-Omani, cited in Kabasakal and Bodur, "Arabic Cluster," 481–82.

39. Najm, "Arab Culture Dimensions," 424.

40. Kabasakal and Bodur, "Arabic Cluster," 46.

of employee value scores collected within the IBM computer company between 1967 and 1973. The data covered more than seventy countries.[41] "Ever since his first cross-cultural research studies, [Hofstede] has continued exploring alternative sources of data to validate and supplement his original, accidental IBM employee data set."[42] Later this research was expanded to include seventy-eight countries and was updated by Hofstede and others up until 2010.

Hofstede's research included the countries of Egypt, Iraq, Lebanon, Libya, Iran, Israel, Turkey, Morocco, Saudi Arabia, and UAE. In his original study, he looked at four cultural dimensions: power distance, individualism versus collectivism, masculinity versus femininity, and uncertainty avoidance. These dimensions were later expanded to include two more: long-term versus short-term orientation and indulgence versus restraint. Hofstede's research shows the Arab group to be high in power distance, collectivist, and uncertainty avoidance and slightly masculine. Arab countries score low on long-term orientation, meaning they tend to prefer time-honoured traditions and norms and view societal change with suspicion. Arab countries generally fall into the bottom half of the indulgence or restraint dimension, meaning they tend to restrain natural human drives to indulge and gratify desires through strict social norms.[43]

We will focus on three cultural factors that have significant impact on the educational process in the Arab region: power distance, uncertainty avoidance, and collectivism. These three provide us with keys to what hinders and what helps promote transformational learning. Studies have shown that Arab culture is characterized by high power distance and a low tolerance for ambiguity (high uncertainly avoidance) and is collectivist or group oriented.

High power distance means that an unequal distribution of power is readily accepted and even expected in the culture. Those without power in the family, business, or society are content for those in power to be in that position. In teaching and training, this cultural dimension impacts the teacher's position in the classroom and the interaction between the teacher and the students.

Uncertainty avoidance describes a society's comfort with uncertainty and ambiguity, which impacts how well and how fast people will accept change. If a teacher or trainer introduces change into the classroom, the degree and pace of the acceptance of the change will depend on the students' comfort with the change and the ambiguity it creates in them.

---

41. Hofstede, *Cultures and Organizations*.

42. Hofstede, *Cultures and Organizations*, Kindle location 254.

43. Hofstede.

Uncertainty avoidance is different than risk avoidance. Rather than leading to reducing risk, uncertainty avoidance leads to a reduction of ambiguity. People in uncertainty-avoiding cultures shun ambiguous situations. They look for structure in their organizations, institutions, and relationships that makes events clearly interpretable and predictable. Paradoxically, they are often prepared to engage in risky behaviour in order to reduce ambiguities, such as starting a fight with a potential opponent rather than sitting back and waiting.[44]

Collectivist societies are more tightly knit than individualistic societies. They think in terms of "we" instead of "I." People's life is defined by their "in-group" to which they pledge allegiance in return for unquestioned loyalty.[45] In the context of training, this cultural attribute impacts interaction between students and how threats to the in-group are perceived.

The GLOBE Report

The research of the GLOBE study included sixty-two countries and grouped the data from these countries into ten specific clusters that shared cultural dimensions but were different from each other.[46] One of those clusters is the Arabic cluster composed of Egypt, Morocco, Turkey, Kuwait, and Qatar.[47] It will be noted that Turkey is not part of the Arab region, but it is included in this grouping due to cultural similarities. This study does not include all countries from the Arab region as we have defined it. Although there are differences between countries in the Arab cluster, these countries do share cultural characteristics that allow them to be grouped together.[48]

The GLOBE report affirms Hofstede's findings in all three dimensions.[49] According to the GLOBE research, the Arabic cluster rates high on group and family collectivism and power distance, and it rates in the middle range for uncertainty avoidance. The cultural traits of collectivism and high power

---

44. Hofstede, 148.

45. Hofstede.

46. Cornelius Grove, *Worldwide Differences in Business Values and Practices: Overview of GLOBE Research Findings* (New York: Grovewell, 2005).

47. Robert House, *Culture, Leadership and Organizations: The GLOBE Study of 62 Societies* (Thousand Oaks, CA: Sage, 2004).

48. Najm, "Arab Culture Dimensions."

49. "Societal practices in the Arabic cluster are rated as high on Group and Family Collectivism (5.58) and Power Distance (5.23) and low on Future Orientation (3.58) and Gender Egalitarianism (2.95). Uncertainty Avoidance falls in the mid-range at 3.91." Kabasakal and Bodur, "Arabic Cluster," 46.

distance (PDI) are apt descriptors of the Islamic-Bedouin culture of the Arab region. The communal nature of Arabs is Bedouin and Islamic (*ummah*). That the leader in the Arab region is allowed to wield a high degree of authority is both a Bedouin and Islamic trait. Hofstede's research and the GLOBE report affirm the predominance of these traits in the region. As we will see from both the GLOBE report and Bedouin practice, the interaction between leader and community honours both the communal nature and high power distance practice of the culture. This interaction and the practice of leadership was studied more deeply in the GLOBE report.

In addition to cultural dimensions, GLOBE identified twenty-one different leadership dimensions that are common across all cultures.[50] These dimensions were ranked from most to least desirable in the respondents' culture and were statistically analyzed to derive universal rankings of most to least desirable.[51] These twenty-one dimensions were then reduced to six major leadership styles that are more or less universally desired. The six styles are charismatic/value-based; team oriented; participative; humane oriented; autonomous; and self-protective.[52] These styles provide us with some helpful insights into what successful leadership looks like in an Arab context, which in turn will help us as we look at how the teacher or trainer can successfully lead and teach their students.

Two leadership styles are most effective in the Arab culture. "Among the different leadership styles, team-oriented (5.47) and charismatic (5.35) are perceived to be most effective in the Arabic cluster."[53] Groves provides descriptions of each style. "The Charismatic/Value-based leader . . . seeks to inspire people around a vision; creates a passion among them to perform; and does so by firmly holding on to core values. The Team-oriented style instils pride, loyalty, and collaboration among organizational members; and highly values team cohesiveness and a common purpose or goals."[54] These findings

---

50. The GLOBE study was not just a study on culture. It also asked 17,300 middle-managers what they valued in a leader, in GLOBE's terminology, "what should be." The "should be" was defined as the values that people in societies and organizations consider important. Based on the survey responses, the team was able to identify twenty-one primary leadership dimensions that people in all cultures view to some extent as contributing to a leader's effectiveness or lack of effectiveness. Grove, *Worldwide Differences*, 3.

51. Grove, *Worldwide Differences*, 6.

52. Globe 2020, "An Overview of the 2004 Study: Understanding the Relationship Between National Culture, Societal Effectiveness and Desirable Leadership Attributes," Beedie School of Business.

53. Kabasakal and Bodur, "Arabic Cluster," 49.

54. Grove, *Worldwide Differences*, 3.

are consistent with a Bedouin style society that looks to their leaders to be strong and yet inclusive in their leadership.

After team-oriented and charismatic leadership styles, participative (4.98), and humane oriented (4.80) leadership styles were found to be desirable in the Arabic cluster. "The Participative style encourages input from others in decision-making and implementation; and emphasizes delegation and equality. The Humane style stresses compassion and generosity; and it is patient, supportive, and concerned with the well-being of others."[55] Humane orientation points to the care and provision that the leader is expected to provide followers in an Arab context. Darwish Al-Moharby states that this is the *shura* style of leadership.[56] Although the influence of these two styles is less than the first two, it is still positive and can be built upon as we look at leadership in the classroom.

The findings on team-oriented leadership promote a team-oriented style of teaching. Participative leadership can provide a model for how to conduct teaching and training according to the proven educational principles in section 2. The charismatic leader has the same concerns as the humane-oriented leader. "Outstanding leaders in the Arabic cluster frequently consult their subordinates in matters that interest them, yet the final decision belongs to the leader."[57] As we will see below, these characteristics are consistent with Arab cultural patterns as well as effective for teaching and training.[58] As we develop fruitful training methods, we can build on these desired leadership traits for teachers in the classroom.

Hall's High Context Communication

The research of anthropologist Edward Hall helped define how cultures differ in their reliance on the surrounding context when communicating with others.[59] High context cultures rely heavily on the surrounding context to understand what is being said because communication in high context cultures is not only by the words expressed, but also through cultural clues including body language, common cultural knowledge, cultural norms, etc. High context

---

55. Kabasakal and Bodur, "Arabic Cluster," 49.

56. Almoharby, "Clarifying Islamic Perspectives," 149.

57. Kabasakal and Bodur, "Arabic Cluster," 53.

58. The "should be" values and leadership attributes are influenced by underlying cultural dimensions that are part of the Arabic cluster and provide important touch points for using effective adult educational practices in the Arab world.

59. Edward T. Hall, *Beyond Culture* (Garden City, NY: Anchor, 1976).

communication is often indirect and requires the ability to "read between the lines."

Low context cultures, which includes many Western cultures, rely very little on the context to communicate and understand what is said because communication is primarily the facts with very little of the message being implied. Low context communication is therefore more direct. For example, Germans and Americans tend to be more direct or low-context. By contrast, Arabs tend to communicate more indirectly or high-context.[60]

"High context people are deeply imbedded in the immediate world around them."[61] They think and communicate more concretely and less abstractly than people in low-context cultures. As people in a high-context culture, Arabs tend to be more concrete and holistic in their thinking and communication. As a result, they use holistic approaches to learning that rely on experience-based knowledge rather than on abstract logic, as in low-context Western cultures.[62] Holistic learning is generally fostered in a collective society.[63] The learning styles of people in high-context, holistic cultures are also generally more concrete. "Holistic learning has a tendency to be praxis-oriented."[64] Yamazaki connects this characteristic to Kolb's concrete experience learning style, saying that people in holistic cultures "rely upon the tangible, felt qualities of here-and-now experience through sensory perception. Their immediate environments rather than universalistic conceptual symbols are so important to learning acquisition."[65] This supports the idea that the Arab learners are more concrete and practically oriented by nature.

We see from the above cultural descriptions that the Arab learning context is influenced by Islam and Bedouin culture, is characteristically collectivist with high power distance and uncertainty avoidance, and is more concrete than low-context Western cultures. These are the primary cultural factors that influence the interactions between leaders and followers and thus the interactions between teachers and students. These are the cultural aspects of the prior learning experiences of our students and what influences the effectiveness of using adult learning principles that we will look at in our next chapter.

---

60. Hall, *Beyond Culture*.

61. James Plueddemann, *Leading across Cultures: Effective Ministry and Mission in the Global Church* (Downers Grove, IL: InterVarsity, 2009), Kindle location 721.

62. Nisbett, "Culture and Systems of Thought," 291–310.

63. Enns, "Now I Know in Part," 251–269.

64. Enns, 268.

65. Y. Yamazaki, "Learning Styles and Typologies of Cultural Differences: A Theoretical and Empirical Comparison," *International Journal of Inter-Cultural Relations* 29 (2005): 529.

12

Practice, Culture, and Learning Expectations

Culture plays an important role in the learning process. In this chapter, we will explore how culture is manifested in learning situations. Our examination of educational principles in light of cultural dynamics will provide confidence to know what adult ELT principles to use and how best to use them in an Arab setting. I believe there are ways to apply effective teaching practices that are culturally and contextually relevant. To do so we must filter our teaching assumptions and methodologies through Middle Eastern and North African culture.[1] We also need to heed the warning from Sidani and Thornberry that "it is difficult to introduce change, not just in schools, but to lead the student or students into new and effective educational methods."[2]

Culture as a Bridge

Adult learning principles and practices do work in Arab settings, and using them is crucial for deep and transformational learning. The question facing us is *how* these theories and resultant teaching activities can be effective in an Arab context, because uncritical adaptation of these practices will not produce the desired results. As Burt states, "Students from teacher-centered educational systems are unfamiliar with active learning and frequently have problems adapting to the new mode of learning."[3] Using ELT methods without any

---

1. Jacqueline Prowse, "Teaching across Cultures: Canada and Qatar," *Canadian Journal of Higher Education* 40, no. 1 (2010): 31–52.

2. Sidani and Thornberry, "Current Arab Work Ethic," 42.

3. John Burt, "Impact of Active Learning on Performance and Motivation in Female Emirate Students," *Learning and Teaching in Higher Education: Gulf Perspectives* 1 (2004): 1–15.

adjustment for culture can cause students to feel frustrated and unmotivated because these methods differ from those used in their primary and secondary schools. Therefore when new methods are used, students "perceive that they are learning less than would be learned through traditional lectures, even with what they feel is an excessively high workload."[4]

It is also important to consider cultural differences when transferring educational practices from one culture to another.[5] Simple one-to-one adaptation of teaching methods, particularly from West to East, is not effective because as Mahrous states, "there are still sharp contrasts between the teaching and learning styles of the Middle Eastern and Western countries."[6] Amira Khattab and David Wong write, "Both Androgogy and Self-Directed Learning exist in stark contrast to Arabic learning traditions where individual autonomy is regarded as potentially damaging to the development of individuals and their relations to others."[7] Western curriculum and teaching methods need adaptation before being employed in the MENA region.

For making these adaptations, we can see value of understanding cultural influences on education. Understanding the prior learning experiences of our students also informs how to adapt and implement different practices. In short, it is important to evaluate both the method and how it is introduced into the context.

The diagram below summarizes the role culture plays in informing our understanding of prior learning, what ELT practices can be used, and how to use them.

**Culture Is the Bridge that Connects Understanding
Prior Learning and How to Use ELT**

---

4. Burt, "Impact of Active Learning," 3.

5. Burt.

6. Mahrous, "Cross-Cultural Investigation," 292.

7. Amira Khattab and David Wong, "Integrating Western and Arab Leadership Development Practices: An Example of the Challenge Bridging Global and Local Adult Learning Perspectives," *Adragoske Studije* 0354–5415, broj 11 (Dec 2018): 67.

We must look at how culture shapes prior learning because this step is critical in shaping expectations, which in turn influence how and what adult ELT practices will be effective. Skipping over understanding prior learning through culture contributes to uncritical use of adult ELT and will make our teaching and training less fruitful at best and counter-productive at worst.

Applying Culturally Appropriate ELT

Arab culture is primarily a product of Islam and Bedouin communal relationships. "The Arab culture seems to be most influenced by two main dimensions which are: (1) the religious dimension (or faith) and (2) family and tribal relationships."[8] These dimensions manifest in culture through family and group collectivism, high power distance (PDI), uncertainty avoidance (UAI), and high-context communication. These elements provide insight into what happens in the classroom and why it happens as well as teacher-student relationships. It also shines light on how students perceive truth or facts, what communication looks like to them, how they accept change, and how they interact with each other.

These cultural factors are manifested in *shura* leadership that seeks the good of followers, listens to them, and serves to protect and provide for them. In turn, followers provide loyalty to their leaders and trust them to seek their good. In our examination of culture and its effect on learning, I suggest that the principle of *shura* can be used to describe the cultural dynamics that shape the learning process, including both prior learning and the learning we hope to offer in our training.

How can the bridge of culture help us use ELT principles that are agreeable with MENA cultural factors? The GLOBE study provides us a guide vis-a-vis adult education principles by describing effective leadership characteristics in the Arab cluster. These include charismatic leadership which conforms to high power distance, team or group orientation that aligns with the communal nature of Arab culture, and humane leadership which is how charismatic leaders use their power and authority for the good of their followers. Together these describe *shura* leadership.

The ideal view of leadership is one of strong, charismatic leaders who are providers and protectors of their followers. This concept can be characterized as servant and guardian leadership.[9] These leaders are consultative using

---

8. Najm, "Arab Culture Dimensions," 426.

9. Samier, "Ethics of Islamic Leadership," 188–211.

the principle of *shura* and seek the good of the community *umma*. They are expected to be unique or set apart,[10] yet consult with followers while guarding the harmony of the group.[11]

Some have described this type of leader as "sheikhocratic," combining the authority of the tribal sheikh with a more democratic view of leadership.[12] "The sheikh is not necessarily the autocratic leader to whom everybody listens."[13] On the contrary, he is a person who continuously seeks the advice of his followers and interacts with them. These interactions signify what is termed "shiekhocracy." He is both autocratic and consulte.[14] As a style that protects and provides for its followers, sheikhocratic is both visionary and committed to the growth of followers.[15] It is what Perry Shaw calls theocratic servant leadership that leads with vulnerable authority.[16]

I call this a *shura*-based approach to leadership. It is charismatic and humane. It is directive while seeking the good of followers and listening to their input. The *shura* aspects that arise out of the Bedouin community culture relate in very direct ways to effective adult learning practices. These are most clearly related to the Power Distance and Collectivist dimensions in Hofstede and GLOBE.

This *shura* interaction between the leader (sheikh) and follower has positive implications for the teacher who uses adult ELT to interact with their students. They point to a way that adult ELT principles and practices can be used in an Arab setting. Team-oriented leadership provides a helpful pattern for interaction between the educational leader and learners. Participative leadership offers us guidance for how to conduct teaching and training according to proven educational principles studied above.

Shura interaction is consistent with both cultural patterns in the Arab Middle East as well as effective teaching and training principles and practices. It is how we can use ELT principles that are agreeable with MENA cultural factors.

---

10. Mansour Javidan, "In the Eye of the Beholder: Cross Cultural Lessons in Leadership from Project GLOBE," *Academy of Management Perspectives* 20, no. 1 (2006): 80.

11. Stephen Robbins, Mary Coulter, Yusuf Sidani, and Dima Jamali, *Management: Arab World Edition* (London: Pearson Higher Education, 2012), 389.

12. See Robbins, Coulter, Sidani, and Jamali, *Management*, and Farida Saidi, "Study of Current Leadership Styles."

13. Robbins, Coulter, Sidani, and Jamali, *Management*, 390.

14. Robbins, Coulter, Sidani, and Jamali, 287.

15. Robbins, Coulter, Sidani, and Jamali, 295–296.

16. Perry Shaw, "Muslim Education: An Introduction to Philosophy, Curriculum and Methodology with Reflections on its Impact on the Evangelical Churches of the Arab Levant" (EdD preliminary paper, Pacific College of Graduate Studies, 1995), 131.

Shura-Based Educational Leadership

From my experience in the Arab world, I have observed that the characteristics that describe successful Arab leaders are similar to the characteristics of effective teachers and trainers. The practice of *shura* offers many keys to what a fruitful learning environment looks like in Arab cultures. The idea of *shura* also incorporates the elements needed in a culturally effective adult ELT approach to teaching and training. We can call this *shura*-based learning or education.

Shura-based learning respects the idea of the sheikh-type leader (high power distance) and the communal nature of students (collectivism). In *shura*-based teaching, teachers consult and seek what is best for those they lead while students honour and respect their teacher. *Shura*-based learning also incorporates Arab world experiences into Arab adult education. *Shura*-based learning coalesces the streams of education, culture, and practical experience into a model that I believe will produce transformational learning in the lives of regional leaders.

Below we will look at how the four cultural factors of PDI, collectivism, UAI and high context shape students' prior learning, how *shura* education plays out in the adult learning process, and what tensions must be balanced in employing *shura* education. As we look at these factors, I will mention some particular behaviours that manifest in the classroom and raise some questions to consider, both of which will help us use experiential learning in culturally effective ways.

Teacher as Authority: Prior Learning

People in societies exhibiting a high degree of power distance, like the Arab cluster, accept the idea that the teacher or professor is rightfully the authority in the classroom. This reality has both positive and negative implications that need to be addressed when developing teaching and training. The parent-child relationship in a high-power distance culture is translated to the teacher-student relationship in the classroom.

> In the large power distance situation, the parent-child inequality is perpetuated by a teacher-student inequality that caters to the need for dependence well established in the student's mind. . . . In the classroom there is supposed to be a strict order, with the teacher initiating all communication. Students in class speak up

only when invited to; teachers are never publicly contradicted or criticized and are treated with deference even outside school.[17]

The teacher is the authority, the sage, and the answer giver who has wisdom to impart to students.[18] Strong uncertainty avoidance also helps us understand the teacher as authority. "Students from strong uncertainty-avoidance countries expect their teachers to be the experts who have all the answers. Teachers who use cryptic academic language are respected."[19] What teachers impart is personal wisdom that is to be memorized and accepted almost without question. The job of the students is memorize what their teachers or professors say, to respect them, and demonstrate their loyalty.

This is a teacher and information-, or pedagogy, not andragogy focused learning environment. Students are not encouraged to think or analyze outside the box of the teacher's imparted wisdom. This is why teaching methods tend to emphasize repetition and memorization rather than creative thinking and lifelong learning. Memorization as learning is connected to the teacher as authority. The teacher is also the one who directs and initiates what happens in the class. Students speak when allowed to speak, which lessens give-and-take interaction.

Changing the teacher as authority or other accepted norms will often be met with reluctance[20] because serious aspects of learning are viewed as being at stake including the role of the teacher, the role of the students, the very purpose of learning, how learning happens, and the source of truth or facts.

Some implications of this way of relating can be seen in the following questions: How does the teacher view the students, and how do students view their teacher? What are the strengths of this method that help facilitate fruitful learning in the classroom? Does it have weaknesses that hinder successful adult learning? Because high power distance and strong uncertainty avoidance are salient characteristics of the Arab cluster, these and other questions must be addressed in forming a fruitful adult learning environment.

---

17. Hofstede, *Cultures and Organizations*, Kindle location 1379.
18. Hofstede, Kindle location 1382.
19. Hofstede, Kindle location 3574.
20. Mahrous, "Cross-Cultural Investigation," 301.

Shura *Education in Practice*

Teachers are the authority, and they impart wisdom that resides with them. This is a personal truth[21] and is in contrast with the low power distance of Western cultures where truth is detached from the teacher and is viewed more abstractly as a set of facts that exist "out there." The high-power distance nature of the classroom in Arab cultures negatively impacts the learning process in many ways. However, this characteristic needs to be understood and respected in an adult learning situation because respectfully guarding this teacher-student relationship can contribute positively to the learning process.

That the truth resides with the professor honours the high-power distance relationship. That the truth is personal can help to foster a warm *shura*-like relationship between the learner and the teacher. Just as the father is the authority who guards the cohesiveness of the family unit, so also the teacher as authority provides stability for the group and the structure that the students desire. This in turn solidifies the teacher's position as the authority. Both parties in the learning process prefer this situation, so a *shura*-like relationship can contribute positively to a fruitful learning environment.

The idea of *shura*-based teaching can include teachers involving their students in the teaching process and encouraging them to discover the truth themselves in groups. However, maintaining a healthy balance between valuing ideas generated by the student group and those communicated by the teacher as authority is critical to developing a culturally appropriate adult learning model.

Balance the Tension Between:

Teacher as Authority ←————————————→ Collaborate with Students

The *shura* view of leadership tempers the idea of only the teacher having authority or possessing all the answers. It pushes against a teacher-centred approach in the classroom and allows for discussion in the classroom that gives the students a voice in the educational process. In a sense, it consults with the students to listen to what they want, which is a foundational adult education principle. Yet it does not release the entire process into the hands of the student. The teacher's role is key. *Shura* teaching honours the principle that adults like to take the initiative in the learning process. Yet it also realizes that the teacher

---

21. Geert Hofstede, *Culture's Consequences: Comparing Values, Behaviors, Institutions, and Organizations across Nations* (Thousand Oaks, CA: Sage, 2001), Kindle location 1386.

or mentor leads the students and has much to offer them. The group (student) oriented leader is both charismatic (authority) and participative (*shura*).

Shura teacher-trainers practice servant leadership that seeks the good of their students. Teachers who lead in a *shura* way will teach for the benefit of their students. They will think how the subject can be taught in ways that meet these needs and will craft both the subject as well as the manner of teaching to benefit their students.

Shura leadership listens to followers and directs followers. *Shura* teachers hear from their students to define their needs. They allow students to express their thoughts as part of the learning process. Yet teachers offer the final thought on the subject, which is both culturally acceptable and educationally effective. Valuing the adult learner and their experience is important to successful adult learning. Forming curriculum goals and methods based on students' needs and input combines both culturally appropriate and educationally effective principles. We see here that educationally effective means of teaching can be employed in culturally appropriate ways.

Interaction and Consensus

The cultural dimensions of collectivism and high-power distance play out in Arab culture through the principle of *shura* or consensus. The power granted authority figures, whether in the family or society, is a "social contract,"[22] and they are unable to lead without the tribe's loyal commitment[23] which requires consulting them on decisions. As we saw above, even Muhammed was instructed to "consult with his followers."[24] In return for their loyalty, they expected the leader to protect, guide, and provide for them.

Viewing students as the followers and the teacher as the sheikh helps us understand the interaction between the two. Students only speak when called upon by the teacher. As well, students find their identity in the group. The collective nature of the students seeks to guard the status quo described above. They want to protect their group coherence. They as a group may be threatened when the *shura* sheikh relationship is challenged, which points to the importance of the group in the classroom. The students remain loyal to each other over against an individual shining above the rest.

---

22. Samier, "Ethics of Islamic Leadership," 195.

23. Sarayrah, "Servant-Leadership in the Bedouin-Arab Culture," 58–79. See also Javidan, "In the Eye of the Beholder," 81.

24. *Al-Qur'an: A Contemporary Translation*, Al Imran 159.

This interaction has implications for the classroom. Is there tension between the teacher as authority and the idea of *shura* where the authority consults their followers? If *shura* is intrinsically Arab, how can it play out in the learning context? What value is placed on ideas generated by the group versus those communicated by the teacher-authority? These are important issues we will address as we develop a culturally appropriate adult learning model.

Shura *Education in Practice*

Shura education turns the focus of teaching away from the teacher to the group, the learners and allows them to discover truth and to learn from each other. Students find their identity in the group. This group identity has positive implications for group work because the students will work together to come to a conclusion that as a group they share with the class. Because individuals find safety in the group and the collective opinion, they can be encouraged to think and contribute to the group process as a tribal member. Yet fruitful teaching requires the collectivist needs of students to be balanced with the teacher as authority.

As we saw above, the *shura* view of leadership tempers the idea of only the teacher having authority or possessing all the answers. It also pushes against a teacher-centred approach in the classroom and allows for discussion that gives the student a voice in the educational process. In a sense, it consults with the student to listen to what they want, which is a foundational adult education principle. Yet it does not release the entire process into the hands of the student. *Shura* teaching honours the principle that adults like to take the initiative in the learning process but also realizes that the teacher or mentor leads the student and has much to offer them. This group-oriented leadership is both charismatic (authority) and participative (*shura*).

Shura leadership is participative in that it listens to followers before directing followers. *Shura* teachers will listen to their students define their needs and allow students to express their thoughts as part of the learning process. Valuing the adult learner and their experience is important to successful adult learning, and forming curriculum goals and methods based on students' needs and input combines both culturally appropriate and educationally effective principles.

Again we must maintain a balance. Effective teaching and training must balance the authority of the teacher with the need to include adult learners in the learning process. Teacher-trainers will need to move between the two based on prior learning expectations and their students' tolerance for change.

Balance the Tension Between:

Truth from Authority ◄────────────► Truth Discovered by Students

A more collaborative approach to teaching and training appeals to the *communal* nature of Arab learners. For example, doing work in small groups, which helps students develop critical thinking and reasoning, appeals to the communal nature of Arabs. As learners work in groups and discover new truths, it would be wise to have groups report their conclusions. Although the group will state their collective conclusion, the individual members of the group will own this conclusion because each is encouraged to think and contribute to the process, which exercises their thinking and reasoning.

To maintain this balance and guard the teacher as authority, it would be beneficial to have the teacher conclude the small group learning session by summarizing and defining the correct conclusions. Thus the teacher as authority provides the structure students are used to, reducing the increased ambiguity created by more student-centred small groups.

Small groups, case studies, class discussions, and other unstructured learning activities contribute to critical thinking and reasoning skills. These can all be facilitated in small group settings which are in harmony with the communal nature of Arab learners. In many cases, it is more fruitful to conduct learning activities in a group setting rather than as individual assignments because the group discovers truth and learns within the safety net of the teacher's authoritative knowledge.

Culture, Educational Structure, and Content

Many of the needs of our students are based in their culture. As we saw above, maintaining the position of teachers and their relationship to students reduces ambiguity in the learning process which in turn reduces students' anxiety. These relate to the cultural factor of uncertainty avoidance.

Need for Structure: Prior Learning

Students who have not been exposed to the type of teaching we are proposing may be slow to accept it due to a low tolerance for ambiguity, also called uncertainty avoidance. Sidani and Thornberry state, "This is why it is difficult to introduce change, not just in schools, but to lead the student or students into new and effective educational methods."[25] High UAI means that students prefer structure within the classroom. This includes both the teacher's authority, as well as the teaching style they use. Students prefer structured assignments, meaning precise instructions and detailed assignments.[26]

Uncertainty avoidance is the extent to which people are made anxious by situations they view as unstructured or unclear and how secure people feel about knowing what to do or when to do it. Through my own observations in the classroom, Arab students prefer prescriptive learning environments where they are told exactly what to do and directed along a single path. The research of others supports these observations.[27] Thus active learning methods with the teacher as facilitator, which is currently being promoted in the Higher College of Technology (HCT), often produces anxiety and disengagement.[28]

As we adjust learning for students who have a low tolerance for ambiguity, these are some questions to address. Since change is adapted to more slowly, will adult learners accept new teaching methods? Will new methods be effective? If so, how can these changes be introduced so they are not perceived as threatening? How will perceived changes in the accepted power distance relationship between teacher and student be accepted? What is the role of the teacher in introducing new learning exercises? Will these exercises be a source of stress to students and thus counter-productive? What methods will be more easily accepted by students versus others?

Shura *Education in Practice*

Many teachers find it hard to employ modern educational techniques with students who are used to extreme disciplinary measures within their families and schools. To address these issues, new forms of teaching "need to be expressed in forms and cultural and religious language that can be understood and internalized in Arab countries."[29] For example, uncertainty avoidance has particular implications for using group work as a teaching method. If the teacher is not controlling the process, then the students can become uncertain and may not trust what is said or value the process as real learning.

---

25. Sidani and Thornberry, "Current Arab Work Ethic," 42.

26. Wursten, and Jacobs, "Impact of Culture," 11.

27. Hitt, "Secondary Implementation," 13–15. See also Prowse, "Teaching across Cultures," 31–52; Huib Wurston and Carel Jacobs, *The Impact of Culture on Education* (Helsinki: ITIM International, 2016), 11.

28. Richardson, "Possible Influences of Arabic-Islamic Culture," 429–436.

29. Samier, "Ethics of Islamic Leadership," 204.

While cultural traits must be considered when introducing new methods, to teach and train effectively requires both challenging and building upon these cultural traits. So we must balance the tension between need for structure due to high uncertainty avoidance and the need to introduce less-structured adult learning activities.

Balance the Tension Between:

Structure ◄──────────────────────────────► Ambiguity

Balancing this tension is important when addressing students' expectations about the role of the teacher, the role of the students, the very purpose of learning, how teaching happens, and the source of truth, and challenging these expectations is difficult. In introducing change in educational practices, care must be taken to consider students and what is best for them, which aligns with *shura* leadership. The ambiguity created by using new learning methods can be lessened by explaining the learning activities, slowly introducing these activities, and showing students the payoffs of these activities such as being better able to lead others, improved relationships, getting a job, etc. Because of *shura*-style leadership, students are used to having a voice in decisions. So introducing *shura*-style discussion and group activities should be effective.

Desire for Concrete Learning: Prior Learning

People in Arab cultures are concrete learners.[30] What they know, they know practically and not theoretically,[31] and they learn from experience. These learners are also holistic, meaning they relate what they learn to a whole and not in isolation.[32] Their learning is more practical or related to the here and now, so their immediate environment rather than universalistic conceptual symbols are important to learning.[33] In short, the Arab learner is concrete and praxis-oriented.

This preference for concrete learning has implications for how information is presented and how teachers and trainers can help their students process information. Understanding this cultural issue helps us address questions like

---

30. Yamazaki, "Learning Styles and Typologies," 521–548.
31. Hofstede, *Cultures and Organizations*.
32. Hall, *Beyond Culture*, 91.
33. Yamazaki, "Learning Styles and Typologies," 529.

these. How can information be presented and processed in a way that avoids the abstract? How can experience and story be used in our teaching? What methods can be used to help students apply what they learn, solve concrete problems they face, and connect what they learn to their life and work?

We saw above that Western thinking is more abstract while Arab thinking is more concrete. Both have advantages to learning and should be utilized in our teaching. Abstract thinking allows for learning a principle and how to apply it in different situations. Yet it sometimes can be theoretical and not applied to real life situations. Concrete thinking is practical and applicable to specific situations. Although it addresses some circumstances, it can be too problem focused and doesn't seek to apply principles across different situations.

Shura *Education in Practice*

In Kolb's learning cycle, abstract conceptualization is an important part of the learning process. Although not a primary feature of Arab culture, it is key to how adults learn and will help shepherd-leaders learn concepts and how to apply them to different situations in life, which is deep learning. Thus the teacher-trainer must move between the learner's tendency toward concrete thinking and the development of more conceptual thinking.

Balance the Tension Between:

Concrete Thinking ◄────────────────► Conceptual Thinking

Balancing between concrete, practical teaching and methods that encourage reasoning and critical thinking takes advantage of the strengths of each. Our goal is concrete application of our teaching and training. At the same time, some of our teaching will be conceptual. But as we balance between these, we will see real change in those we train, particularly in their ability to apply what they learn to concrete situations.

Balancing Four Tensions

The characteristics of successful leadership in Arab culture contexts – consultative, group oriented, compassionate – mirror successful adult education practices. However, teacher-trainers should balance the high-power distance view that the teacher is the authority (charismatic leadership) with high collectivism which is consultative (participative leadership) in including students in the learning process. Teachers also need to balance a structured (low ambiguity tolerance) approach with a student-initiated approach that encourages creativity and critical thinking and changes the passive nature of the learning process. These practices honour both the culture of the region and fruitful adult education principles.

Effective educational leaders employ a servant leader[34] approach that allows them to be the charismatic authority, but also to seek the good of the learners and include them in the learning process. Teacher-trainers need to balance the expectation to be the authority with the reason-developing practice of involving students collaboratively in the learning process.

Summary of *Shura* Educational Leadership

I define *shura*-based learning as the interaction between the discipler (teacher, trainer, etc.) and the disciple (learner, leader, etc.) that incorporates the elements of adult ELT in a way that honours and challenges the educational and cultural makeup of the Arab learner by respecting the role of the teacher while seeking what is best for the learner to produce transformation in the disciple's thinking, affections, and actions.

Shura-based learning is how biblical, educational, and cultural principles can be effectively applied in training leaders in an Arab context. Fruitful adult-education practices align with successful MENA leadership practices and regional cultural characteristics. Wisdom and sensitivity are needed to apply these principles in ways that are acceptable and effective.

Shura-based learning facilitates the interaction between the teacher as authority and desire of students to share in the learning process, including both planning what will be done and the learning process. Because this approach values students, it utilizes their experience and seeks to help them address the problems and challenges they face.

Shura-based learning also provides learners the opportunity to reflect on both what they have learned and their experiences. Teacher-trainers play an important part in this process by using their experience and knowledge to ask questions and provide perspective. They also support students by giving them practical opportunities to experiment and apply what they have learned.

Shura-based learning helps us manage the cultural tensions of concrete and conceptual thinking; teacher as authority and collaboration with students; ambiguity and structure; and truth from authority; and truth discovered by

---

34. Sarayrah, "Servant-Leadership in the Bedouin-Arab Culture," 71–72.

students. It honours the important role of the teacher-trainer while valuing the student. It presents truth in a way that is personal and practical. It supports the student while introducing new learning methods. *Shura*-based learning keeps the above tensions in balance.

To this point we have woven together principles from the Scriptures, education, and culture to form a culturally appropriate learning paradigm. I believe there is good reason to trust that this paradigm, when applied wisely, can produce the deep learning we seek for shepherd-leaders of God's church in the Arab world. We should have confidence that adult ELT principles and Arab culture are compatible. We will next consider how specific adult ELT practices can work in an Arab setting and how best to introduce them in light of the prior learning experiences and culture of our students. To buttress our confidence, we will listen and learn from educators in the Arab Gulf who have used adult ELT principles and practices successfully.

Section IV

Implementing ELT in MENA Adult Education

In this final section, I seek to offer some guidance on how to implement *shura-based* principles in our Arab context. In the introduction, I noted three (there are no doubt more) challenges specific to training leaders in an Arab context. These were issues related to security, Western and Arab learning practices, and the difficulty of many in accessing seminaries and Arabic materials for the growing Arab church. Just as making adjustments for culture facilitates more effective training, we need to adjust for contextual issues in which the Arab church exists.

Contexts differ from country to country, and even within the same country. The need for privacy varies. Some groups meet openly; others are extremely careful. Some groups have up to one hundred believers; others are quite small, even three to twenty believers. Some places are able to provide training and seminary courses in country; some are not. Leaders differ in maturity. Some need to focus on character development; some need deeper knowledge of God's word.

Our contexts include leaders desperate to develop people within their church to serve the body. They need both elders and mature leaders. The people to be developed are often new to the faith and have little knowledge of the

Scriptures or understanding of the church. So the church is overwhelmed by the need to care for the many new believers in their midst. Other leaders want to develop and train a team of church planters to send to different areas of the country to start new churches. These church planters have a basic knowledge of Scripture and have shown themselves faithful in serving. They already possess a certain level of proven knowledge, character, and ministry skills. But they need more training.

I have seen the principles presented in this book used in a variety of situations, including in training church planters, pastors of established churches, other wanting to revitalize churches ravaged by violence, and groups trying to identify and develop leaders for new believers. The specific situations are many and diverse, which is why implementing these principles takes a lot of discussion, trial, error, listening, and learning. Nonetheless, the paradigm is applicable in each of these different contexts.

In stating that this paradigm works, I am reminded of our first principle – God's sovereignty. Ultimately it is God who builds his church and raises up shepherd-leaders to care for her. I believe God uses our wise efforts, but am sure he works beyond them for his purposes. Resting in God's good promise to build his church, I do believe that this paradigm can be used to develop training appropriate to our context. In the first chapter of this section, we will look at how the educational theories and principles of Bloom, Knowles, and Knob can be applied in Arab cultural contexts. Next, we will see how their theories and principles are currently being used in adult education in the Arab Gulf. To help us think about our particular context, I will then suggest some critical issues to consider for developing and implementing training and then present a three-part development process for implementing *shura*-based leadership education.

13

ELT Principles in Cultural Practice

In the last chapter, we looked at some of the ways cultural factors play out in the classroom. In this chapter, we will evaluate adult experimental learning theory (ELT) principles through the lens of cultural values and practices. Specifically, we will spell out how the principles from Knowles, Kolb, and Bloom can be adapted for use in our Arab context and what adjustments may be needed to apply them effectively. This will move us toward our goal of using adult experiential learning in culturally appropriate ways to produce deep learning.

We can understand cultural values and the practices influencing Arab education as building blocks toward an effective use of ELT. Experimental learning theory is not strictly a Western concept. It is a collection of adult teaching principles that do work in an Arab context.

> Sustainable development is built on what people have, and not on what people lack. The most valuable asset every person/ group has is their experiences and what they do. Reflecting on one's practice and expressing what people do are, thus, the most valuable abilities/habits one can acquire in relation to learning. In addition, they are crucial in building authentic Arab discourse and thought concerning education, and in contributing to current discussions concerning education around the world.[1]

The experiences and practices of the Arab culture are the building blocks for constructing a fruitful training programme that incorporates adult ELT principles and practices. As with any culture, some issues will need to be addressed. But our examination of Arab culture has revealed the assets for constructing a fruitful and culturally appropriate training model.

---

1. Richardson, "Possible Influences of Arabic-Islamic Culture," 435.

Our goal is deep, transformational learning that develops new ideas, new abilities, and new affections in learners. Because Arab culture is amenable to fruitful adult ELT, we should find a number of other touch points between the principles of Knowles and Kolb and Arab culture and experience. We will also see how ELT education principles can be used in culturally appropriate ways, which move us toward our goal of deep learning in Bloom's three domains.

Knowles and Arab Culture

Below we will examine Knowles's five adult education principles vis-á-vis MENA culture which will help us as we seek to apply these principles in our context.

Independent Learning

First, learners must value being self-directed and independent. The cultural attribute of high power distance has produced a highly teacher-directed and dependent learning environment. As a result in a formal classroom setting, adult learners tend to take a more dependent role in the learning process. That adults in Arab cultures are able to learn independently can be seen in practical and informal education. But we will need to support them to be more self-directed in the learning process. Based on my experience, as adult learners see the benefits of taking ownership of the learning process, they are internally motivated to learn and become more independent.

Experience-Based Learning

For MENA learners, past experiences are stories from their life that have meaning and significance to them and are a part of who they are. Their experience is contained in their story. People in Arab cultures learn in story and communicate concepts in story. I have noticed this in interacting with students in the region. When I ask students to explain what they know, they often share a story or a situation that demonstrates their knowledge. They don't answer in concepts but in stories. This cultural attribute fits with their concrete, holistic nature of learning. "Stories draw us into an experience at more than a cognitive level; they engage our spirit, our imagination, our heart, and this engagement is complex and holistic."[2] "The eliciting of personal stories makes

---

2. M. C. Clark and M. Rossiter, "Narrative Learning in Adulthood," *New Directions for Adult and Continuing Education* 119 (Fall, 2008): 65.

the curriculum content more real, more immediate, and more personal."[3] So their experience is a tremendous resource in our teaching and training.

Inclusion of concrete experience as a part of the learning process is supported both by Kolb's learning cycle and the cultural makeup of Arab learners. These learners also desire practical knowledge that addresses the issues they face in life. We should assist students in learning by helping them reflect on their experiences and also build upon their experiences by giving them more, including ministry assignments in the church.

Learning in Life and Work Categories

The education experience of MENA learners has been learning theoretical information that is separated from real life, but they live life in the practical. We can open up new venues of learning and develop an appreciation for acquiring knowledge and skills if we appeal to this practical and concrete nature by connecting learning with the life and work of our shepherd-leaders. Adults desire to learn what is relevant and helpful for their immediate role or task. This desire creates an appreciation for acquiring new knowledge and skills as they understand how what they learn is connected to what they do. They do not want theoretical information but teachers' personal wisdom connected to their experience. Thus training should be a transfer of practical information, and in this type of training there is cultural and andragogic educational alignment.

Problem-Centred Learning

Knowles tells us that adult learners are not mainly content centred but problem centred. Adult MENA learners want to solve problems and address the challenges they face. They innately adapt to better ways of doing their work, and they readily imbibe new experiences that speak to their everyday life situations and help them grow because their practical desire to solve problems is part of their culture.

In our context, teacher-trainers will have to lead learners in thinking about how to transfer what they learn to solve the problems they face because transferring principles to practical life situations is not how they learned in school. Also, adult Arab students naturally learn concepts and principles from concrete examples, so it will be crucial to give them concrete examples and

3. M. C. Clark and M. Rossiter, "'Now the Pieces Are in Place . . .': Learning through Personal Storytelling in the Adult Classroom," *New Horizons in Adult Education and Human Resource Development* 20, no. 3 (Summer 2006): 31.

support them in applying the abstract principles they must learn to various work and life challenges. Students are ready, but the process of how-to needs to be modelled and guided.

Internal Motivation

Throughout their childhood education experience, the motivation for Arab learners was primarily external. The teacher directed the learning process, and learning was primarily motivated by the externally determined need to pass a test. But as adult learners see fruit from application of the first four principles – as they learn from their experiences while doing, from solving problems, and from seeking new ways to work – their internal motivation to learn will grow. Also, the practical nature of MENA learners and their need to know should motivate them to learn more. Learning and growth should beget more learning and growth.

Kolb and Arab Culture

Below we will examine what Kolb's four parts of the learning cycle look like in Arab culture which will help us as we seek to apply them in our context.

Concrete Experience – Active Learning

Most education praxis for adult education in the MENA context reproduces the educational experience of content and not experience-based learning. However, Knowles's principle that adults bring a pool of experience to the learning process should be combined with Kolb's experiential learning theory as the starting point of the adult education process. In a sense, the knowledge of MENA learners is already experiential knowledge, and much of their continued learning results from their experience.

It is not just that learners have experience to build upon, but much of their learning results from their experience. Arabs are primarily concrete learners.[4] What they know, they know really and practically and not theoretically.[5] In a sense, their knowledge is already experiential knowledge. Starting with this

---

4. Y. Yamazaki and D. C. Kayes, "An Experiential Approach to Cross-Cultural Learning: A Review and Integration of Competencies of Successful Expatriate Adaptation," *Academy of Management Learning and Education* 3, no. 4 (2004): 362–379.

5. Hofstede, *Cultures and Organizations*.

assumption and building upon experience is a natural, culturally appropriate part of learning. Starting with these assumptions and building upon experience is a natural and culturally appropriate approach to learning.

Need to Emphasize Reflection

Helping students reflect on their experiences is a key component in deep learning[6] because this crucial step turns experiences into real understanding and change. The reflective process helps students develop conclusions about their experiences and benefit from them. Reflection has not been a significant part of the learning experience of most MENA adults. The teacher is seen as an answer giver, so learning was not related to the students' previous experience.[7] Also, the focus was on memorization for test taking, so little or no emphasis was given to relating the information to the real-life issues and challenges. Reflection is a skill that needs to be developed. It is here that the mentor's role is key. Mentors can guide and support learners as they develop their reflecting skills. After understanding their experience, whether positive or negative, students can be helped to reflect on, learn from, and develop observations about their experience.

Including reflection in the learning process communicates that past experience is valuable. Robert Clinton describes the early phase of a growing leader's experience as sovereign foundations. Clinton recognizes that *all* of the leader's life, including childhood, is part of God's sovereign developmental plan and thus valuable.[8] This valuing helps students see their experience as a learning resource and communicates that the teacher is not the sole source of learning: learners also bring something to the learning process. Further, reflection gives students tools to benefit from their experiences. Finally, it models a *shura*-oriented learning process for the benefit of the followers.

The role of mentors should be two-fold. First, they need to help students become comfortable with reflection,[9] which includes addressing a mindset of shame in students who see their experiences as positive or negative. In their thinking, assigning a negative value to an experience is a way of assigning a negative value to their person. This important hurdle will need to be overcome

---

6. Kolb, *Experiential Learning*.

7. Sidani and Thornberry, "Current Arab Work Ethic," 35–49.

8. Robert Clinton, *The Making of a Leader: Recognizing the Lessons and Stages of Leadership Development* (Colorado Springs: Navpress, 1994), 44.

9. Hitt, "Secondary Implementation," 17.

so that learners are able to reflect, develop observations, and then seek change based on those observations. Teacher-trainers facilitate this by knowing learners and helping them successfully integrate reflection into their learning process.

Second, mentors can use their own experience to ask questions that will help the student reflect. For example, why was the experience successful? Why was the experience not successful? Did you change your understanding or practice because of the experience? What did you change? These and other questions will help learners develop reflection skills.[10]

Reflecting on experiences in groups can also be helpful. The communal nature of the students makes groups a natural environment for reflection. Individual students can learn from the observations of others that challenge, affirm, or expand their own observations of an experience. Having the group answer the above questions also challenges individuals to understanding their experience from different angles. One danger with group reflection is the reluctance of people in Arab cultures to share negative experiences because of honour and shame issues, which could inhibit learners from fully benefitting from all of their experiences. Again, we see the need to introduce learning experiences wisely.

Abstract Conceptualization

Two factors inform the inclusion of abstract conceptualization in an MENA adult education model. A number of studies indicate that all learning styles exist in the region,[11] which tells us that abstract conceptualization is part of the learning make-up of adults in our context. On the other hand, Arab adult learners are concrete in their orientation, which pushes against them thinking abstractly. Also, many adult learners have not been encouraged to think abstractly in their previous learning experiences. These two opposing factors need to be appreciated.

Arab learners do think abstractly; however, they generally do not begin with the abstract principle and apply it to different concrete situations. Instead, they begin with concrete situations and derive abstract principles from those situations. This practice should direct how we combine concrete experience and abstract principles in our teaching and training. In most instances, we should begin from concrete experiences and extract principles from them, which fits with Kolb's experiential learning theory.

---

10. Komives, *Leadership for a Better World.*
11. Zualkernan, Allert, and Qadah, "Cross-Cultural Comparison of Learning Styles."

Active Experimentation

Because of past teaching experiences and high uncertainty avoidance, adult Arab learners may not be familiar with learning via trial and error. In school they were not encouraged to experiment and instead were told to apply exactly what they learned. High uncertainty avoidance in an honour and shame culture results in thinking it is better to not try than to try and fail.

However there is little doubt that in life outside of school, students in Arab cultures have learned much via trial and error. So role of trainers is twofold here. One is to help adult students experiment with new ways of doing things, which we can model by using new teaching methods in class. Second, we can help them see the value of learning from their mistakes. Both of these practices will serve to support and encourage them to experiment in applying what they are learning in different situations both inside and outside of the classroom – even if they fail in their application.

Bloom and Arab Culture

The ELT principles of Knowles and Kolb can be implemented in MENA contexts to achieve the goals of Bloom's educational taxonomy: higher-level thinking in the cognitive domain, life transformation in the affective domain, and advanced development of ministry skills in the psychomotor domain as we applied it to teaching shepherd-leaders.

The Cognitive Domain

The educational experience most adult MENA learners has included primarily memorization of information and comprehending the meaning of that information, the lowest skills on Bloom's cognitive learning ladder. ELT principles can be effectively used to advance students up the ladder to the higher-level thinking skills they need to be fruitful in ministry. For example, Bible studies that challenge students to think more deeply about not just what a text means but how to apply it to a specific situation in their life helps students advance to the application level. Learning experiences followed by reflection encourages and also develops the higher-level thinking skill of applying as well as analyzing, synthesis, and evaluation. Knowles's problem-centred learning in particular requires using these advanced cognitive skills and enables students to reach the highest level, creating, or coming up with new ways of doing things for better results.

Higher-level thinking is abstract thinking, which fits with Kolb's abstract conceptualization. MENA students can and should be encouraged to develop these skills, and we need to keep cognitive development in mind when creating our educational model and assignments.

The Affective Domain

Bloom's affective domain involves motivation for learning, engaging in the learning process, valuing and organizing information, and internalizing values to change thinking, attitudes, and behaviour. It is deep learning for transformation, our primary goal. Several of the ELT principles can be used to promote advancing in the affective domain from receiving information to life transformation. MENA learners are used to teacher-focused education with students taking a passive role of absorbing information from the teacher, which is the lowest level of Bloom's affective ladder, receiving phenomena. ELT practices that encourage student interaction in the classroom, experiential learning, and experimental learning moves students up to the next level, responding to phenomena.

When students reflect on experiences and experiments and see for themselves how information can be applied to solve problems and deal with challenges in life, they begin to value information, organize it, and prioritize some information over other information, the next two levels on Bloom's ladder. This valuing also promotes the learners' inner motivation to learn more and to take ownership of their learning, becoming independent learners. The more students see the value of the truth they are learning – from the teacher, from other students, and from their own experiences – the more likely they will be to internalize the truth and change their values and attitudes to align with it. When this is biblical truth, the process is growth in Christ-likeness, which is transformation of thinking and behaviour.

Moving students up the ladder of the affective domain can be more difficult that moving them up the cognitive domain, and care must be taken when introducing new ways of learning and thinking to learners in uncertainty avoidance cultures. Negative experiences could move them backward. But as with the cognitive domain, fruitful learning can be achieved if we keep the goal of affective transformation in mind as we develop our education model and determine the learning goals of individual assignments.

The Psychomotor Domain

Experiential learning and mentoring tie directly into Bloom's ladder of developing skills, the psychomotor domain, which we have applied to ministry skills. Pragmatically oriented MENA adult learners want to learn the skills they need to be fruitful in ministry. Thus, following Bloom's psychomotor domain can aid in bringing their skills to the highest levels. First when teachers use a *shura*-leadership style in the classroom, students learn from watching their teachers model servant leadership that provides the authority and structure students desire but also consults and involves them in the learning process (perception). Their teachers model good teaching styles that students can imitate when they teach others. Shepherd-leaders may also learn by observing mentors in ministry until they are ready to act themselves (readiness).

Tying together learning in the classroom with church ministry helps to advance the students to imitation and doing ministry under supervision, then up the ladder to more advanced ministry roles and ministering in different situations. Again, reflecting on these experiences helps learners evaluate their skills, see areas for improvement, and be motivated to continue developing their skills. Actively using the ELT principles of experiential learning in church ministry under wise and supportive mentors will enable MENA learners to develop their skills, and also appeals to their desire for practical education.

Summary

Our goal is deep, transformational learning, moving students from "rote to realization."[12] We saw above that adult ELT principles and practices as described by Knowles and Kolb are amenable to the learning of adults in Arab cultures. We also have an indication that a teacher-student relationship characterized by *shura* can facilitate successful practice of ELT principles. Some adjustments will have to be made in how they are applied, but overall, our adult learning principles and practices will work in an Arab context. This gives us confidence to push forward with new learning methods. Yet we need patience as students slowly leave behind their old comfort zones, and their negative experiences melt away. We need to apply new learning methods at a pace that is appropriate for students and accompanied by explanations of their benefits because we need to help adult learners feel comfortable with a self-directed learning process.

Part of this process is not just communicating knowledge or a skill, but modelling what self-directed learning looks like. We will need to help learners see that this process can actually help them address the challenges they face as a leader. This modelling not only serves to promote transformational teaching

---

12. Lawrence Richards, *Creative Bible Teaching* (Chicago: Moody, 1998), 121.

and training, but it also helps developing leaders see how they can use these practices to teach and train other leaders in the future.

Arab culture contains the building blocks needed to construct effective teaching and training. In the next chapter, we will look at how educators in the Arab Gulf have used ELT principles in adult education and learn from their experience.

14

Current ELT Use in Gulf Adult Education

A s we seek to form a picture of what *shura*-education looks like, we have the benefit of seeing its use in an Arab setting. The Arab Gulf is home to a number of universities that use adult ELT principles in some way. The advantage of this setting is that professors have used a wide variety of adult ELT principles in their classrooms. The students are Arab adults who have been educated in the prior learning situation described in section 3. Universities in the Arab Gulf provide us with real-life cases of adult ELT used in an Arab setting.

These actual examples are invaluable as we work toward our goal of employing effective adult education principles and practices that contribute to transformational learning. Yusuf Sidani and Jon Thornberry remind us that this isn't a simple task. "After many years of learning in this manner [memorization, et al] – it becomes extremely difficult to break such habits. It goes without saying that such teaching limits students' ability to connect ideas, analyze, solve problems, synthesize, and think critically."[1]

Keeping the caveat of Sidani and Thornberry in mind, we need to push forward with using new learning methods. This will require patience because it will take time to allow old comfort zones and experiences to melt away – both ours and our students! To successfully overcome these cultural hurdles and walk learners forward, time and support is vital because our goal is not only to teach and train them transformationally, but also to model for developing leaders how they can use these practices to teach and train other leaders in the future.

---

1. Sidani and Thornberry, "Current Arab Work Ethic," 42.

How to Introduce Adult ELT in an Arab Educational Context

Based on their research and experience working with Arab adult students, professor George Hitt and others tell us that new learning methods need to be applied at a pace appropriate for the students and with explanations of their benefit because we need to help adult learners feel comfortable with a self-directed learning process. This requirement affirms our need to be acquainted with the previous educational experiences of the students. "When students are socialized in different ways from their school expectations, they have to adjust themselves to the culture of school."[2] Abeer Mahrous relates this to business training stating that it is important to understand "how students from Middle Eastern countries respond to the various teaching tools employed in business classrooms."[3] This is our first step in applying new learning activities.

To get a glimpse of how new learning activities have been used, we will learn from the experiences of professors using adult ELT methods with Arab university students and their reflections on their experiences. We will look at what ELT methods they used and how they introduced and adapted these methods. But first we will look at a model for how these methods were introduced and adapted and then at what specific methods were employed successfully.

How Educational Practices Are Transferable

Hitt, Mahrous, and others affirm the need for a different way of teaching MENA students to produce the true learning they need. These professors understand the emphasis in Arab schools on memorization and the teacher as the authority and answer-giver. Their research tested the usefulness of Knowles' adult learning principles and Kolb's experiential learning theory. They did not specifically test these principles but investigated their usefulness and how to introduce them into an Arab context, but their findings are helpful in determining what learning elements are fruitful.

Hitt took a model for teaching physics, Physics Education Researched (PER), that was developed in the US, and sought to use it with his college students in the United Arab Emirates (UAE). Hitt makes a number of suggestions on what does and does not work in an Arab culture. In regards to the physics curriculum, he concluded that "prior classroom experiences, and not broader cultural expectations about education, are the more significant

---

    2. Pegah Omidvar and Bee Hoon Tan, "Cultural Variations in Learning and Learning Style," *Journal of Distance Education* 13, no. 4 (2012), 275.

    3. Mahrous, "Cross-Cultural Investigation," 290.

cause of expectations that are at odds with the classroom norms of well-functioning PER-based instruction."[4] The key factor in the effectiveness of utilizing adult learning practices across cultures is how the theories and practices are implemented.

Hitt provides a helpful model of how Western teaching practices can be successfully introduced to Arab students. Understanding how students will respond to various teaching methods informs whether, how, and at what pace we use proven adult education methods. "PER-based innovations can be implemented across great changes in cultural context, provided that the method is thoughtfully adapted in anticipation of context and culture-specific student expectations."[5] There are a number of key words in Hitt's summary: thoughtful, anticipation, context, culture, and expectations. Each is key to fruitful use of adult ELT with Arab students.

We will look at Hitt's classroom use of experiential learning methods with his university students to understand some principles on how to introduce these methods to Arab learners. First, Hitt tested a number of teaching methods used to teach physics in US universities. Then he applied these methods to a university setting in the UAE. The US is the place of primary implementation (PI), and the UAE is the place of secondary implementation (SI). Hitt compared the transfer of teaching methods from PI to SI and sought to discover,

> If one of the broader contexts mentioned above is very different to that of the original developing institution, are there criteria in these contexts that can help faculty who are planning a SI to predict possible risks for their reform project? Following from this, in terms of the implementation, how and to what extent can the original instructional strategy be changed in anticipation of these failure risks to better match the contexts of the implementing institution without compromising core functions and principles of that strategy?[6]

Hitt's question is central to our purpose. The type of evaluation he used defines criteria to determine what elements of the original learning process can and cannot be changed without losing the effectiveness of the lesson, but also be culturally amenable to the learners. Hitt says this evaluation process "presents a design-based methodology for choosing and changing these

---

4. Mahrous, 1.

5. Hitt, "Secondary Implementation," 1.

6. Hitt, 1.

instructional strategies based on an analysis of the cultural expectations of its users (students)."[7]

At the core of transferring educational practices from one culture to another is understanding the educational context of the students. "Educational context includes student expectations about the nature of instruction, interactions, and learning and that those expectations, accommodated (or violated), contribute causally in the performance of a SI (Secondary Implementation of a teaching method)."[8] Here again we see the link between students' prior learning and their expectations and acceptance of what good teaching looks like.

When trying to determine how best to implement adult learning principles and practices, Hitt tells us that "the level of context and its associated expectations [are] important for addressing each choice."[9] Later he states, "The goal is to keep the learning concept and its core, but change its implementation based on cultural expectations."[10] For example, a group activity was conducted via email, and a number of steps were performed over a period of time in the US version of the curriculum activity. Each person did their part individually, and then the work was combined to form a single, final group result. This process was adjusted for the Emirate setting. The activity was conducted in a group. All of the steps were performed together in one sitting, rather than individually through email over a period of time. However, the activity and its goals remained the same.

The core of the process, done by a group and including a number of steps, was kept intact, but adjustments were made for cultural differences between the original and target culture. As MENA culture is more communal than individualistic, doing the exercise as a group was more culturally acceptable to the Emirati students. Also introducing this new method under the instructor's supervision rather than having individual students try to figure it out on their own increased the students' comfort and provided their needed structure. Since the Emirati culture's educational background did not employ this method, adjustments needed to be made so the students with high uncertainty avoidance would not reject it because of its unfamiliarity. Hitt found that it is not only possible to transfer teaching methods but they achieved "improvement in comprehension and deeper conceptual understanding."[11]

---

7. Hitt, 6.
8. Hitt, 2.
9. Hitt, 17.
10. Hitt, 17.
11. Hitt, 1.

Understanding the culture behind learners' expectations will help us know what practices we can use and at what pace they can be introduced. As we introduce new teaching activities, we will need to patiently support students, help them adapt, and demonstrate the benefits of these activities. Having understood and thoughtfully considered how we can introduce new learning activities, we will now look at what learning activities might be used successfully.

Which Educational Practices Are Transferable

In deciding what practices to include and exclude, the recent growth in the use of different educational practices in the Arab Gulf can be helpful. Within the past few years, some countries in the Arab Gulf have begun to use active learning practices at the university level.[12] The advantage of learning from these universities is two-fold. First, the students have a shared culture and prior educational experiences. Second, we gain from the actual classroom experience of those who have employed adult learning methods. Adult students in the UAE who have been exposed to experiential learning methods describe them as acceptable or highly effective.[13] This feedback provides insight into the feasibility of using these methods in other parts of the MENA region. They are also helpful in discerning what practices have been helpful. Below is a summary of practices used in the classroom.

Cooperative Group Problem Solving

Hitt successfully used cooperative group problem solving by adjusting the process to account for contextual differences and culture-specific student expectations.[14] He introduced group-based and hands-on learning, equity in student-teacher interactions, sense making over answer making, and informal learning. These norms align with what both Knowles and Kolb say contribute to deep learning. The result of using this method "has improved problem

---

12. United Nations Development Program. 2014. "Arab Knowledge Report 2014: Youth and Localization of Knowledge. Dubai, UAE: Mohammed bin Rashid Al Maktoum Foundation (MBRF) and The United Nations Development Programme/Regional Bureau for Arab States (UNDP/RBAS)."

13. Hitt, "Secondary Implementation," 167.

14. Hitt, 17.

solving performance and deeper conceptual understanding relative to lecture centred instruction."[15]

In his example, Hitt had to address the students' uncertainty of working in groups rather than learning from a professor's lecture. When the group had to decide how to perform tasks for a science lab, Hitt had to address students who "expect tasks with sure outcomes that involve following instructions and no risks."[16] Despite the fact that group work fits with the students' communal culture, students were anxious about the learning methods used that were unfamiliar to them. Hitt notes that added structure aided greatly in managing student anxiety toward reformed pedagogy. Structure includes the planning of lesson delivery that carefully considers the students' prior learning experience. It includes taking time to explain *why* we use experiential learning exercises and *how* to use them. It includes introducing these exercises slowly and supporting students as they adjust to these new learning experiences. Hitt provided structure for three learning tasks by communicating a clear routine and sequence of tasks so that students encountered uncertainty about these tasks in small, controlled doses.[17]

This structure enabled students to adapt to teaching methods that were not just different, but difficult for them to accept. Hitt used this structured approach to address sense making over answer making and equity in student-teacher interactions. These were substantially more difficult to overcome in the Khalifa University: "the importance of sense making over answer making . . . is in direct conflict with our students' emphasis on learning how to do over learning how to learn."[18] But by providing structure, Hitt noticed a change in student acceptance of group collaboration as a teaching method. Feedback from the students showed that "Reaction went from Negative to Positive in 3–4 weeks after getting used to the differences."[19] Overall use of these methods saw failure rates drop from 50 percent to 24 percent.[20]

---

15. Hitt, 1.
16. Hitt, 16.
17. Hitt, 13.
18. Hitt, 15.
19. Hitt, 10.
20. Hitt, 17.

Effectively Using Case Studies

Mahrous also noticed that case studies are helpful teaching tools.[21] At first the students were confused about what was expected of them.[22] But with explanation and guidance in using this method, students benefited from the practical aspect of applying what they learned to real life situations. Jacqueline Prowse reports that professors in Qatar "used student presentations, group work and class discussion to encourage analytical thinking."[23] She noted that students enjoyed group work, but affirmed the need to provide a structure to allow students to get used to these new teaching methods because of their high uncertainty avoidance. Here we see the merging of adult education principles and MENA culture for a beneficial result.

Group Class Discussion

Mahrous suggests encouraging group discussions that involve the entire class.[24] This is difficult for two reasons. First, it moves the focus away from the teacher as the authoritative answer giver. Second, speaking up in class involves the risk of saying something wrong and losing face in front of one's colleagues. An intermediate step to open class discussion could be small group discussions that report back to the entire class. This lessens the risk of losing face and makes what is reported a product of the group and not the individual. This intermediate step can facilitate the move toward a full class discussion.

Concrete/Practical Learning

Mahrous found that providing a link between topics in a subject helped students understand the topics as related to each other and not just theoretical disconnected truths. He suggests that it is important to develop skills and not just cover materials.[25] The focus here should be on learning how to learn and how to use the material covered. Though this differs from what students are

---

21. Mahrous, "Cross-Cultural Investigation," 299. See also Brian Bielenberg and Maxine Gillway, "Adapting Problem-Based Learning to Meet the Life-Long Learning Needs of Developmental Students," *Learning and Teaching in Higher Education: Gulf Perspectives* 3, no. 2 (2006): 2–16; Sonleitner and Khelifa, "Western-Educated Faculty," 1–21.

22. Mahrous, "Cross-Cultural Investigation," 299.

23. Prowse, "Teaching across Cultures," 42.

24. Mahrous, "Cross-Cultural Investigation," 302.

25. Mahrous, 302.

used to, it appeals to their concrete nature while at the same time implementing the adult learning principle of applying what is learned to real life situations.

Real-Life Examples

Eugenia Samier argues that the use of active teaching methods is effective in making the teaching of Islamic ethics and leadership more practical and less theoretical. She suggests using case studies, role-playing and story-telling as teaching tools,[26] and states that studying the lives and situations of historical Islamic figures and actual situations helps students apply what they learn. Story telling links the lives of Islamic leaders to the lives of the students. Case studies help students learn what they can actually apply to their work and leadership. Both stimulate thinking and "serve as a catalyst for changes in thinking,"[27] which is a part of deep learning.

Reflection

From his experience in the UAE utilized group work and reflective exercises in his teaching, John Burt notes that active learning "decreased [students'] confidence due to their unfamiliarity with the approach."[28] But he goes on to say that "with exposure, confidence grew as students became comfortable with the learning style, until it exceeded high-school levels."[29] All in all he noticed that students "improved their communication skills, use of information technology, and ability to work in teams."[30] Despite their initial reticence, students grew in their ability to work with others and to transfer the skills they learned to other contexts.

The results of using active learning are in line with our goals for transformational deep learning. "In all, the students' comments indicate that active learning has fostered a strong development of higher-order learning skills."[31] Burt concludes, "As a result, the relative proportion of the intrinsic

---

26. Samier, "Ethics of Islamic Leadership," 202.
27. Samier, 203.
28. Burt, "Impact of Active Learning," 7.
29. Burt, 1.
30. Burt, 6.
31. Burt, 6.

reinforcement has increased with active learning, while extrinsic reinforcement has decreased."[32]

Sharing Differing Points of View and Opinions

Salah Saafin used a variety of teaching methods in his classroom in the UAE. He recommends giving students the "chance to speak and ask questions."[33] He says it "gives the students the chance to express their opinion and participate in class discussions."[34] Immediate implementation of active teaching methods "may misread student's readiness for independent work. Some students may become anxious when given autonomy."[35] Yet he concludes that the use of discussion and problem-solving activities helps students retain information better because they are doing something with the information, making sense of the information, and not just passively receiving the information.

Active Learning

Nancy Sonleiter and Maher Khelifa summarize the experience of a number of professors who discovered that working in small groups "stimulated student interest" and was used with great success. Small groups helped students "focus on the class material and produce quality projects."[36] Finally some professors noted that students' understanding of their learning goals contributed positively to their success.[37] Understanding the reason for studying is tied to student motivation which is an important adult learning principle.

Students who clearly understood the reason they were taking a specific class were more motivated to learn and better able to link what they learned to their life goals. This aligns with Knowles' concept of intrinsic motivation for learning and the need to connect learning to real-life challenges.

Sarah Al-Haj summarizes students' reflections from the UAE. When the professor opened up the class for discussion, the students were eager to

---

32. Burt, 10.

33. Salah Saafin, "Arab Tertiary Students' Perspectives of Effective Teachers," *Learning and Teaching in Higher Education: Gulf Perspectives* 5, no. 2 (2008): 7.

34. Saafin, "Arab Tertiary Students," 7.

35. Kristine Joy Manalo, "Science Teachers' Teaching Styles, Students' Learning Styles and Their Academic Performance," *International Journal of Social Science and Humanities Research* 5, no. 2 (April–June 2017): 404.

36. Sonleitner and Khelifa, "Western-Educated Faculty," 11.

37. Sonleitner and Khelifa, 2.

participate, which encouraged their participation in the learning process. Also, the professor would propose open questions that called on the students to apply the theory they had been discussing. The students reported that it "increased our critical thinking skills and also incorporated the topics to us personally."[38] Active learning practices were appreciated and effective. Students valued learning activities outside of the classroom as "just as important and integral as topics covered in the classroom."[39]

Problem-Based Learning

Within a classroom setting, problem-based learning (PBL) can be a useful teaching method provided it is carefully introduced and used. PBL can draw students into a real-life, experience-oriented way of learning. The problem should be drawn from a real-life situation that learners face. "PBL problems are developed based on concerns raised by students."[40] Here we see the need for evaluation to understand the challenges learners face.[41] The advantage of PBL is that it is practical, can be done in groups, helps to develop critical thinking skills, and can be self-directed. It removes the teacher from the role of answer-giver and places students into the role of answer-seekers. However as Bielenburg says, "students may require some additional scaffolding to support their early efforts to work in groups, access and analyze information and participate in the problem solving process."[42] Because PBL focuses on real-world problems that are relevant to their lives, it grants students more ownership over their learning and helps them acquire knowledge and skills that will benefit them after university life.

---

38. Sarah Al-Haj, "Lighting the Fire: Teaching Is about Learning," *Learning and Teaching in Higher Education: Gulf Perspectives* 2, no. 2 (2005): 2.

39. Al-Haj, "Lighting the Fire," 4.

40. Bielenberg and Gillway, "Adapting Problem-Based Learning," 5.

41. Bielenberg and Gillway, 5.

42. Bielenberg and Gillway, 4. Scaffolding is the process of guiding the learner from what is presently known to what is to be known. Thus, constructive instructional designers must situate cognition in real-world contexts. Situated cognition suggests that knowledge and the conditions of its use are inextricably linked. J. S. Brown, A. Collins, and P. Duguid, "Situated Cognition and the Culture of Learning," *Educational Researcher* 18, no. 1 (1989): 32–41. Learning occurs most effectively in context, which becomes an important part of the knowledge base.

Summary

From research and use in MENA adult education, we see the benefit of using active learning in our context. Adaptation of these practices should happen as follows: introduction of the method, explanation of the method and support in using it, fuller acceptance of the method by the learners, and finally successful learning. Deep learning does happen when using these methods as long as proper support is provided. Mahrous states that "students, who are rarely exposed to such active learning activities as case studies and projects, may be reluctant to participate in them. Therefore, explaining the benefits of using active learning tools, after preparing students to participate through earlier coursework and maintaining a balanced workload, would improve students' perceptions of active learning tools."[43]

The above examples of learning practices that have been used successfully in an Arab context are only a sample of possible activities. Along with the activities, some cultural adaptations have been suggested that might help in introducing these activities. Having confidence that these and other practices can be successfully employed, we should take the time to understand learners before us. What is their prior learning situation? What expectations has this situation created about learning? What learning practices are they comfortable with, and uncomfortable with? What cultural factors contribute to their expectations and comfort? How can we move them out of their comfort zone? Answering these questions will help us to patiently introduce fruitful learning practices and support learners to benefit from these practices.

---

43. Mahrous, "Cross-Cultural Investigation," 301.

15

Elements of a Contextual Leadership Development Programme

The educational principles above should be incorporated into a leadership development programme designed and driven by the local church. The programme should take advantage of seminary and other resources that address the call, the heart, the skills, and the knowledge of shepherd-leaders. The varied situations demonstrate the need for wisdom in applying these principles to our unique context. Below are suggestions to consider for how to make teaching and training appropriate for the church in the MENA region. Thinking through these issues will help individual churches and leaders decide how to best implement these principles in their unique context.

The Church as Context for Training

We have seen that the regional educational models are insufficient to produce the deep transformation needed in shepherd-leaders. Also much of the training of shepherd-leaders in the West has become focused on seminary-based education, and the church has relied heavily on the seminary to develop its leaders with little church involvement. This model has been exported throughout much of the world. When this model is combined with the prestige awarded with a degree in many places, the idea of seminary as the main way of preparing leaders is solidified.[1] For reasons related to both the educational principles we have studied – the importance of addressing not only the mind,

---

1. Brent Fulton, "Beyond Theological Education" (2 March 2016), ChinaSource.

but the character and skill of a leader – and contextual needs in the region – difficulty of attending seminary, small group churches, etc. – current teaching-training models don't adequately include the role of the church in training leaders that the church needs.

Biblical models and examples from church history including Origin, Augustine, Calvin, Wesley, etc. tell us that for pastors to be spiritually and practically prepared, seminaries must be closely connected to the church.[2] It is important to understand that seminaries exist to serve churches: "pastoral training is uniquely related to local church ministry."[3] The movement of ministry preparation away from the church or disconnecting from the church leads toward abstract, academic training that has little or no connection to the actual practice of ministry. Victor Nakah says that seminaries are too irrelevant to the competencies needed for ministry, too inaccessible, and too intellectual.[4] So training of shepherd-leaders needs to be closely tied to the ministry of the local church body. Even more, the training and development of shepherd-leaders should be driven by the local church. This does not mean that the seminary does not have a role; it does. But the church should primarily determine the overall curriculum needed for training, not primarily the seminary.

Regional leaders strongly emphasized the importance of the church in the process of developing leaders because the church is where young leaders learn about the realities of leadership – serving others, conflict, sacrificing for others, etc. Also, leaders pointed out that relationships in the church are the door through which ministry happens. For young leaders, the church is both a place of testing as well as support.

What should church-based leadership development look like? One important step is to create a culture of developing leaders in the church. By this I mean helping the members of the church see the benefits of developing leaders and that they are an important part of this process. We do this by communicating to the body that we value their different gifts and perspectives and encouraging them, especially older and more mature believers, to share their wisdom and experience with developing leaders. This sharing can be done informally, but it might be helpful on a regular basis to have older believers sit with the group of developing leaders and share their experience. Developing

---

2. See John Frame, "Proposal for a New Seminary" (23 May 2001); Lausanne Committee for World Evangelization, "Occasional Paper 57: Effective Theological Education for World Evangelization" (2004); Victor Nakah, "The Capetown Commitment as a Missional Framework for Theological Education," Personal copy of presentation (2010).

3. Lausanne Committee for World Evangelization, "Occasional Paper 57."

4. Nakah, "Capetown Commitment."

leaders can ask questions and afterwards could be asked to reflect on what they learned.

Training in the church includes giving the developing leaders different responsibilities. For example, they can be asked to disciple a new believer. They can be charged with teaching young people a short series on a specific topic or book of the Bible. Start small and support them by reflecting with them on positive aspects of their teaching and also ways they need to improve. When young leaders encounter conflict in the church, don't solve the problem for them, unless it is a harmful issue, but help them think of ways to resolve the conflict and help them see their heart in the midst of the conflict. Knowing the development needs of the leaders should determine what areas of responsibility they can be given. From my experience in helping with training, because the leaders spend most of their ministry time with others, they come to training times full of questions. Leaders naturally confront challenges and issues that need answers by serving in the midst of community.

Communicating to the congregation the vision and process to develop leaders helps to include them in the journey. The members of the body, even a small body, have resources that can help young leaders. Including them in the process encourages the whole body to share in developing leaders for their church or to start other churches. Remember as well, that leadership development applies not just to a few, but to all in the church. Though not all will be pastors or elders or church planters, all are called to minister. A culture of leadership development develops leaders at all levels of the church.

In my experience, small churches of ten to twenty people often include the entire church in whatever training is offered. This may mean that new believers will be sitting next to more mature believers and the young leaders being developed. We have had unbelievers join teaching and training that was intended for more mature leaders. This is the beauty of a group-oriented culture. They don't want anyone to be left out. My advice is not to resist this. In one way, it exposes everyone to the idea of leadership and what we as a church want our leaders to know and be. For the leaders you are focused on developing, make time after the training to debrief and reflect on the training with these leaders. To keep our training connected to the church, it will be helpful to think through some issues. For example, what does our church need in leaders? How will we balance the young leaders' participation in church and in formal learning settings? How can we connect what they learn outside the church to actual ministry within our church?

Theological Training in Context

The security situation affecting the church in the region is another reason why the model of seminaries as the primary trainers is not always practical. Because all of the countries in the MENA region are majority Muslim, starting and maintaining formal seminaries is not always possible. Egypt, Lebanon, and Jordan have minority Christian populations and do have seminaries that serve the Christian population. In North Africa and other places, small theological colleges are being formed and are beginning to be formally recognized in their country in some ways. These schools are tremendous resources for the growing church in the region. However for some, attendance at these institutions is against the law and problematic for many reasons, which still leaves the majority of countries in the region without seminaries.

Existing seminaries are making great efforts to accept students from these other countries, and their desire to serve these brothers and sisters is commendable. But even this solution, as wonderful as it is, is impractical due to inability to travel, obtain visas, and other issues. Beyond this, seminary leaders are finding that removing leaders from their context for one to three years severely undermines their ability to fit back into their culture and context. So the small theological colleges in North Africa are a valuable resource. One immediate advantage is the closeness of the institution to the students who attend, which makes accessing necessary biblical and theological training much easier. However even with these advantages, both contextual and educational reasons prohibit these schools from being the primary place for teaching and training of shepherd-leaders because as we discussed above, training should be rooted in the local community.[5]

Formal teaching and training can include teaching on doctrinal issues, books of the Bible, practical ministry skills, culture and society specific issues, and many other topics. The local shepherd-leader of the body should work with leaders and outside mentors to determine what topics that developing leaders need most. Whatever is taught, formal teaching times should be combined with times for reflection and application (Kolb). Any teaching should include time for young leaders to sit together to discuss and reflect on the teaching. The shepherd-leader should sit with them as a group and as individuals to help them connect what they learn to practical ministry.

---

5. Nakah, "Capetown Commitment"; David Esterline, Dietrich Werner, Todd Johnson, and Peter Crossing, *Global Survey on Theological Education 2011–2013* (Geneva: World Council of Churches, 2013).

For example if you are having someone teach on pastoring God's people, don't let the formal teaching time be all you offer. Build a learning exercise out of the topic. Discuss the subject beforehand to discover what questions the leaders have about the topic. Ask them what they struggle to know and do. After the teaching time, make time for reflection and discussion about the topic. Create practical opportunities to apply and practice what has been spoken. Even "academic" topics like the Trinity and the doctrine of grace can include exercises that help leaders think how these doctrines make a difference in our life and ministry. These exercises illustrate the importance of reflection and discussion as part of the overall learning process. Below are examples of how this method has been used with leaders in the MENA region.

One group that we had the privilege to work with had a team of ten to twelve leaders who gathered together for training every two to three months. This time was focused on developing other leaders and ministry planning. About half of the leaders were evangelists and working to start churches. As we got to know them, instead of offering our programme of teaching, we sought to discover what they needed. We asked what needs they had in developing their leaders. In our discussions, we saw that we could help them with both biblical-theological teaching and training in practical ministry skills.

Each time this group met, they would invite someone to teach them. They determined the topic to be discussed based on their overall training plan. These topics had included the Trinity, Christology, peacemaking, shepherding, grace in Romans, evangelism, and leadership, among others. The key parts of the process were conducting training in the midst of ministry, teaching sessions, and time away for teaching and reflection. The teaching time would be two to three days. After the guest teachers left, the group would stay another two days to discuss the teaching. They didn't just listen to the teaching and then return to their ministry. They included time to reflect on the teaching and discuss how it related to the struggles they faced in their ministry. Because they determined the teaching topics, no doubt based on their needs, the teaching was relevant to them. They were motivated to learn and to apply what they learned. The teaching topics were the product of their needs, and they were the ones who worked through how to apply the teaching to their context.

Another group we worked with was already offering some training, but this training was unfocused with random topics being offered based on whoever they could find to teach. Before starting to teach and train, we took a couple of visits to describe what transformational learning looks like and ways to offer this type of teaching and training. This initial training was conducted with a group of leaders in the country. Much more time was spent with an individual who had a vision to train pastors and leaders in his country. With him we discussed adult ELT principles in detail, and I was able to model these principles for him in different training sessions over a period of a year or so. Finally, he developed materials and training that allowed him to test out these principles and allowed us specific opportunities to reflect on and learn from his experience. Thus we continued to discuss the topics and how they would be presented and ways to produce deep learning in the leaders.

This leader established a training programme centred around quarterly training times that included teaching and peer mentoring groups. The leaders were given assignments and would meet in peer mentor groups between meetings. The programme leader would follow up with each of the leaders between teaching times as well. This programme differed from the one above in that the programme leader determined the topics to be covered based on his personal knowledge of the struggles and issues the leaders faced. Topics covered included apologetics specific to their context, servant leadership, various books of the Bible, marriage and family, and social ministry in their society. Teaching was practical and oriented to address these issues. Training happened in the midst of ministry. Leaders were not removed from their ministry contexts but continued leading in their churches. Although "academic" topics were taught that included notes and even occasional tests, the teaching and training was related to their needs as leaders in the church. The local leader continues to direct the programme with periodical support from me.

Some questions to address include the following. How can we keep our leaders connected to our culture and context while they learn? How relevant to our culture is the teaching content and method? What teaching and training do young leaders need to address issues in our culture and context?

Learning Conducted in Community

Just as leaving their context to study at a seminary does not fully prepare shepherd-leaders, neither does studying alone. Growth happens best in community. Our Saviour modelled the importance of community in learning, which informs learners' interaction with professors and with each other.[6] In 2 Timothy 2:2, Paul affirms the importance of community and learning in the presence of others (see also Phil 4:9; 2 Tim 3:10).

In Ephesians 4, Paul is addressing the body of Christ, and verses 11–16 focus on how this body is built up. As he discusses growing to "the stature of

---

6. Frame, "Proposal for a New Seminary."

the fullness of Christ" (v. 13), Paul asserts that the body of Christ edifies itself. It is the ministry of brothers and sisters in Christ to each other that causes us to grow up and become like Christ (vv. 15–16). In other words, the body "builds itself up in love" (v. 16). When the body is working together, all members grow.

The local church provides a ready-made community for ministry training because it is where the biblical ethos is lived out among others. The local church community provides opportunities for practical ministry in teaching, caring for, reconciling with, and ministering to others and enables learners to apply what is taught. It is also where growing shepherd-leaders can find the support they need in the midst of struggles and provides different voices for feedback.

When the congregation is part of the development process, they should understand that young leaders are learning in the midst of the family. Members share in training by being patient while young leaders learn new skills like preaching, leading meetings, etc. Members can help encourage younger leaders by accepting their leadership even when, not if, they make mistakes and can offer their affirmation for successes. Members should also pray for developing leaders and let them know they are praying for them. Finally, members should offer ideas on how to improve in a gracious manner.

Leaders in the region recognize the importance of community in developing leaders, the local church as well as other growing leaders. These other leaders also supply fellowship, support, advice, confrontation, and learning about how to relate biblically. Their community is one where "iron sharpens iron" and where burdens are shared. God developed the interviewed regional leaders in the context of community, and they are committed to training leaders in this way as well.

Learning along with other leaders is critical as well. In the examples above, leaders were trained in groups. They were from different parts of their country but would gather to study together. They took the course together, and they would debrief and discuss the teaching together in a group. The second group of leaders also met together in peer mentoring groups to discuss assignments. They would share their challenges and questions as well, and the group would offer their wisdom and support. These groups can be fifteen people or two people. When possible, create opportunities for leaders to learn together.

Some questions to address in this area include the following. How do we create a culture of development and growth as a body? What is the body's role in developing and sending new leaders? How can our young leaders learn together? How can we maximize the personal interaction of learners with teachers and trainers, versus taking a course mainly online? How can we integrate being part of a community of other leaders into the training process?

Selecting and Training Mentors

As previously discussed, I have found the role of mentors to be critical in the development of young leaders. More mature believers are needed to disciple younger leaders in all facets of life and leadership, including sharing their experience and knowledge, helping young leaders with reflection and conceptualization, and providing them with opportunities for gaining ministry experience and experimenting. Regional leaders testify to the central role of a mentor in helping the young leader grow and develop.

I use the term "mentor" quite often in this book. A better term might be "discipler," although this term isn't as natural to say nor as easy to define. Because our paradigm is rooted in the idea of discipleship, older or more mature leaders should mentor younger ones. The process isn't complicated. In a very real sense, we can all disciple or mentor others. The models of Christ and Paul presented at the beginning of the book offer guidance on what areas to focus on and how to go about the process. To help you think through how you can better mentor those you disciple, take time to read the passages about Jesus and Paul and think through what they did and how you can replicate their methods in your context.

Jesus loved his disciples. He laid down his life for them. He served them. This is the attitude we should have toward those we mentor or disciple. To better serve those we disciple, we should seek to grow in our ability to serve them in our mentoring. Mentoring skills can be learned and developed, but the basics of discipling another go a long way in helping us understanding how to mentor others. I have hinted at how we can disciple young leaders throughout the book. We should think about how we can develop their call, their doctrine, their character, and their ministry skills. Within each of these categories, we should take time to get to know our disciples and evaluate their needs. Good mentors ask good questions to discover the needs of those they disciple. They also ask good questions to help the disciples discover gaps in their understanding, abilities, and Christ-likeness. Disciplers ask good questions, like Jesus did, in the midst of ministry and the pressures of life. They use questions to help young leaders benefit from their ministry and life experiences. You can use the questions on page 86 from Susan Komives to get started.

This book is designed to help in developing a plan for growing leaders and mentoring them. Having said this, we need to always be ready to teach. Life is full of unexpected challenges, blessings, and opportunities. Never waste a crisis, a trial, a failure, or a success. If we believe that God is sovereign in this process, then we will view these events as God-sent opportunities to teach.

Finally, remember that we disciple, train, and teach in the midst of the body of Christ. You don't have all the resources, time, or knowledge to teach, train, mentor, and disciple every leader. We mentioned above the benefit of including your local body in the mentoring process. We aren't only part of our local body, but the larger body of Christ. Other leaders from your city or country can serve as co-mentors as well. For example, if a young leader has the gift of evangelism, and you know another leader who is a gifted and fruitful evangelist, connect this young leader with that evangelist. You won't be asking the other leader to do all of the mentoring, but just to mentor specifically in evangelism. Maybe for a limited time of one to six months, the young leader can spend one day a week or a couple of days a month learning from the more experienced leader. Our desire to love and serve disciples should move us to help them grow even if we aren't the ones who do the teaching and training. Ultimately it is God who develops shepherd-leaders.

Questions to address when selecting and training mentors include the following. Who will be the primary mentor for our young leader or leaders? Who should mentor young leaders in different areas including personal life, how to evangelize, how to pastor, etc.? How can we make regular conversations with mentors a part of our training programme? What support can we provide mentors to help them successfully mentor young leaders?

Centred on the Word in Content and Application

"Above all theological education must serve to equip pastor-teachers for their prime responsibility of preaching and teaching the Bible."[7] The word of God is the main tool of the pastor-teacher (2 Tim 2:15; 3:16–17) and the agent by which the Holy Spirit transforms us (Ps 19:7–11; John 17:17; 2 Tim 3:15; Heb 4:12; 1 Pet 1:23). Thorough knowledge of God's word is also needed to refute the lies of the devil and false teaching (Luke 4:5–8; 1 Tim 1:3–5; 5:5–7; 6:3–5). Regional leaders are clear that the Bible is the foundation of our faith and practice. The separation of seminary and church can create an unhealthy separation of biblical-theological knowledge and application to life and ministry. However when seminary is eschewed as a part of training pastor-leaders, they have a much harder time gaining a deep knowledge of God's word. This is the strength that the seminary provides.

First Timothy 4:14–16 calls for a full-orbed development of the entire person. Formal learning programmes, like a seminary, play an important

---

7. Lausanne Committee for World Evangelization, "Occasional Paper 57."

role in this process, but are not designed to address all aspects of leadership development. Relationships, modelling, and practice are best carried out in the church. As we saw with Calvin's academy, cooperation between the academy and the church provides the best model for leadership development.

If leaders are going to act right, they must first know what God's word says. I have found that using stories and characters from the Bible facilitates communication of concepts and roots teaching and training in the Scriptures. I am not opposed to the social sciences as a source of truth. This book contains two sections based on educational and cultural research. But when we use Scripture as the foundation of our teaching and training, it makes what is taught more acceptable to Arab believers, especially those from a majority context. I have found that these brothers and sisters have a strong and deep allegiance to the Scriptures, and they are leery of ideas from the social sciences which they see as Western and not always relevant to their context. Because this chapter is about contextual application of principles, and some from the social sciences, rooting them in Scriptures will prove to be helpful.

Also, using leaders from the Bible and historical figures from the church can serve as models for teaching and training. For example, I have used David as a model for trusting God in the midst of persecution by Saul. After he spent forty years in the wilderness, Moses teaches us that God's timing in raising us up as leaders is always perfect. Paul's ministry in the book of Acts provides instruction on courage, boldness, evangelism, and the importance of the church. As often as possible, I use quotes and stories from believers from the MENA region, for instance Origen and Augustine who are discussed above. These and other stories of faith are a ready curriculum that is rooted in the Scriptures.

Questions to address about biblical content include the following. Do the training programmes we use have their foundation in the Scriptures? Are issues of teaching, character, and skills from Scripture or more from a worldly point of view? Does our teaching and training have the goal of biblical change in the mind, heart, and actions of our leaders?

Summary

Successful development of shepherd-leaders should take place in the context of the church in partnership with seminaries or other theological training institutions. Seminaries should be in service to the church. Victor Nakah summarizes our approach saying that training should be "scholarly engagement" rooted in the "formation of Kingdom-oriented character and competency" within the leaders.[8]

To address issues of security, educational appropriateness, lack of seminaries, and the need for training within the context, the elements of the training and development of shepherd leaders can be summarized by the following three questions: Where should we train? How should we train? and What should be included in the training?

Where Should We Train?

1. Local church based – Training leaders for the local church is the goal and should be the primary setting of training.

2. In the local context – Training should be done as close to the local context as possible.

3. In community – The church community and peer leaders are both critical for learning.

How Should We Train?

4. Mentoring – Wise and spiritually mature mentors provide guidance and support to growing shepherd-leaders. This includes modelling through mentor-learner interaction (Phil 4:9; 2 Tim 2:2; Heb 13:7–8).

What Should Be Included in the Training?

5. The Word of God – Deep knowledge of Scripture and the ability to teach it accurately are primary goals in training shepherd-leaders.

6. Character formation – The importance and priority of the heart (discussed in chapter 1).

7. Skills – Practical on the job training (discussed in chapter 1).

It is clear that context determines the means of leadership training in many ways. But we have a faith that is translatable to different cultures and contexts. As we translate the training of shepherd-leaders for God's church and adapt

---

8. Nakah, "Capetown Commitment."

means of training them, we don't want to lose the biblical core of content and method, and we should use proven adult education principles.

16

Implementing
Shura-Based Education

We have looked at educational, cultural, and contextual factors that contribute to deep, transformational learning. We have heard from experienced leaders in the region on what these factors looked like in their development process as leaders and have defined a *shura*-based training paradigm that uses adult education principles in culturally appropriate ways. Finally, we have examined some contextual factors that need to be considered in the delivery of teaching and training. These are the biblical, educational, cultural, and experiential pieces that can be used in forming training to develop leaders in the church. Being aware of these principles will help us design programmes that are appropriate for our context and will help us evaluate what materials and programmes will contribute to our goal of training shepherd-leaders.

Building the Designer: The Leader of Leaders

You are the designer. The principles we have studied are what you can use to build a training programme for your leaders. You know best what type of leaders you need. You are the one who knows your context and understands best what works in your context. You know the type of teaching and training your leaders need. You are the best person to work with your young leaders to help them grow in godly character, ministry skills, and knowledge of God's word. Each of the pieces we have looked at is important and ought to be included in your leadership development programme. But you are the one who decides how these pieces best fit together in your context.

Although you are the best person to develop your leaders in your church, you don't have to be the one to do all of the teaching and training. In fact, you aren't able to do all of this. God has provided other leaders, teachers, programmes, and churches to help in the process. By understanding the principles we have discussed, you will be able to evaluate the many programmes, teachers, trainers, and curriculums that are available, discern if they are based on proven adult education principles, know if they are appropriate for your culture and context.

Below are the pieces of *shura*-based learning that you can use to develop the training you need for your leaders. We will highlight the salient principles for each of the pieces and then look at ways to connect them to design and deliver training. Our goal should be to build these principles into leaders who can in turn use them to design and deliver training for other leaders. I said in the introduction that the "build the designer" process is the long road to leadership development. But I believe it is the road that leads to a leadership development paradigm that can be owned by MENA leaders and allows you to build training for your leaders that fits your situation.

Overview of the Three-Part Development Process

Below are steps for building *shura*-based learning into MENA leaders and empowering them to use this paradigm. This brief overview will be followed by a more detailed explanation of each step.

1. Three Foundational Considerations – These key issues need to be understood before embarking on training shepherd-leaders. (1) God is the one who calls and develops leaders; (2) primarily through the process of discipleship; (3) in the context of the local church where leaders live and serve. These foundational considerations are an introduction to the paradigm. The first two can be communicated in a one-day session, and of course should be reinforced throughout leadership development. The third consideration should involve consultation with those who understand the constraints and opportunities of their context. Consideration and discussion of the context and the best ways to facilitate training will provide the framework for delivering leadership training.

2. One Core Competency – This is the heart of what the designer needs to understand and be able to put into practice. It is understanding and being able to practice *shura*-based learning that employs adult

ELT principles from Knowles, Kolb, and Hall to produce the deep transformation we see in Psalm 119 and that is summarized in Bloom's taxonomy. Although this is one core competency, it includes principles from each area. Communicating this competency will take a lengthy period of time and involve modelling, mentoring, experience, and reflection. It is the core of the paradigm, so it is imperative that it is built into the designer who will design and deliver training for their leaders.

3. Three-part Training Framework – The actual training involves three parts: (1) assessment; (2) educational activities; and (3) support. The designer determines the content and length of the training, which depends on the goal of the training, what is being taught, and what resources are used in the training.

Detailed Steps of the Three-Part Development Process

Before implementing the three parts of training, it is important to take time to explain and understand the model's principles. The explanation of the principles below can be provided as part of a formal training course or in consultative discussions with the teacher-trainers and mentors about goals for leadership training. Helping these leaders understand the principles is crucial for successful implementation of a training programme of *shura*-leadership employing experiential learning.

In designing the programme, the role of mentors in assessing future leaders should be well defined. I've offered some guidance in the previous chapter. Their roles of providing ministry challenges, facilitating reflection, and giving support are vital to the overall process. After these foundational principles are communicated, we can begin the process of defining the needs of the leaders to be trained. I have provided the principles from this project that support this, including each element. The four principles are biblical, educational, cultural, and interview themes. In the below steps, I use the term "teacher-trainers" for leaders who are seeking to develop other leaders and designing the course. I use "leaders" for the people who are to be trained and developed.

Three Foundational Considerations
God's Sovereign Work

God's sovereign hand prior to belief and during the growth and development of young leaders is recognized as the primary agent of change beginning with calling to becoming a fruitful leader. Regional leaders strongly affirmed this in their testimonies.

1. Helping young leaders see that God has been at work and is at work even when they don't feel he is or aren't aware of his working highlights this truth. Reminding them throughout the training process of God's work encourages them to continue.

2. God's sovereign work includes the following:

   a) God loves his church (Eph 5:25).

   b) God develops shepherd-leaders for his church.

   c) God has been at work in his leaders from the beginning of their life.

   d) God is working in potential leaders right now.

   e) God gives us characteristics that he wants in the shepherd-leaders of his church in his word (1 Tim 3:1–13; Titus 1:5–16; 1 Pet 5:1–11).

Discipleship

It is important to define the goals, principles, and practices of leadership development from the Bible and to root our training in the Scriptures. Leadership development is simply an extension of discipleship, and of which Jesus, Paul, and leaders throughout church history provide tangible examples. Regional leaders also overwhelmingly affirm this principle. Discipleship is the overarching paradigm of leadership development and should be woven into every part of the training process.

The following describe what should be the goals of developing leaders through discipleship:

1. Leader discipleship should involve deep learning in the cognitive, affective, and psychomotor (doing) domains. In other words, discipleship should encompass the mind, the heart, and the actions of leaders.

2. Leader discipleship should involve true change in the life of the believing leaders, including growing deeper and more mature in the Lord in every area of life.

3. Leader discipleship should involve learning God's word as a key component. Much more than just head knowledge, this learning should result in a depth of understanding that enables leaders to discern true from false teaching, apply truth to life, live it out, and accurately teach the Scriptures.

4. Leader discipleship should involve growth in Christ-likeness. Leaders learn from the Bible and observing the actions and character of more mature leaders, from which they form ideas of what true Christianity looks like and what it means to be faithful to Christ.

Contextual Setting

As we seek to develop leaders, we need to create a process that is appropriate for our context, that will work in our situation and is realistic for us. We don't want to just copy and paste someone else's programme into our situation. Beyond the factors mentioned below, being realistic includes administrative issues such as where we do the training, what it will cost, what resources are available, etc. Here are five contextual factors with questions to consider:

1. Church-based – How do we keep our programme connected to our church?

2. Contextually Close – How can we train our leaders where we live? As much as possible, how can we develop them in our country, our city, and our church body?

3. Conducted in Community – How can we connect young leaders to other young leaders in the same stage of development?

4. Roles of the Mentor – How does our cultural context determine what the mentoring relationship should look like and the roles of mentors? Who can be effective mentors in our context?

5. Bible Centred in Content and Method – How are we depending on the Bible for what we include in our training? Are we using methods that are based on biblical principles?

One Core Competency

Shura-based learning using adult ELT principles should promote what Psalm 119 clearly teaches us, that true growth happens when thinking, affections, and actions are changed. This is real change at the heart level, what we call deep, transformative learning. As we consider how we will teach and train young leaders, we need to consider how best to use *shura*-based learning principles to reach this goal.

Below is a summary of the educational principles we have looked at with questions to help you think through how to make these principles a part of your training.

Knowles's Adult Learning Principles

Knowles's adult learning principles help us understand leaders and how they learn and remind us that adults learn differently than children. Understanding these principles will make our teaching and training of adult leaders more effective.

1. Adult learners are independent and self-directed, as opposed to dependent. How can we include leaders in the planning process? In what ways can we give them responsibility for their own learning?

2. Adults bring experience as a resource to the learning experience, as opposed to children who have little or no life experience. From our assessment, what positive experiences can we build on for our training? What negative experiences need to be addressed or corrected? How can we help leaders learn from their previous experience?

3. Adult readiness to learn is determined by the tasks of life and work, as opposed to preparing for life. What are the leaders' responsibilities and roles in life such as family, job, society, and church? How can we connect what we teach to these roles? What do leaders need to learn to succeed in these roles?

4. Adult learning is problem-centred, as opposed to subject centred, thus more immediate in application. What challenges in life and ministry are leaders facing? How can what we teach help address or solve these problems or challenges? How do these challenges help us decide what is important to teach?

5. Adult motivation for learning is internal, as opposed to external. They are motivated by the need to know. How can we take advantage of this desire to learn? How can we deepen this desire to learn more and encourage leaders to be life-long learners?

Kolb's Experiential Learning Theory (ELT)

Kolb's experiential learning theory (ELT) describes the four stages of learning that must happen to produce deep learning. Especially relevant to our teaching training is how experience is processed, so we need to include time for and training in reflection on experiences. Training should also include opportunities for experimentation and hands-on experience in ministry.

The steps in Kolb's learning cycle are followed by questions we should ask:

1. Concrete experience – Leaders' current or new experience, including learning. What experiences do learners bring to the learning process? How can we give learners concrete experience in the classroom and church ministry?

2. Reflective observation – Leaders' thoughts and evaluation of the experience as being good, bad, helpful, etc. How can we create ways for leaders to reflect on their experiences? What is our role in helping them reflect? Do each of their learning activities include reflection?

3. Abstract conceptualization – Based on reflection, what modifications in thinking, attitudes, or actions do leaders think should be made, for example changing the way they do something or reject a teaching they now see as wrong. How can we help leaders imagine new ways of doing ministry?

4. Active experimentation – Leaders try to apply their new way of thinking or doing in real life. They experiment and see if what they thought works or is true. How can we give the leader opportunities to actually do ministry? What challenges and opportunities can we give them to test their new learning? How can we encourage them to try new ways of doing things and not be afraid to fail, or not do it perfectly the first time?

Bloom's Learning Domains

Bloom's three domains of learning are the cognitive, affective, and psychomotor. Deep learning, growth, and change happens when leaders advance up the learning levels in each domain.

Bloom's three domains of learning are followed by questions we should ask:

1. Cognitive – Thinking that advances from basic comprehension to advanced application and using information in problem solving. How can we encourage students to advance to higher-level thinking

skills? How can we teach them to evaluate and use the information they have learned to face ministry challenges and solve real-life problems?

2. Affective – Engagement with learning that progresses from being willing to listen to being willing to prioritize values and change thinking and behaviour. How can we engage leaders in the learning process so that they want to learn more on their own? How can we show leaders that what we are teaching from the Bible is true, that it really does make a difference in real life, and encourage them to desire biblical truth to transform their thinking, values, and behaviour?

3. Psychomotor – Developing skills that advances from observing another to the ability to apply skills in different situations. What do leaders need to be able to do? How can we help grow in ministry skills such as preaching, conflict resolution, and leading small groups? What opportunities can we create to help them practice and improve their skills?

Hall's High-Context Culture

Leaders in the MENA region are members of high-context cultures, and we looked in particular at how being in a high-context culture impacts communication and thinking. Here are some aspects of high-context culture and questions we should ask:

1. Communication is highly dependent on the surrounding context. What are we communicating by the way we teach or train? How should we use the communication practices of our culture in the classroom and in mentoring?

2. Thinking tends to be concrete rather than abstract. Does our teaching include concrete examples? How can we start from the concrete and move to abstract principles?

3. Learning tends to be holistic and praxis oriented rather than departmentalized and abstract. How can we teach using case studies and real-life examples from our region, our own ministries, and even situations in the lives of learners?

Three-Part Development Framework

The overall training programme should be developed within the framework of assessment, challenges, and support (ACS).[1] This framework will be applied in light of the principles of how adults learn via reflection and active experimentation presented by Knowles and Kolb.

Assessment

The teacher-trainer should conduct an initial assessment of the leaders. What are their needs, and what resources do they bring to the training process? The teacher-trainer should also understand the prior learning situation of the leaders. This initial assessment should be conducted through interaction with leaders, providing them ownership of the process and making the learning partially self-directed. Each of these steps can be done with individual leaders as well.

Assess the Learners

1. Assess the leaders' call and spiritual gifts and their need to grow in understanding these. Calling will be clarified and confirmed, as much as possible, through discussion with potential leaders.

   a) Develop teaching on the biblical explanation of calling.

   b) Discuss their internal call to serve.

   c) Discover their spiritual gifts based on their personal enjoyment of ministry and the testimony of others on their strengths.

2. Assessment should include an inventory of the experience leaders bring to the process. What life experiences do they have, including previous learning, business or other experience, and leadership in life or work? What experience do they have serving in the church?

3. Assess leaders' life situations including their stage of life, roles, etc. Ministry challenges should take place in the context of leaders' life situations as much as possible.

4. Assess the leaders' learning needs. Where do they need to grow in their character, knowledge, and ministry skills? What are the gaps

---

1. ACS is a framework for training from the Center for Creative Research (CCL). Regina Eckert and Simon Rweyongoza, *Leadership Development in Africa: A Focus on Strengths* (Greensboro, NC: Center for Creative Research, 2010).

between where they are and where they need to be in order to be fruitful shepherd-leaders?

5. As a result of this assessment, the teacher-trainer and the leaders should discuss and define the goals for learning and development as shepherd-leaders.

Assess the Learners' Context

To ensure the proper use of ELT, it is important to understand the prior learning experience of leaders and to use this information to inform the teaching and training process so that training elements and methods are both effective and culturally appropriate. Training should begin where leaders are and leads them toward accepting and benefitting from ELT. Here are some questions to consider:

1. Prior Learning Situation. What is their cultural, educational, socio-economic situation? How did they learn in school? How does our culture teach, for example through stories, doing, etc.?

2. Cultural Considerations. Based on the culture of the leaders, what are the best learning activities to use? In what ways will our and their culture make it easier to use ELT principles in training? In what ways will it make it harder?

3. Introduce New Learning. Understanding the factors that influence how change can be introduced to the learning situation. Determine what are the best ways to introduce ELT and how fast can we introduce ELT practices.

Based on the above assessment, the teacher-trainer will define ELT learning activities that will contribute to the defined learning goals. Depending on the teacher-trainer's level of understanding and ability to use ELT, it might be beneficial to train the teacher-trainer on how to use ELT practices. The teacher-trainer will need to determine the most appropriate setting and the curriculum for the teaching and training process.

Challenges or Training Experiences

Challenges are activities, tasks, courses, and experiences that will be used in developing leaders. These are the elements of the overall leadership development programme you will use to train shepherd-leaders in your context. These training elements fall under the categories given in 1 Timothy

4:14–16: character, teaching, and skills related to ministry. (Calling is included under assessment.) These should be developed in the context of experience and support using ELT adult education principles. The teacher-trainer should develop a programme that seeks to grow the leaders in each of these categories, integrating the categories with each other as much as possible.

The teacher-trainer should assign ministry tasks that test and develop character and ministry skills. They should select teaching courses that provide required biblical knowledge and address the character and skills that need to be developed. They should seek to connect teaching, character, and skills and help leaders understand how they inform each other.

Following are questions to ask and more detailed recommendations for integrating each category given in 1 Timothy 4:14–16 – ministry skills, character, biblical knowledge – into a teaching and training programme.

Ministry Skills (1 Tim 4:15)
Based in the assessment, what are the skills leaders will need to develop, such as evangelism, church planting, discipleship, handling persecution, leading a small group, handling conflict, teaching, prayer, etc. The teacher-trainer should recognize God-ordained opportunities and challenges that will help leaders grow in ministry skills and abilities and create opportunities to be involved in different ministry situations. Then provide training in the areas where leaders have needs via a combination of teaching and hands-on experience, along with evaluation and reflection. Studying the biblical basis and pattern for ministry activities provides biblical guidance on what we do and how we do it. Practical involvement with the direction and support of mentors will help leaders grow in the skills needed for ministry.

Character (1 Tim 4:16)
Character and how God develops character in his leaders is key. For example, are they caring for their family in the midst of the pressures of ministry? How do leaders respond to criticism and conflict? Other character areas are loving people including our enemies, communion with God, integrity in handling money, patience and endurance, humility and a servant heart, and courage in the face of trials.

Teacher-trainers should identify ministry assignments that will test the character of leaders. They should also teach the biblical reasons for and standards of godly character for a leader, using the pastoral epistles in particular, as well as examples from the lives of Moses, David, and others along with historical figures and examples of MENA leaders. Teacher-trainers should also cover related character issues including the role and responsibility of a husband and father, how Christ responded to conflict, how to be a peacemaker, etc.

As part of training, teacher-trainers should observe the character of each leader in the midst of life and ministry, evaluate it, and discuss how the leader's life compares to biblical standards. For example, in what situations have they exhibited the fruit of the Spirit? Where have they failed to do this on a regular basis? How does the leader handle personal attacks? Does the leader trust God and have peace in the midst of trials and challenges? Does the leader exhibit faith and trust in God's timing? Knowing the areas young leaders need to develop helps to identify gaps in their character and helps the teacher-trainer establish situations to observe and develop their character through trials, reflection, and support.

Biblical Knowledge (1 Tim 4:16)

The teacher-trainer should identify courses and learning programmes that will help leaders obtain a level of understanding of Scripture and doctrine that will enable them to teach others in their context. In-person instruction and learning in community should be encouraged as much as possible.

1. The leader needs a deep knowledge of the Bible including understanding the Old and New Testaments, what the Bible teaches about the Godhead including the individual members, salvation by grace and faith, living the Christian life, and more. The teacher-trainer should also include context-specific topics to be covered such as Islam, marriage in MENA cultures, child raising, etc.

2. Teacher-trainers will most likely use outside sources to provide needed biblical and theological knowledge that they are unable to provide, but they determine the best ways to deliver this knowledge in light of the context. They should also ask, could leaders travel to study for a few days or a week three to six times per year? Could online courses be used in conjunction with in person teaching? Can teachers come to leaders on a regular basis?

3. The teacher-trainer should take time to reflect with leaders on how the biblical knowledge they are studying relates to their personal life and ministry in the church. For example, how does knowing Christ and the gospel help leaders have a balanced life or deal with conflict? What are implications of the Trinity for community? How can leaders explain the Trinity to others in their country?

As much as possible, these three areas should be connected and inform each other. For example, biblical and theological studies should be applied to real-life ministry situations and interactions with people, and the scriptural foundations of ministry activities should be explained.

Support

To make the learning process transformative, the teacher-trainer should support leaders through reflection, encouragement, challenges, and teaching. They provide the right word at the right time. Growth and development of leaders is done best in the context of community. Members of the church can also provide support and encouragement to developing leaders, and young leaders can also help to support each other.

Training should include a close relationship between a more mature leader who serves as a mentor and the developing leader. The supporting role of the mentor is vital to the process.

The mentor needs to consistently reflect with the leader to help them learn from their experiences, both positive and negative, and help them form new ideas. They should connect learning to experience and help the young leader benefit from experiences both positive and negative. Ministry tasks or challenges should be assigned by the mentor under the supervision of the teacher-trainer. Mentors should encourage leaders to take risks by trying new challenges as well as encourage them in the midst of struggles. In the midst of this process, the mentor should share timely words of reassurance, wisdom and inspiration.

To summarize, as much as possible, the teaching and ministry assignments should complement and reinforce each other. For example, training on evangelism should include the biblical basis for evangelism and models from Scripture as well as encouragement to develop a love for the lost and a passion for lost souls, both character traits. But it should also include opportunities to do evangelism with reflection on the process. In another example, studies on the nature of Christ should be expanded to helping leaders understand how this knowledge strengthens their faith in the midst of trials and how it produces appreciation for the wonder and beauty of our Saviour.

These examples illustrate the importance of designing teaching and training with the three categories from 1 Timothy 4 in mind and show how an issue can be addressed from all three perspectives at the same time. Doing so serves to reinforce the teaching and training and produces deep learning that is transformational.

A Scenario for Our Region

God has blessed the Brand New Faith Church (BNFC), and the body has grown deeper in the love and knowledge of the Lord. They sense the need to develop leaders to serve as elders. They also have a heart to start another church in a nearby city. They are a small church but have identified two men to serve as elders and one church planter to send from their body. To prepare these shepherd-leaders, they began looking at training programmes, seminaries, and trainers to help them. They found a multitude of training seminars and seminary programmes from both inside and outside the region.

Before deciding on the programme to use, BNFC took time to understand the leadership development principles that God develops leaders for his church and that the leadership development process is part of the biblical paradigm of discipleship. After understanding these principles, BNFC defined the type of training needed and how it would be delivered. They thought through categories for training from 1 Timothy 4:14–16 to determine the call of the leaders and their needs in knowledge, character, and skills based on their type of ministry and the general needs of leaders.

The pastor of BNFC sought to include these three potential leaders in the planning throughout the development process. So he sat with the three to begin assessing their gifts, their calling, and their needs as shepherd-leaders as well as their prior learning situations. After the pastor took time to understand the potential leaders, what they needed, and how the church wanted to offer their training, he assessed available programmes and determined that courses from Serving Seminary (SS) could be used as part of the development process.

The pastor established a six-month programme that would integrate knowing, feeling, and doing. Training for BNFC leadership at a residential seminary was impractical. However, SS was willing to send professors to teach the courses BNFC requested. So the pastor decided to use a combination of SS professors and local leaders to offer one course each month to cover Old Testament, New Testament, who God is, salvation by grace, and the Bible and the church. The teachers and professors agreed to adapt their teaching style to include case-studies from the leaders' cultural context to stimulate discussion as well as give an assignment that is related to their ministry in their church.

BNFC's pastor would mentor all three shepherd-leaders, helping them to reflect on what they learned and how it applied to ministry in the church. The presence of outside teachers to teach the courses presented an opportunity for further mentoring and reflection. The church planter would also spend two days each month with another pastor who had recently planted a church. The three leaders met together once a week to encourage each other, drink tea, and discuss issues from their ministry and from their classes.

All three leaders were involved in ministry as they were being trained. They were each asked to teach a three-part lesson on one of the courses they had completed. The church planter was also asked to preach once per month. Their training included regular times of reflection and feedback with the pastor as well as interaction with members of the church. Throughout all of this training, the church body was encouraged to see their part in developing leaders.

As these leaders served in the church, it became clear that each of them struggled with different issues such as their response to criticism, ability to learn from failure, and need for greater faith when they didn't see immediate fruit in their ministry. Training in the midst of the community of the church provided many challenges which the pastor used to help these young leaders learn and grow.

The process actually took eight months instead of six. At the conclusion of the training, the church gathered to recognize these three men as elders. They celebrated God's work in these leaders and gave thanks for their own role in the process. They understood the challenge the church planter faced in starting a new church in a neighbouring city but were confident in God's promise to build his church and provide her the shepherd-leaders she needs to care for her.

BNFC is already thinking about how to create ongoing ways to grow and develop leaders in their church and who they could develop to plant the next church.

Appendix

Report of Research Results

The research conducted for this book included interviews with MENA regional leaders and an extensive survey of studies in Arabic culture and adult education. This research was part of my dissertation.[1]

Interviews with MENA Leaders

An important part of this book is learning from the experience of church leaders in the region, including how God developed them as leaders and what they have found fruitful in developing leaders. Comments from the leaders who were interviewed for this project have been included throughout the previous chapters. I had the privilege and joy to sit with thirty-six leaders in the region and ask them a simple question: "What are the most significant experiences that contributed to your formation as a leader?"

The interview subjects consisted of thirty-one men and five women. I conducted four group interviews of ten, five, three, and three persons respectively. The remaining fifteen interviews were conducted one on one. Experience in leadership ranged from two to forty-two years, with an average of eleven and a median of twelve. Leaders were defined as those who are pastoring a church or leading others in a ministry setting. Most were pastors of small house churches, and all were involved in discipleship. Most worked with adults and some with children. These leaders provided almost three hundred and fifty comments in answer to my basic question, though some were duplicate. Much of the conversations consisted of leaders explaining what they meant by certain answers. These answers were recorded and compared for patterns. Below is a summary of answers, insights, and wisdom.

---

1. Joseph Nehemiah, "A Contextual and Cultural Adult Education Model for Leadership Development in the Arab Middle East" (Doctoral dissertation, 2018).

Interview Results

Overall, twelve themes were evident in the interview responses of the thirty-six leaders.

- 5 Major Themes: Discipleship, Learning through Doing, Involvement with Others, Teaching Relationship with God
- 3 Minor Themes: Character, Calling, God's Sovereign Work
- 4 Individual Themes: Inner Desire, Ministry Skills, Self-Development, Vision

The five major themes had strong support across the thirty-six leaders interviewed. The three minor themes were mentioned less frequently, but were nonetheless considered important in God's work in developing leaders. Both calling and character were mentioned in individual and group interviews, but not in high numbers. God's sovereign work was not mentioned in the group interviews but had a high frequency in the individual interviews. Finally the four individual themes were only mentioned in the group or the individual interviews but not both, and the frequency was small.

The interview results were placed in twelve categories. Seven are common to both group and individual interviews. Three are unique to group interviews, and two are unique to individual interviews. Table 1 reports the numbers for each type of interview, and Table 2 summarizes the leaders' definitions of each theme.

Table 1: Number of Mentions of the Twelve Themes in Group and Individual Interviews

Themes	Group Interviews 4 groups totalling 21 people	Individual Interviews with 15 people
Major Themes		
Discipleship	18	41
Learning through Doing (Challenge)	13	44
Involvement with Others	18	33
Teaching	18	24
Vision	10	0
Relationship with God	16	19

Minor Themes		
Character	3	30
Calling	18	5
God's Sovereign Work	0	24
Individual Themes		
Inner Desire to Serve	5	0
Ministry Skills	3	0
Self-Development	0	3

Table 2: Consensus of the Definitions of the Twelve Themes from Interview Responses

Theme	Summary of Definitions Given in the Interviews
Discipleship	A deeper knowledge of the Lord through personal and spiritual discipline in all its forms. Addresses teaching and behaviour and implies multiplication. Overall formation through support, encouragement, and modeling by someone more mature in the faith.
Learning Through Doing	Learning through experiences and challenges in ministry given by another or from personal trials and mistakes, both of which are how we learn skills and verify gifts.
Involvement with Others	Support through fellowship, accountability, and encouragement. Growth through being related to and involved with others (church) including the leader's spouse.
Teaching	Learning Christian doctrine and practice to be able to discern right and wrong teaching, including a previous religion's teaching and culture, so that you can evangelize and disciple others. Need for continuous study.
Vision	Working out one's calling.
Relationship with God	A continuous communing with and knowing God through the Bible, prayer, and reflection on life and ministry. An intimate and sincere commitment and zeal for God.
Character	Growing in Christ-likeness expressed through obedience and wise living out of faith. Not just talking or teaching about Christ, but applying God's work to life and living it.

Calling	Hearing God's call directly and made sure by others and the church. Certainty of a call is crucial.
God's Sovereign Work	God's sovereign personal provision and awareness of such prior to and following conversion.
Inner Desire to Serve	An inner drive and sense of responsibility to serve devoid of personal motives.
Ministry Skills	Learning and gaining skills to be able to interact with, impact, and confront others. We gain skills for the sake of serving others and building the church.
Self-Development	Being responsible for your own spiritual and ministerial development.

Expansion of Interview Results

The responses of interviewed leaders for each of the twelve categories are given in expanded form below. They are not external definitions of the concepts, nor are they interpretations of the leaders' answers but represent the words of the leaders who were interviewed when they were asked to explain or describe each theme.

1. Discipleship

Discipleship best summarizes the interaction between leaders and those they are developing and includes teaching and modelling in both groups and one on one. So discipleship encompasses a number of the other themes. Without discipleship it is impossible to be a fruitful Christian or Christian leader. It is what the Lord did and what he commanded us to do, so is an assumed activity. When I asked one group what they meant by discipleship, they just stared at me silently as if to express, "Don't you know what it is? It is so foundational to Christianity."

According to the leader responses, discipleship encompasses going deep into the word of God, and they emphasized that this study should be done in a group. The purpose of discipleship is knowing our Lord personally and more deeply. It also helps leaders know themselves and understand their strengths and weaknesses. It is learning all that God wants to teach, and helps leaders be more rooted in their faith, and addresses and corrects behaviour that is not in line with the Bible.

Discipleship happens when a more mature leader teaches someone younger in the faith. The majority of responses in this category mentioned mentoring and role models as significant in helping them grow as a leader. The presence of someone "in front of me" made a critical difference in their development. Mentors helped them make sense of and benefit from the challenges of life and ministry. Mentors helped them see the big picture, make sense of the Bible and their trials, and understand how to relate the Scriptures to their life. Mentors also confirmed the leaders' gifts and calling. They provided assessment, support, encouragement, correction, and shepherding and inspired them to be greater than they were.

According to the interviews, role models give growing leaders a tangible picture of what godly leaders look like and model godly character in the midst of life. Examples given included showing what forgiveness and patience look like. As one leader said of his mentor/role model, "He lived the gospel in front of me." Role models loved their wives and families and even invited the growing leaders into their family to see how to live out biblical precepts in a family. However, leaders cannot give what they do not have. If leaders are not living out what they have learned, then they will not be able to affect others.

Role models also showed young leaders how to develop the skills they need to minister, how to study the Bible in depth, how to lead a small group, and how to start a church. Leaders benefitted greatly from seeing someone practice the skills they need in front of their eyes. For these leaders, mentoring and modelling were the primary means of discipleship. They also explained that before any leader disciples another person, they must first be discipled. Without discipleship, fruitful ministry leadership is impossible, and ministry is the natural outgrowth of discipleship. Discipleship and growth should be continuous in the life of a leader.

The overarching theme includes the deep learning or real transformation that is our goal in developing leaders. It is aimed at the heart, involves others, includes knowledge of God's word, and leads to lives conformed to Christ and the Scriptures. Discipleship defines both the goal and the process of developing leaders. So that leadership development should be included even in the early stages of discipleship.

2. Learning Through Doing (Challenge)

Being involved in ministry helps to develop a sense of responsibility. Ministry challenges give young leaders the opportunity to practice ministry and develop their gifts and skills. These include serving in the community, outreach, and providing shepherding and support to people in the church. Practical ministry opportunities are the way leaders learn and grow in ministry, wisdom, and know-how. Engagement in ministry should happened in relation to one's call. It is based on their call and part of verifying their call and gifts. The goal is to develop their gifts and abilities to minister.

Many leaders said they grew when a more mature leader recognized them as a potential leader and challenged them with a task to help them grow in their gifting and ability to minister in the church. They grew by being challenged to take on more responsibility. When their leaders saw that they had been faithful in the small responsibilities, they gave them more responsibility. Facing problems and challenges actually served to help leaders grow in their passion to serve and their ability to minister to others and to develop others and form teams. Exercising responsibility early in their faith served to confirm their gifting and calling.

Leaders said they grew through "on-the-job training" or "field-work," ministry responsibilities being delegated to them and being given ownership of ministry tasks. In one country, when the first wave of ministers from outside left, the local believers had the chance to try to do ministry "in a way that was culturally appropriate." The model of watch, practice with oversight, and then do it on your own allowed one leader to start and lead his own small church.

Leaders also grew as they encountered trials in life and ministry. It should be noted that these trials were mostly negative. Yet they make up an important part of God's work in developing them as leaders. Trials and pressures served to make these leaders stronger and wiser and enabled them to endure more and know better how to respond in the future. Often these trials are hardships that happened to them because of others including family and government. God used trials in their life to test their faith so that they would learn to trust God to provide for their needs. As well, God used trials to reveal and develop their heart and to teach them perseverance.

The leaders also described how they learned from mistakes they made as they led others in ministry and how they learned to love others and trust God through conflict and negative behaviour in people who led them. A repeated phrase was "being in over their heads in ministry." Because of the great needs, many of these leaders were "thrown into ministry." But God used ministry challenges whether they were given to young leaders or they encountered them as they ministered.

3. Involvement with Others

Leaders expressed the importance of being supported and helped by others in the church as crucial for growth. Developing leaders must see themselves as part of the group. Because of the importance of the family in their culture and its subsequent loss after their faith, the church group became the life support for many of these regional leaders. They see themselves in the context of the group, the "we" and recognize that they need fellowship, support, advice, confrontation, and help for learning how to relate biblically.

Leaders expressed that the importance of others includes the idea that iron sharpens iron. Different points of view need to be shared, appreciated, and learned from. Relationships provide both support and accountability, and leaders should be open to being impacted by others. The leaders also expressed that one's relationship with the Lord is demonstrated through relationships with others, and that good relationships are a must in the church. Relationship is the door through which ministry happens. It happens through communication and should happen regularly, almost daily. The group models Christ to one another in word and deed, but it is also important to recognize that as a group, they serve as a light to society and witness to others. Whatever the size, Christian groups are generally viewed as the church, and their godly relationships are how the world knows they are disciples of Christ.

In the church, leaders see the "good, the bad and the ugly" and learn how to love, forgive, act humbly, and accept others. The church is a place of testing, but it should also be a place of support because it is a leader's family.

4. Teaching

The regional leaders stated that early learning created a hunger in them to learn more about God's word and how to live out the Christian life. As they learned more, they came into contact with different teaching, and their former religion challenged some of the basic tenets of their new faith.

The word of God should be the main focus of teaching, in contrast to training, which the leaders did not consider to be the same. For these leaders, right teaching is a priority to guarantee doctrinal fidelity and necessary for church growth. It is a responsibility for which we will have to give an account. If leaders do not rightly understand the word of God, they will lead others into error, which could be disastrous for their soul. The church determines right and wrong teaching.

Christ said that those who love him will keep his commandments. One group rightly stated that we can't love Christ if we don't know his commandments, so leaders need good and true teaching to properly live out their faith and rightly teach others. Knowledge of God's word is also needed to evangelize well and answer the questions seekers have.

When leaders encountered someone to teach them, they developed a deeper understanding of both doctrine and practice of their new-found faith. They received this teaching both directly and as part of a study programme. Participation in formal or semi-formal study programmes helped them learn how to study the Bible and how to systematize their knowledge. Having categories through which to understand biblical teaching helped them to better discern truth from error. This formalized teaching also included training in leadership skills such as how to develop others and how to disciple. One leader stated that "formal training is very beneficial in the life of the leader to develop him," and along with a continuous programme of reading helps leaders to keep growing.

Finally, the MENA regional leaders stated that teaching should include study of the Islamic religion. This study is important for equipping leaders to answer the questions of new Muslim-background believers and for enabling them to provide apologetic answers to inquirers. Knowledge of Islam can also help leaders create an atmosphere where fellow believers feel comfortable.

The inclination is to learn until one becomes a leader and then stop. But the regional leaders stated that leaders need to continue learning all of their life. Despite leaders defining learning as mainly a cognitive activity, they stressed the need to practice and to live out what one learns. One leader recognized that if a leader does not know what is right, they won't be able to do what is right. The teaching and doing that encompasses real learning should be done in the context of life and should be a life-long process.

5. Vision

Leaders expressed the need to understand the big picture of what they are doing and why. This includes the general vision of what the Christian faith is about. But also understanding the vision for a particular ministry helps leaders understand the reasons they do what they do and how they support the overall work.

6. Relationship with God

In the interviews, regional leaders emphasized the importance of intimacy with the Lord that is characterized by constant communication that enables leaders to trust God and wait for his timing. Leaders should have a commitment and a zeal for God and should seek teaching and training to develop this depth of relationship with the Lord.

This intimate relationship is cultivated by spending time alone with God, reflecting on the issues of life and sitting at God's feet to gain wisdom through God's word which is alive and speaks his words to us. Leaders should view this time as a "vacation with God." The basics of Christian growth, particularly prayer and the word (Acts 6:4), are crucial in leader development. Leaders must read the Bible to know about God but more importantly to know God, to be inspired, and to respond to God in prayer.

According to regional leaders, it is crucial to understand that sitting before God is a dialogue. First we need to hear what God says, and not what we think, by reading and reflecting on his word. It is through the Bible that we know God. The Bible is a spiritual instrument that God uses to speak to us and to change our life according to his will. The Bible gives us wisdom and answers the doubts of the scoffer. It is also a weapon that helps us in the midst of spiritual warfare. Reading and reflecting on the Bible is how we gain wisdom in the face of trials and know what God wants us to do. Leaders learn by seeing their experiences, both success and failures, in the mirror of God's word.

Second, leaders gain more wisdom and intimacy with God by applying his word through reflective prayer. The regional leaders stressed the importance of filling up and relating intimately with God before seeking to lead others in his ways and regularly examining and improving their personal relationship with the Lord as they lead.

7. Character

Character was a difficult category to define. In some ways it is the characteristics of godly leaders, what they should be, their character, and should be doing, obeying God. It is vital to not just talk or teach about Christ, but to live out the teaching of Christ. The life of leaders must align with what the Bible teaches, which requires applying God's word to every area. Examples given by the regional leaders included being disciplined in thinking about life and money.

In this category, the leaders interviewed emphasized integrity, living by principle and not compromising one's principles, having faith in God, and loving him and others. The leaders believed that God matures them and others by developing godly character that is marked by truth, faith, and love, which is foundational for Christian leaders.

The leaders also emphasized obedience. Their simple definition of obedience was to "do what God's word says." For example, God develops leaders who give from what they have even from the very beginning of their faith. Obedient shepherds are humble before those they lead which creates trust between them and their flock. They grow by developing wisdom in applying God's word and discerning how to interact with others. They exhibit their faith by being bold in proclaiming Christ and working faithfully even if they don't understand all the reasons for their service. In the interviews, the leaders explained that obedience or doing flows from being, and doing affects our being. They are connected; therefore leaders grow by developing both of these areas.

8. Calling

The leader's discernment of their call from God is foundational to a proper start in ministry. The interviewed leaders recognized both internal and external aspects to discerning and confirming their call. One group was adamant that, "There must be a call, and that God is the one who gives the call." Regional leaders believe that God's call has priority over a calling from groups outside of the country. One group was clear that it is the church who confirms the call.

A leader's call comes before being set apart for ministry, but is in many ways dependent upon others recognizing their Christ-like character. Leaders pointed to the fact that character worthy of a leader only happens if the leader is called by God. An inward, self-generated desire to serve is insufficient to supply perseverance in the midst of trials and conflict. Leaders recognize God's work as producing the character worthy of that call.

According to the interview responses, an important step in understanding one's call is to be deployed in ministry by leaders who can evaluate call and gifting. The verification of one's call is a step-by-step process. Leaders begin to sense and clarify their call through prayer and by reading the Bible. Then the young leader tries ministry and is assessed, supported, and confirmed by others in the church especially other leaders.

The regional leaders stated that calling should not be confused with a personal desire to minister. It is more than a personal desire. It is also not to be confused with working in any other type of job because leadership in the church is not a job. It is a calling, a stewardship, and a responsibility. This is why affirming the call is so important. If leaders have not adequately verified their call, they will find ministry a hardship, and their impact on others will be negative instead of being a blessing. But being sure of their call will allow them to do the hard work and endure the trials and hardships of ministry.

The presence of an inner motivation to serve, the commitment to ongoing personal growth, and the development of ministry skills for the sake of others can be used to evaluate a call and vision for ministry, an understanding of how and where they fit in God's work. Here we have the coalescence of God's work and our role in calling, developing, and helping shepherd-leaders serve fruitfully in God's church.

9. God's Sovereign Work

Many leaders spoke of the work of God's Spirit in building his church and providing her with shepherds. This mirrors closely what we find in the Scriptures and God's work in history. Leaders recognized the priority of God's Spirit, his word, and the body of Christ as means God uses to raise up faithful shepherds for his church. Having said this, the clear recognition of God's sovereign hand in so many different aspects of developing them while building his church points to God's glory. Though this study focuses on the instruments God uses to develop leaders, regional leaders remind us that God is the one who created, uses and directs these instruments.

A number of the interviewed leaders testified to God's direct provision for them in their growth as a believer and as a leader. As they read the Bible, apart from any formal studies or another person teaching them, leaders learned by relying on the Holy Spirit to teach them. "God was my main teacher," some said. They were also able to discern false teaching without any formal teaching because they were guided by the Holy Spirit to respond biblically to trials and hurts from others. God's direct work in them created a hunger to know him more deeply and to study and learn his word more fully.

God also provided directly for various needs and guided these leaders by helping them know what to do at that right time. They were enabled to recognize God's timing and what he was doing. Sometimes God provided a song in the midst of a severe time of persecution. He sovereignly provided material needs, ministry blessings, a person to guide at the right time, and energy and perseverance to minister.

Leaders also testified to the Holy Spirit's work in breaking and changing them. Their arrogance was stripped away, and one leader testified to God removing hatred for his family that had ruled his heart even after coming to faith. One young leader learned the hard lesson of being "the least of these" as a servant of Christ when the Holy Spirit applied his word and changed her heart. Leaders sometimes recognized God's hand when he intervened, but were more able to recognize his working for them as they looked back.

Finally, some leaders became aware of God's presence and work in their lives even before their faith in Christ. They had a positive impression of Christianity and were aware of God's care for them. They saw how God was preparing them to lead and teach others even as an unbeliever by developing their abilities, and he used their pre-Christian experiences, culture, and context to enable them to minister to and lead others. These testimonies of God's direct work were more pronounced among those who were among the first believers where they lived and is a good reminder that God keeps his promise to build his church.

10. Inner Desire to Serve

If leaders are called, have become mature, and have sought spiritual discipleship, it is natural that they will have the desire to serve. According to the regional leaders, this isn't just a personal desire but a sense of responsibility and stewardship of the message. Spiritual maturity creates the feeling of responsibility to serve that needs to be void of any personal motives, interests, and ambitions like being recognized or holding a position. If leaders lack this mature desire, they will serve the desires of their flesh and will shrink back when challenges arise in their ministry. Leaders must have a sense of responsibility and drive to help through the hard times.

11. Ministry Skills

A few leaders interviewed mentioned the need for leaders to grow in skills that enable them to interact, impact, and confront others. They also stated that we need to gain skills for the sake of serving others and building the church, not just to learn a new skill for ourselves.

The unique category of ministry skills was mentioned by only one of the four groups, one with three people. However as I listened to leaders, the idea of ministry skills was present in the categories of teaching, discipleship, and learning through doing (challenge). So the idea was prevalent in leaders' thinking. I decided to break it out as a separate category for two reasons. One is that it was mentioned by one of the four groups, so that gives it some importance. The other is the leaders' recognition of the need to be able to minister and serve. They focused more on the process of developing ministry skills with the understanding that possessing these skills is imperative to fruitful ministry. For these reasons I included ministry skills as a separate category.

12. Self-Development

A few interviewed leaders stated that leaders have to be responsible for their own spiritual and ministerial development. Although they need others, they need to know how to "find their sanctuary" in the Lord and not have to depend on others for spiritual refreshment. They are also responsible for their behaviour, to watch themselves to ensure that they are walking with the Lord and living out his word. Finally, leaders need to constantly seek to grow in their abilities and skills because they can only lead others as far as they have traveled. They must be self-motived and self-directed in developing their life with the Lord and with others.

Summary

The practical experience of leaders in the region is a valuable resource for forming leadership development principles and practices. The regional leaders interviewed provide real life examples of how God has worked in developing leaders for his church. From their experiences, we recognize the three areas of character, skills, and teaching from 1 Timothy 4. We see God's sovereign hand in calling and developing leaders. We see the importance of the church as the context of learning.

The experience of leaders also affirms the effectiveness of adult ELT learning in an Arab context. Their experience shows us that real learning does not just inform the mind, but transforms the person. We learn from them the importance of reflection with God and with older leaders. Leaders also tell us the importance of being able to experiment and learn as they try new ministries, which reminds us that experience is an important part of the development process and for facing the challenges of life and ministry.

Research Results and Adult ELT Principles

Table 3 summarizes how each of the twelve themes that emerged from the interviews of regional leaders relate to specific adult ELT principles.

Table 3: Shared Characteristics of Interview Themes and Education Principles

Themes	Bloom	Kolb	Knowles
Discipleship	✓	✓	
Learning Through Doing	✓	✓	✓
Involvement with Others	✓	✓	✓
Teaching	✓		✓
Vision	✓		
Relationship with God	✓	✓	
Character	✓		
Calling		✓	✓
God's Sovereign Work			
Inner Desire to Serve	✓		✓
Ministry Skills	✓	✓	✓
Self-Development			✓

Results from interviews confirm conclusions from our research of adult ELT principles, that they are appropriate and effective in a MENA cultural setting.

Bloom

The responses of the regional leaders interviewed reveal the importance of Bloom's focus on deep learning that produces real change in the life of leaders. They recognize the importance of teaching leaders and learning through doing in the development process, as well as the importance of character development. What is most helpful to us is their stress on the need for deep learning that is more than just casual knowledge, and their understanding of the progression of learning from observation to trying to doing, which mirrors Bloom's psychomotor domain.

Kolb

The elements in Kolb's learning theory were well represented in the ways the leaders described how God developed them. Experience and reflection were an important part of their growth. They also identified the importance of experimenting and learning from mistakes. All steps in the Kolb cycle can be seen in the leaders' responses. Having a mentor was identified as important for making reflection and experimentation fruitful in producing real learning.

Knowles

The interview responses indicated that Knowles's principles for adult learning were used in the leaders' development. Those interviewed recognize the importance of internal motivation and the need for leaders to have some ownership in their learning process. A number of leaders mentioned the value of experience in their growth and development and that they benefitted from experiences both positive and negative. The leaders also stressed the importance of applying what one learns to life. Their learning was problem focused, and not merely subject oriented. In short, the regional leaders interviewed confirmed the usefulness of adult learning principles in adult learning situations, which increases our confidence that these principles will be effective in a workable model.

The Twelve Themes and the Three Agents of Leadership Development: God, Church, Self

Table 4 indicates the relationship between the twelve themes that emerged from the interviews and the three agents of leadership development: (1) the work of God; (2) the role of the church; and (3) the responsibility of the leader. These three agents point to the reality that the discipleship process is a partnership between God, the church community, and the leader.

Table 4: Agents and Elements of Leadership Development

God	Church	Self
Discipleship	Discipleship	Discipleship
	Involvement with Others	
	Learning Through Doing (Challenge)	
	Teaching	
	Vision	
		Relationship with God
	Character	Character

God	Church	Self
	Calling	Calling
God's Sovereign Work		
		Inner Desire to Serve
	Ministry Skills	
		Self-Development

Summary

Leadership development involves the sovereign work of God, involvement with others in the church, and leaders taking responsibility for their development. This is the paradigm that regional leaders described as how God developed them as leaders. Their experiences confirm that adult ELT principles were effective in their preparation and development. The real-life outworking of these principles in the lives of leaders gives us confidence that adult ELT principles are practical and useful to inform the design and practice of how we train leaders.

Bibliography

Abdalla, Ikhlas. "Exploring the Implicit Leadership Theory in the Arabian Gulf States." *Applied Psychology: An International Review* 50, no. 4 (2001): 506–531.

Abu-Asba, Angela, Hazita Azman, and Rosniah Moustafa. "A Match or Mismatch between Learning and Teaching Styles in Science Education." *International Journal of Education and Research* 2, no. 3 (2014): 1–14.

Abul-Faris, Ahmad. *The Political System of Islam.* Amman, Jordan: Library of the Modern Message, 1980.

Akkari, Abdeljalil. "Education in the Middle East and North Africa: The Current Situation and Future Challenges." *International Education Journal* 5, no. 2 (2004): 144–153.

Al-Dabbagh, May, and Christine Assaad. *Taking Stock and Looking Forward: Leadership Development in the Arab World.* Abu Dhabi, UAE: NYU Institute, 2010.

Al-Haj, Sarah Abdulla. "Lighting the Fire: Teaching is About Learning." *Learning and Teaching in Higher Education: Gulf Perspectives* 2, no. 2 (2005): 1–4. http://www. zu.ac.ae/lthe/vol2no2/documents/lthe02_02_05.htm.

Al-Omani, Jehad. *Understanding the Arab Culture: A Practical Cross-Cultural Guide to Working in the Arab World.* 2nd edition. Oxford, UK: How to Books, 2008.

Al-Qur'an: A Contemporary Translation. Translated by Ahmed Ali. Princeton, NJ: Princeton University Press, 1993.

Al Suwaidi, Muhammed. "When an Arab Executive says 'Yes': Identifying Different Collectivist Values that Influence the Arabian Decision-Making Process." Masters dissertation, University of Pennsylvania, 2008.

Aldajah, Saud, Yousef Haik, and Kamal Moustafa. "Compatibility of Teaching Styles with Learning Styles: A Case Study." *European Journal of Educational Sciences* 1, no. 1 (March, 2014): 50–58.

Ali, Abbas. "Islamic Perspectives on Leadership: A Model." *International Journal of Islamic and Middle Eastern Finance and Management* 2, no. 2 (2009): 160–180.

———. "Management Research Themes and Teaching in the Arab World." *International Journal of Educational Management* 6, no. 4 (1992): 7–11.

Ali, Abbas, and R. Camp. "Teaching Management in the Arab World: Confronting Illusions." *International Journal of Educational Management* 9, no. 2 (1995): 10–17.

Almoharby, Darwish. "Clarifying Islamic Perspectives on Leadership." *Education, Business and Society: Contemporary Middle Eastern Issues* 6, no. 3/4 (2013): 148–161.

Arnold, V. "Leadership Assessment and Development in the Mid-East." In *Advances in Global Leadership*, edited by W. Mobley, Y. Wang, and M. Li, 273–295. London: Emerald, 2009.

Banks, Robert. *Paul's Idea of Community: The Early House Churches in Their Cultural Setting*. Peabody, MA: Hendrickson, 1994.

———. *Re-envisioning Theological Education: Exploring a Missional Alternative to Current Models*. Grand Rapids, MI: Eerdmans, 1999.

Banu-Yucel, T., and A. Ok. "Incorporating Critical Thinking in the Pedagogical Content of a Teacher Education Programme: Does it make a Difference?" *European Journal of Teacher Education* 35, no. 1 (2012): 39–56.

Barakat, Halim. *The Contemporary Arab Society: An Exploratory Research*. Beirut, Lebanon: Center for Arab Unity Studies, 2004.

Barmeyer, Christopher. "Learning Styles and Their Impact on Cross-Cultural Training: An International Comparison in France, Germany and Quebec." *International Journal of Intercultural Relations* 28 (2004): 577–594.

Barrett, N. C. "The Alexandrian Catechetical School of Clement and Origen as a Postmodern Model for the Contemporary Church and Theological Academy." MA thesis, Hardin-Simmons University, 2011. Accessed 12 July 2017. http://www.scielo.org.za/scielo.php?script=sci_arttextandpid=S2074-77052015000100028.

Beekun, Rafik Issa, and James A. Badawi. *Leadership: An Islamic Perspective*. Beltsville, MD: Amana, 1999.

Bell, Skip. *Servants and Friends: A Biblical Theology of Leadership*. Berrien Springs, MI: Andrews University Press, 2014.

Bielenberg, Brian, and Maxine Gillway. "Adapting Problem-Based Learning to Meet the Life-Long Learning Needs of Developmental Students." *Learning and Teaching in Higher Education: Gulf Perspectives* 3, no. 2 (2006): 2–16.

Blanchard, K. H., and P. Hodges. *Lead like Jesus: Lessons from the Greatest Leadership Role Model of All Times*. Nashville, TN: Thomas Nelson, 2005.

Bloom, B., M. Englehart, E. Furst, W. Hill, and D. Krathwohl. *Taxonomy of Educational Objectives: The Classification of Educational Goals. Handbook I: Cognitive Domain*. New York: Longmans, 1956.

"Bloom's Taxonomy: The Affective Domain." 12 January 2015. http://www.nwlink.com/~donclark/hrd/Bloom/affective_domain.html.

"Bloom's Taxonomy of Learning Domains." 12 January 2015. http://www.nwlink.com/~donclark/hrd/bloom.html#intro.

"Bloom's Taxonomy: The Psychomotor Domain." 12 January 2015. http://www.nwlink.com/~donclark/hrd/Bloom/psychomotor_domain.html.

Boyle, Helen. "Memorization and Learning in Islamic Schools." *Comparative Education Review* 50, no. 3 (2006): 478–495.

Brown, Francis, S. R. Driver, and Charles A. Briggs. *Hebrew and English Lexicon, Unabridged*. Electronic Database. Biblesoft, Inc., 2006. https://biblehub.com/bsoft2.htm.

Brown, J. S., A. Collins, and P. Duguid. "Situated Cognition and the Culture of Learning." *Educational Researcher* 18, no. 1 (1989): 32–41.

Bruce, Alexander. *The Training of the Twelve*. Grand Rapids, MI: Kregel, 1971.

Burt, John. "Impact of Active Learning on Performance and Motivation in Female Emirate Students." *Learning and Teaching in Higher Education: Gulf Perspectives* 1 (2004): 1–15.

Călin-Ştefan, Georgia. "Rules and Hofstede's UAI: A Study on the Arabic Muslim and European Christian Cultures." *Journal of Global Politics and Current Diplomacy* 1, no. 1 (2013): 79–90.

Campbell, Regi. *Mentor Like Jesus: His Radical Approach to Building the Church.* Nashville, TN: RM Press, 2017.

Chapman, Anne, and David Pyvis. "Identity and Social Practice in Higher Education: Student Experiences of Post-Graduate Courses Delivered 'Offshore' in Singapore and Hong Kong by an Australian University." *International Journal of Educational Development* 25, no. 1 (2005): 39–52.

Cheng, K. M. "Can Educational Values Be Borrowed? Looking into Cultural Differences." *Peabody Journal of Education* 73, no. 2 (1998): 11–30.

Clark, M. C., and M. Rossiter. "Narrative Learning in Adulthood." *New Directions for Adult and Continuing Education* 119 (Fall, 2008): 61–70.

———. "'Now the Pieces Are in Place . . .': Learning through Personal Storytelling in the Adult Classroom." *New Horizons in Adult Education and Human Resource Development* 20, no. 3 (Summer, 2006): 19–33.

Claxton, G., and Margaret Carr. "Framework for Teaching Learning: The Dynamics of Disposition." *Early Years* 24, no. 1 (2004): 87–97.

Claxton, G., T. Atkinson, M. Osborn, and M. Wallace, eds. *Liberating the Learner: Lessons for Professional Development in Education.* London: Routledge, 1996.

Clement of Alexandria. *Paedagogus.* Early Christian Writings. http://www.earlychristianwritings.com/text/clement-instructor-book1.html.

Clinton, Robert. *The Making of a Leader: Recognizing the Lessons and Stages of Leadership Development.* Colorado Springs: Navpress, 1994.

Common, Robert. "Barriers to Developing 'Leadership' in the Sultantate of Oman." *International Journal of Leadership Studies* 6, no. 2 (2011): 215–228.

Craig, Peter. *The Book of Deuteronomy. International Commentary on the Old Testament.* Grand Rapids, MI: Eerdmans, 1976.

Creswell, John. *Research Design: Qualitative, Quantitative, and Mixed Method Approaches.* Thousand Oaks, CA: Sage, 2013.

de Bona, Silvia, and Beatrice van der Heijden. *Managing Cultural Diversity.* Aachen, Germany: Meyer and Meyer Fachverlag und Buchhandel GmbH, 2011.

Dejani, Maha, and Mohamed Mohamed. "Leadership Styles, Organizational Culture and Learning Organizational Capability in Education Industry: Evidence from Egypt." *International Journal of Business and Social Research* 6, no. 11 (2016): 42–57.

DeSilver, Drew, and David Masci. "World's Muslim Population More Widespread than You Might Think." 31 January 2017. Pew Research Center. http://www.pewresearch.org

/fact-tank/2017/01/31/worlds-muslim-population-more-widespread-than-you-might-think/.

Dimmock, Clive. *Designing the Learning-Centered School: A Cross-Cultural Perspective.* London: Falmer, 2000.

Dimmock, Clive, and A. Walker. "Globalization and Societal Culture: Redefining Schooling and School Leadership in the Twenty-First Century." *COMPARE* 30, no. 3 (2000): 303–312.

Dudley, Carl, and David Roozen. *Faith Communities Today: A Report on Religion in the United States Today.* Hartford, CT: Hartford Institute for Religion Research, Hartford Seminary, 2001.

Eckert, Regina, and Simon Rweyongoza. *Leadership Development in Africa: A Focus on Strengths.* Greensboro, NC: Center for Creative Research, 2010.

Egger, Roman, and Christian Maurer, eds. "Proceedings of the International Student Conference," ISCONTOUR 2013. Norderstedt: Books on Demand, 2013.

Eldakak, Sam. "The Modern Effects of Teacher Education on the Arab World." 23 June 2010. http://archive.org/details/ERIC_ED510606.

Enns, Marlene. "Now I Know in Part: Holistic and Analytic Reasoning and Their Contribution to Fuller Knowing in Theological Education." *Evangelical Review of Theology* 29, no. 3 (2005): 251–269.

———. "Recovering the Wisdom Tradition for Intercultural Theological Education." *Journal of European Baptist Studies* 5, no. 3 (2005): 5–23.

Esterline, David, Dietrich Werner, Todd Johnson, and Peter Crossing. *Global Survey on Theological Education 2011–2013.* Geneva: World Council of Churches, 2013.

Fasokun, Thomas, Anne Katahoire, and Akpovire Odauran. *The Psychology of Adult Learning in Africa.* Bonn, Germany: UNESCO Institute for Education, 2005.

Floyd, D., and Y. Bodur. "Using Case Study Analysis and Case Writing to Structure Clinical Experiences in a Teacher Education Program." *The Educational Forum* 70 (2005): 48–60.

Fontaine, R. "Problem Solving: An Islamic Management Approach." *Cross Cultural Management* 15, no. 3 (2008): 264–274.

Ford, Leighton. *Transforming Leadership: Jesus' Way of Creating Vision, Shaping Values, Empowering Change.* Downers Grove, IL: InterVarsity, 1993.

Frame, John. "Proposal for a New Seminary." 23 May 2001. https://frame-poythress.org/proposal-for-a-new-seminary/.

Fulton, Brent. "Beyond Theological Education." 2 March 2016. ChinaSource. http://www.chinasource.org/resource-library/from-the-west-courtyard/beyond-theological-education.

Galad, Ahmed. *The Road Not Traveled: Education Reform in the Middle East and North Africa.* Washington, DC: World Bank, 2008.

Globe 2020. "An overview of the 2004 study: Understanding the Relationship Between National Culture, Societal Effectiveness and Desirable Leadership Attributes." Beedie School of Business. https://globeproject.com/study_2004_2007.

Gorveatte, Mark. *Lead Like John Wesley: Help for Today's Ministry Servants.* Indianapolis, IN: Wesleyan, 2016.

Greenleaf, Robert. *Servant Leadership: A Journey into the Nature of Legitimate Power and Greatness.* Mahwah, NJ: Paulist, 2002.

Grove, Cornelius. *Worldwide Differences in Business Values and Practices: Overview of GLOBE Research Findings.* New York: Grovewell, 2005.

Grow, Gerald O. "Teaching Learners to be Self-Directed." *Adult Educators Quarterly* 41, no. 3 (Spring, 1991): 125–149.

Haik, Y. "Thinking and Learning Preferences for a Sample of Engineering Students at the United Arab Emirates University." *Emirates Journal for Engineering Research* 12, no. 1 (2001): 65–71.

Hall, Edward T. *Beyond Culture.* Garden City, NY: Anchor, 1976.

Hamady, Sania. *Temperament and Character of the Arabs.* New York: Twayne Publishers, 1960.

Hawkes, Thomas. *Pious Pastors: Calvin's Theology of Sanctification and the Genevan Academy.* Milton Keynes, UK: Paternoster, 2016.

Heck, Ronald. "Leadership and Culture: Conceptual and Methodological Issues in Comparing Models Across Cultural Settings." *Journal of Educational Administration* 34, no. 5 (1996): 74–97.

Heller, Patricia, and Mark Hollabaugh. "Teaching Problem Solving Through Cooperative Grouping: Part 2: Designing Problems and Structuring Groups." *American Journal of Physics* 60 (1992): 637–44.

Heller, Patricia, Ronald Keith, and Scott Anderson. "Teaching Problem Solving Through Cooperative Grouping. Part 1: Group Versus Individual Problem Solving." *American Journal of Physics* 60 (1992): 627–636.

Hendriksen, William, and Simon Kistemaker. *New Testament Commentary: Exposition of Thessalonians, the Pastorals, and Hebrews.* Grand Rapids, MI: Baker, 2007.

Hitt, G. W. "Secondary Implementation of Interactive Engagement Teaching Techniques: Choices and Challenges in a Gulf Arab Context." *Physics Review Special Topics: Physical Education Research* 10, no. 2 (2014): 1–20.

Hofstede, Geert. "Cultural Differences in Teaching and Learning." *International Journal of Intercultural Relations* 10, no. 3 (1986): 301–320.

———. *Culture's Consequences: Comparing Values, Behaviors, Institutions, and Organizations Across Nations.* Thousand Oaks, CA: Sage, 2001.

———. *Cultures and Organizations: Software of the Mind.* New York: McGraw Hill, 2010. Kindle edition.

House, Paul. *Bonhoeffer's Seminary Vision: A Case for Costly Discipleship and Life Together.* Wheaton, IL: Crossway, 2015.

House, Robert. *Culture, Leadership and Organizations: The GLOBE Study of 62 Societies.* Thousand Oaks, CA: Sage, 2004.

Hull, Bill. *The Disciple Making Pastor: Leading Others on a Journey of Faith.* Grand Rapids, MI: Baker, 2007.

ICETE. "ICETE Manifesto on the Renewal of Evangelical Theological Education." 1990. Accessed 15 March 2017. http://icete-edu.org/manifesto/.

James, Aleya, and Niccole Shammas. "Developing Intercultural Intelligence: Dubai Style." *Journal of International Education in Business* 6, no. 2 (2013): 148–164.

Javidan, Mansour. "In the Eye of the Beholder: Cross Cultural Lessons in Leadership from Project GLOBE." *Academy of Management Perspectives* 20, no. 1 (2006): 67–90.

Jawarneh, Tariq. "Life Skills Teachers' Readiness for their Role: Implications for Higher Education." *Learning and Teaching in Higher Education: Gulf Perspectives* 10, no. 1 (2013): 1–17.

Jenkins, Philip. *The Next Christendom: The Coming of Global Christianity.* New York: Oxford University Press, 2007.

Johnstone, Patrick. *From Seed to Fruit: Global Trends, Fruitful Practices and Emerging Issues among Muslims.* Edited by J. D. Woodberry. Pasadena, CA: William Carey, 2008.

Joy, Simy, and David A. Kolb. "Are There Cultural Differences in Learning Style?" *International Journal of Intercultural Relations* 33 (2009): 69–85.

Kabasakal, Hayat. "Leadership and Culture in the MENA Region: An Analysis of the GLOBE Project." *Journal of World Business* 47, no. 4 (2012): 519–529.

Kabasakal, Hayat, and Ali Dastmalchian. "Introduction to the Special Issue on Leadership and Culture in the Middle East." *Applied Psychology: An International Review* 50, no. 4 (2001): 479–488.

Kabasakal, Hayat, and Muzaffer Bodur. "Arabic Cluster: A Bridge between East and West." *Journal of World Business* 37, no. 1 (2002): 40–54.

Karagiorgi, Yiasemena, and Loizos Symeou. "Translating Constructivism into Instructional Design: Potential and Limitations." *Educational Technology and Society* 8, no. 1 (2005): 17–27.

Karn, Gary. "Learning Style Differences in the Perceived Effectiveness of Learning Activities." *Journal of Marketing Education* 28 (2006): 56–63.

Keil, C. F., and Franz Delitzsch. *Commentary on the Old Testament.* Grand Rapids, MI: Eerdmans, 1971. StudyLight.org. https://www.studylight.org/commentaries/kdo/psalms-119.html.

Khasawneh, Samer, Abdullah Abu-Tineh, and Osamha Obeidat. "The Relationship Between Learning Style Preferences and Academic Achievement of the Hashemite University Students." *Journal of Educational and Psychological Sciences* 7, no. 3 (2006): 7–24.

Khattab, Amira, and David Wong. "Integrating Western and Arab Leadership Development Practices: An Example of the Challenge Bridging Global and Local Adult Learning Perspectives." *Adragoske Studije* 0354–5415, broj 11 (Dec 2018): 65–85.

Knight, George R. *Philosophy and Education.* 4th edition. Berrien Springs, MI: Andrews University Press, 2006.

Knight, George W. *The Pastoral Epistles. The New International Greek Testament Commentary*. Grand Rapids, MI: Eerdmans, 1992.

Knowles, Malcolm. *The Adult Learner*. 7th edition. New York: Taylor and Francis, 2014.

———. *The Adult Learner: A Neglected Species*. Houston, TX: Gulf, 1973.

———. *The Modern Practice of Adult Education*. Englewood Cliffs, NJ: Cambridge, 1988.

Knowles, Malcolm S., Elwood F. Holton, III, and Richard A. Swanson. *The Adult Learner: The Definitive Classic in Adult Education and Human Resource Development*. San Diego, CA: Elsevier Butterworth Heinemann, 2005.

Kolb, David. *Experiential Learning: Experiences as the Source of Learning and Development*. Englewood Cliffs, NJ: Prentice Hall, 1984.

———. *Experiential Learning Theory: Previous Research and New Directions*. Cleveland, OH: Case Western University, 1999.

Komives, Susan. *Leadership for a Better World: Understanding the Social Change Model of Leadership Development*. San Francisco, CA: Jossey-Bass, 2009.

Kronqvist, Eeva-Lissa. "Alfa Course in Oulu: Organization Development and Innovative Project Work." In *Management in Education: An International Teaching Project for Strengthening MA Programmes in Education*, edited by Dietmar Waterkamp, 11–30. Berlin: Waxmann, 2000.

Kruger, Michael. *Christianity at the Crossroads*. London: SPCK, 2017.

Lausanne Committee for World Evangelization. "Occasional Paper 57: Effective Theological Education for World Evangelization." 2004. Accessed 27 March 2017. http://www.lausanne.org/wp-content/uploads/2007/06/LOP57 _IG28.pdf. Forum for World Evangelization. Pattaya Thailand. September 29-October 5, 2004.

———. "The Third Lausanne Congress on World Evangelization." Cape Town, South Africa. 16–25 October 2010. https://www.lausanne.org/gatherings/congress/cape-town-2010-3.

Lawrence, Randee, and Dennis Paige. "What Our Ancestors Knew: Teaching and Learning Through Storytelling." *New Directions for Adult and Continuing Education* 149 (2016): 63–72.

Lightfoot, J. B. *The Apostolic Fathers*. Grand Rapids, MI: Baker, 1991.

Lingenfelter, Sherwood. *Teaching Cross-Culturally: An Incarnational Model*. Grand Rapids, MI: Baker Academic, 2003.

Madsen, Susan. "Leadership Development in the United Arab Emirates: The Transformational Learning Experiences of Women." *Journal of Leadership and Organizational Studies* 17, no. 1 (2010): 100–110.

Mahjoub, M., M. Ghonaim, and F. Shareef. *Studies in the Bedouin Societies*. Cairo: University Knowledge, 2011.

Mahrous, Abber A. "A Cross-Cultural Investigation of Students' Perceptions of the Effectiveness of Pedagogical Tools, the Middle East, the United Kingdom, and the United States." *Journal of Study in International Education* 14, no. 3 (2010): 289–306.

Makhlouf, Asmaa M. El Sayyed. "A Comparison of Preferred Learning Styles between Vocational and Academic Secondary School Students in Egypt." *Institute for Learning Styles Journal* 1 (2012): 1–9.

Manalo, Kristine Joy. "Science Teachers' Teaching Styles, Students' Learning Styles and Their Academic Performance." *International Journal of Social Science and Humanities Research* 5, no. 2 (April–June, 2017): 397–408.

Massialas, Byron, and Samir Jarrar. *Arab Education in Transition: A Source Book.* New York: Garland, 1991.

Mays, James Luther. "The Place of the Torah-Psalms in the Psalter." *Journal of Biblical Literature* 106, no. 1 (1987): 3–12.

McMillan, Sara, Fiona Kelly, Adem Sav, Elizabeth Kendall, Michelle King, Jennifer A. Whitty, and Amanda Wheeler. "The Ideal Healthcare: Priorities of People with Chronic Conditions and Their Careers." *Health Services and Outcomes Research Methodology* 14, no. 3 (2014): 92–108.

Metcalf, Beverly, and Fouad Mimouni. *Leadership Development in the Middle East.* Cheltenham, UK: Edward Elgar, 2011.

Metcalf, Beverly, and Tony Murfin. "Leadership, Social Development and Political Economy in the Middle East: An Introduction." In *The Ethics of Islamic Leadership: A Cross-Cultural Approach for Public Administration*, edited by Beverly Metcalf and Tony Murfin, 1–60. Cheltenham, UK: Edward Elgar, 2011.

Michael. "Mentoring in a Chinese Context." 28 October 2011. ChinaSource. http://www.chinasource.org/resource-library/articles/mentoring-in-a-chinese-context.

Mir, Ali Mohammed. "Leadership in Islam." *Journal of Leadership Studies* 4, no. 3 (2010): 69–72.

Mitsis, Ann, and Patrick Foley. "The Effect of Students' Cultural Values on Their Student-Driven Learning Preferences." Unpublished paper, June 2005. https://researchbank.swinburne.edu.au/file/ec24c33b-ba0a-4d21-9b03-1d6a4d6498ae/1/PDF%20%28Published%20version%29.pdf.

Morris, P., and M. L. Lo. "Shaping the Curriculum: Contexts and Cultures." *School Leadership and Management* 20, no. 2 (2000): 143–160.

Müller, Roland. *Honor and Shame.* Philadelphia: Xlibris, 2000.

———. "Honor and Shame in a Middle Eastern Setting." Nabataea.net, 2000. https://nabataea.net/explore/culture_and_religion/honorshame/.

Muna, Farid, and Grace Khoury. *The Palestinian Executive: Leadership under Challenging Conditions.* Farham, UK: Gower, 2012.

Najm, Najm. "Arab Culture Dimensions in the International and Arab Models." *American Journal of Business, Economics and Management* 3, no. 6 (2015): 423–431.

Nakah, Victor. "The Capetown Commitment as a Missional Framework for Theological Education." Siem Rap, Cambodia, November 2015.

Nathan, Alli, and Margaret Ruggieri. "Challenges in Cross-Cultural Business Education." *American Journal of Business Education* 2, no. 2 (March/April, 2009): 55–64.

Nehemiah, Joseph. "A Contextual and Cultural Adult Education Model for Leadership Development in the Arab Middle East." Doctoral dissertation, 2018.

Netland, Harold, and Craig Ott. *Globalizing Theology: Belief and Practice in an Era of World Christianity*. Grand Rapids, MI: Baker Academic, 2006.

Nisbett, Richard. "Culture and Systems of Thought: Holistic Versus Analytic Cognition." *Psychological Review* 108, no. 2 (2001): 291–310.

Nouwen, Henri J. *In the Name of Jesus: Reflections on Christian Leadership*. Chestnut Ridge, NY: Crossroad, 1992.

Obeidat, Bader Yousef. "Toward Better Understanding of Arabian Culture: Implications Based on Hofstede's Cultural Model." *European Journal of Social Sciences* 28, no. 4 (January, 2012): 512–22.

Oden, Thomas. *How Africa Shaped the Christian Mind*. Downers Grove, IL: InterVarsity, 2007. Kindle edition.

Oliver, Willem. "The Heads of the Catechetical School in Alexandria." *Verbum Eccles* 36, no. 1 (2015): 1–14. https://www.researchgate.net/publication/307847514_The_ heads_of_the_Catechetical_School_in_Alexandria.

Omidvar, Pegah, and Bee Hoon Tan. "Cultural Variations in Learning and Learning Style." *Journal of Distance Education* 13, no. 4 (2012): 269–286.

Pedersen, Johannes. *Israel: Its Life and Culture, I–IV*. London: Oxford University Press, 1973.

Pinnington, A. "Leadership Development: Applying the Same Leadership Theories and Development Practices to Different Contexts?" *Leadership* 7, no. 3 (2011): 335–65.

Plueddemann, James. *Leading Across Cultures: Effective Ministry and Mission in the Global Church*. Downers Grove, IL: InterVarsity, 2009. Kindle edition.

Prowse, Jacqueline. "Cross-Cultural Comparison: Piloting an Analytical Framework." *Learning and Teaching in Higher Education: Gulf Perspectives* 11, no. 2 (2014): 1–14.

———. "Teaching across Cultures: Canada and Qatar." *Canadian Journal of Higher Education* 40, no. 1 (2010): 31–52.

Rahal, Tofi, and David Palfreyman. "Assessing Learning Styles of Students at Zayed University." *Learning and Teaching in Higher Education: Gulf Perspectives* 6, no. 2 (2009): 1–17.

Rajasekar, James. *Culture and Gender in Leadership: Perspectives from the Middle East and Asia*. New York: Palgrave Macmillan, 2013.

Rhem, James. "Deep/Surface Approaches to Learning: An Introduction." *The National Teaching and Learning Forum* 5, no. 1 (1995): 1–5.

Richards, Alan. "Higher Education in Egypt." World Bank Policy Research Working Paper. Washington, DC: World Bank, 1992.

Richards, Lawrence. *Creative Bible Teaching*. Chicago: Moody, 1998.

Richardson, Patricia M. "Possible Influences of Arabic-Islamic Culture on the Reflective Practices Proposed for an Education Degree at the Higher Colleges of Technology in the United Arab Emirates." *International Journal of Educational Development* 24, no. 4 (2004): 429–436.

Robbins, Stephen, Mary Coulter, Yusuf Sidani, and Dima Jamali. *Management: Arab World Edition*. London: Pearson Higher Education, 2012.

Rowdon, Harold. "Theological Education in Historical Perspective." *Vox Evangelica* 7 (1971): 75–87. https://biblicalstudies.org.uk/pdf/vox/vol07/education_rowdon. pdf.

Rugh, William. "Arab Education: Tradition, Growth and Reform." *The Middle East Journal* 56, no. 3 (2002): 396–414.

Russell, Alan. "Zayed University Students' Teaching and Learning Beliefs and Preferences: An Analysis Based on the Surface Versus Deep Learning Approach." *Learning and Teaching in Higher Education: Gulf Perspectives* 2, no. 1 (2005): 1–15.

Saadi, Ibrahim. "An Examination of the Learning Styles of Saudi Preparatory School Students Who are High or Low in Reading Achievement." PhD dissertation, Victoria University, 2012.

Saafin, Salah. "Arab Tertiary Students' Perspectives of Effective Teachers." *Learning and Teaching in Higher Education: Gulf Perspectives* 5, no. 2 (2008): 1–11.

Saidi, Farida. "A Study of Current Leadership Styles in the North African Church." PhD dissertation, Fuller Seminary, 2011. Also published: Carlisle, UK: Langham Monographs, 2013.

Saleh, Amjed, and Samih Al-Karasneh. "Visionary Leadership as an Approach to Social Studies Teacher Preparation Program Reform: Participants' Perspectives." *Procedia: Social and Behavioral Sciences* 1, no. 1 (2009): 877–899.

Salem, Zaneb, and Syed Agil. "The Effects of Islamic Management Ethics on Organizational Commitment of Employees in Libyan Public Banks." *Australian Journal of Basic and Applied Sciences* 6, no. 7 (2012): 260–270.

Sameh, Laneh. *Translating the Message*. Maryknoll, NY: Orbis, 2009.

Samier, Eugenia. "The Ethics of Islamic Leadership: A Cross-Cultural Approach for Public Administration." *Administrative Culture* 14, no. 2 (2013): 188–211.

Sanders, J. Oswald. *Spiritual Leadership*. Chicago: Marshall Pickering, 1986.

Sarayrah, Yasin Khalif. "Servant-Leadership in the Bedouin-Arab Culture." *Global Virtue Ethics Review* 5, no. 3 (2004): 58–79.

Sargent, Benjamin. "The Dead Letter? Psalm 119 and the Spirituality of the Bible in the Local Church." *Evangelical Quarterly* 81, no. 2 (2009): 98–115.

Saucy, Robert. *Minding the Heart: The Way of Spiritual Transformation*. Grand Rapids, MI: Kregel, 2013. Kindle edition.

Shah, S. "Educational Leadership: An Islamic Perspective." *British Educational Research Journal* 32, no. 3 (2006): 363–385.

Shahin, A., and P. Wright. "Leadership in the Context of Culture: An Egyptian Perspective." *Leadership and Organization Development Journal* 25, no. 6 (2004): 499–511.

Shaw, Perry. "Muslim Education: An Introduction to Philosophy, Curriculum and Methodology with Reflections on Its Impact on the Evangelical Churches of the Arab Levant." EdD preliminary paper, Pacific College of Graduate Studies, 1995.

———. *Transforming Theological Education: A Practical Handbook for Integrative Learning.* Carlisle, UK: Langham Global Library, 2014.

———. "Vulnerable Authority: A Theological Approach to Leadership and Teamwork." *CEJ* 3, no. 1 (2006): 119–133.

Shi, Xiumei, and Jinying Wang. "Interpreting Hofstede Model and GLOBE Model: Which Way to Go for Cross-Cultural Research?" *International Journal of Business and Management* 6, no. 5 (2011): 93–99.

Sidani, Yusuf. "Ibn Khaldun of North Africa: An AD 1377 Theory of Leadership." *Journal of Management History* 14 (2008): 73–86. https://www.researchgate.net/publication/242023930_Ibn_Khaldun_of_North_Africa_An_AD_1377_theory_of_leadership.

Sidani, Yusuf, and Jon Thornberry. "The Current Arab Work Ethic: Antecedents, Implications, and Potential Remedies." *Journal of Business Ethics* 91, no. 1 (2009): 35–49.

Simpson, Elizabeth. *The Classification of Educational Objectives in the Psychomotor Domain: The Psychomotor Domain.* Urbana, IL: University of Illinois, 1966.

Smith, Derik. "Teaching Humanities in the Arabian Gulf: Toward a Pedagogical Ethos." *Learning and Teaching in Higher Education: Gulf Perspectives* 8, no. 2 (2011): 1–14.

Smith, Peter, Mustafa Achoui, and Charles Harb. "Unity and Diversity in Arab Managerial Styles." *International Journal of Cross Cultural Management* 7, no. 3 (2007): 275–290.

Smither, Edward. *Augustine as Mentor: A Model for Preparing Spiritual Leaders.* Nashville, TN: B & H Academic, 2009.

Sonleitner, Nancy, and Maher Khelifa. "Western-Educated Faculty Challenges in a Gulf Classroom." *Learning and Teaching in Higher Education: Gulf Perspectives* 2, no. 1 (2005): 1–21.

Spurgeon, Charles. *The Treasury of David.* Pasadena, TX: Pilgrim, 1983.

Tayeb, Monir. *International Human Resource Management: A Multinational Company Perspective.* Oxford, UK: Oxford University Press, 2005.

Tenant, Timothy. *Theology in the Context of World Christianity.* Grand Rapids, MI: Zondervan, 2009. Kindle edition.

Tessmer, Martin, and Rita Richey. "The Role of Context in Learning and Instructional Design." *Educational Technology Research and Development* 45, no. 2 (1997): 85–115.

Thornton, Phil. "Contextual Teaching: Changes in Content and Culture." *Evangelical Missionary Quarterly* (July, 2014): 345–348.

Tienou, Tite, and Paul Hiebert. "Missional Theology." *Missiology: An International Review* 24, no. 2 (2006): 219–238.

Trompenaars, Fons, and Charles Hampden-Turner. *Riding the Waves of Culture: Understanding Cultural Diversity in Business*. London: Nicholas Brealey, 1997.

United Nations Development Program. 2014. "Arab Knowledge Report 2014: Youth and Localization of Knowledge. Dubai, UAE: Mohammed bin Rashid Al Maktoum Foundation (MBRF) and The United Nations Development Programme/Regional Bureau for Arab States (UNDP/RBAS)." http://www.undp.org/content/dam/rbas/report/UNDP-GENERAL-REPORT-ENG.pdf.

Vale, Jordan. "The Healthy Pastor: A Holistic Approach to Pastoral Training." MReligion dissertation, Reformed Theological Seminary, 2014.

Valiente, Caroline. "Are Students Using the 'Wrong' Style of Learning?" *Active Learning in Higher Education* 9, no. 1 (2002): 73–91.

Venema, Cornelius. "Mid-American Reformed Seminary: An Academy with a Vocational Aim." *Mid-American Journal of Theology* 13 (2002): 7–23.

Walker, A., and Clive Dimmock. "A Cross-Cultural Approach to the Study of Educational Leadership: An Emerging Framework." *Journal of School Leadership* 9, no. 4 (1999): 321–348.

———. "Moving School Leadership beyond Its Narrow Boundaries: Developing a Cross Cultural Approach." In *Second International Handbook of Educational Leadership and Administration*, edited by K. Leithwood and P. Hallinger, 167–202. Dordrecht: Kluwer Academic, 2002.

Walls, Andrew. *The Missionary Movement in Christian History*. Edinburgh: T&T Clark, 1996.

Webber, Malcolm. "Leader Development: What Is Our Role?" 18 March 2008. ChinaSource. https://www.chinasource.org/resource-library/articles/leader-development-what-is-our-role.

Weber, Timothy. "The Seminaries and the Churches: Looking for New Relationships." *Theological Education* 44, no. 1 (2008): 65–91.

Weir, David. "Human Resource Development in the Middle East: A Fourth Paradigm." In *Human Resource Development in a Complex World*, edited by M. Lee, 69–82. London: Routledge, 2003.

———. "Management Development and Leadership in the Arab Middle East: An Alternative Paradigm for the Mediterranean Worlds." UFHRD conference paper, 2003. https://www.bam.ac.uk/sites/bam.ac.uk/files/contribution650.pdf.

Weiser, Artur. *The Psalms: A Commentary*. The Old Testament Library. Louisville, KY: Westminster John Knox, 1962.

Westermann, Claus. *The Psalms: Structure, Content, and Message*. Minneapolis, MN: Augsburg, 1980.

Whybray, Richard. "Psalm 119: Profile of a Psalmist." In *Wisdom, You Are My Sister*, edited by Michael L. Barré, 31–43. CBQ Monograph Series 29. Washington, DC: CBAA, 1997.

Wilson, R. "Globalisation, Governance and Leadership Development in the Middle East." In *Leadership Development in the Middle East*, edited by B. Metcalf and F. Mimouni, 61–85. Cheltenham, UK: Edward Elgar, 2011.

Wolff, Hans Walter. *The Anthropology of the Old Testament*. Translated by Margaret Kohl. Philadelphia, PA: Fortress, 1974.

Wu, Jackson. *Reading Romans with Eastern Eyes: Honor and Shame in Paul's Message and Mission*. Downers Grove, IL: IVP Academic, 2019.

Wurston, Huib, and Carel Jacobs. *The Impact of Culture on Education*. Helsinki: ITIM International, 2016.

———. "The Impact of Culture on Education: Can We Introduce Best Practices in Education across Countries?" Academia. 2016. https://www.academia.edu/12349034/The_impact_of_culture_on_education.

Yamazaki, Y. "An Experiential Approach to Cross-Cultural Adaptation: A Study of Japanese Expatriates' Learning Styles, Learning Skills, and Job Satisfaction in the United States." PhD dissertation, Case Western Reserve University, 2004.

———. "Learning Styles and Typologies of Cultural Differences: A Theoretical and Empirical Comparison." *International Journal of Inter-Cultural Relations* 29 (2005): 521–548.

Yamazaki, Y., and D. C. Kayes. "An Experiential Approach to Cross-Cultural Learning: A Review and Integration of Competencies of Successful Expatriate Adaptation." *Academy of Management Learning and Education* 3, no. 4 (2004): 362–379.

Zen-Rufinen, Bernard, and Serif Kaynar. *Business Leadership in the Arab World*. Dubai: Korn/Ferry Institute, 2011.

Zualkernan, I. A., J. Allert, and G. Z. Qadah. "A Cross-Cultural Comparison of Learning Styles: The AUS-UMD Experience." Paper presented at the Second International Conference on Innovations in Information Technology. Dubai, UAE. 16–18 September 2005. http://www.it-innovations.ae/iit005/proceedings/articles/F_2_IIT05_Zualkerna.pdf.

———. "Learning Styles of Computer Programming Students: A Middle Eastern and American Comparison." *IEEE Transactions on Education* 49, no. 4 (2006): 443–450.

Index

Langham Literature and its imprints are a ministry of Langham Partnership.

Langham Partnership is a global fellowship working in pursuit of the vision God entrusted to its founder John Stott –

> *to facilitate the growth of the church in maturity and Christ-likeness through raising the standards of biblical preaching and teaching.*

Our vision is to see churches in the Majority World equipped for mission and growing to maturity in Christ through the ministry of pastors and leaders who believe, teach and live by the word of God.

Our mission is to strengthen the ministry of the word of God through:
- nurturing national movements for biblical preaching
- fostering the creation and distribution of evangelical literature
- enhancing evangelical theological education

especially in countries where churches are under-resourced.

Our ministry

Langham Preaching partners with national leaders to nurture indigenous biblical preaching movements for pastors and lay preachers all around the world. With the support of a team of trainers from many countries, a multi-level programme of seminars provides practical training, and is followed by a programme for training local facilitators. Local preachers' groups and national and regional networks ensure continuity and ongoing development, seeking to build vigorous movements committed to Bible exposition.

Langham Literature provides Majority World preachers, scholars and seminary libraries with evangelical books and electronic resources through publishing and distribution, grants and discounts. The programme also fosters the creation of indigenous evangelical books in many languages, through writer's grants, strengthening local evangelical publishing houses, and investment in major regional literature projects, such as one volume Bible commentaries like *The Africa Bible Commentary* and *The South Asia Bible Commentary*.

Langham Scholars provides financial support for evangelical doctoral students from the Majority World so that, when they return home, they may train pastors and other Christian leaders with sound, biblical and theological teaching. This programme equips those who equip others. Langham Scholars also works in partnership with Majority World seminaries in strengthening evangelical theological education. A growing number of Langham Scholars study in high quality doctoral programmes in the Majority World itself. As well as teaching the next generation of pastors, graduated Langham Scholars exercise significant influence through their writing and leadership.

To learn more about Langham Partnership and the work we do visit **langham.org**

CPSIA information can be obtained
at www.ICGtesting.com
Printed in the USA
LVHW011342100121
675965LV00002B/107